Palgrave Ex

Today's complex and changing business environment brings with it a number of pressing challenges. To be successful, business professionals are increasingly required to leverage and spot future trends, be masters of strategy, all while leading responsibly, inspiring others, mastering financial techniques and driving innovation.

Palgrave Executive Essentials empowers you to take your skills to the next level. Offering a suite of resources to support you on your executive journey and written by renowned experts from top business schools, the series is designed to support professionals as they embark on executive education courses, but it is equally applicable to practicing leaders and managers. Each book brings you in-depth case studies, accompanying video resources, reflective questions, practical tools and core concepts that can be easily applied to your organization, all written in an engaging, easy to read style.

Poornima Luthra · Sara Louise Muhr

Leading Through Bias

5 Essential Skills to Block Bias and Improve Inclusion at Work

Poornima Luthra
Copenhagen Business School
Copenhagen, Denmark

Sara Louise Muhr
Copenhagen Business School
Copenhagen, Denmark

ISSN 2731-5614 ISSN 2731-5622 (electronic)
Palgrave Executive Essentials
ISBN 978-3-031-38573-5 ISBN 978-3-031-38571-1 (eBook)
https://doi.org/10.1007/978-3-031-38571-1

© The Editor(s) (if applicable) and The Author(s), under exclusive license to Springer Nature Switzerland AG 2023

This work is subject to copyright. All rights are solely and exclusively licensed by the Publisher, whether the whole or part of the material is concerned, specifically the rights of translation, reprinting, reuse of illustrations, recitation, broadcasting, reproduction on microfilms or in any other physical way, and transmission or information storage and retrieval, electronic adaptation, computer software, or by similar or dissimilar methodology now known or hereafter developed.
The use of general descriptive names, registered names, trademarks, service marks, etc. in this publication does not imply, even in the absence of a specific statement, that such names are exempt from the relevant protective laws and regulations and therefore free for general use.
The publisher, the authors, and the editors are safe to assume that the advice and information in this book are believed to be true and accurate at the date of publication. Neither the publisher nor the authors or the editors give a warranty, expressed or implied, with respect to the material contained herein or for any errors or omissions that may have been made. The publisher remains neutral with regard to jurisdictional claims in published maps and institutional affiliations.

This Palgrave Macmillan imprint is published by the registered company Springer Nature Switzerland AG
The registered company address is: Gewerbestrasse 11, 6330 Cham, Switzerland

Paper in this product is recyclable.

We would like to thank everyone who was a part of making this book come to life—

the companies we collaborate with, the many leaders and employees we have worked with in our workshops and talks, and our families for the incredible support for the work we love doing. We wouldn't have been able to do this without you. We would also like to thank Copenhagen Business School for supporting the publication of this book.

No part of this book has been created by ChatGPT

Foreword

I am a woman with power. I am also often the person in meetings who holds the most senior position in the room. Unfortunately, I am also one of the very few women at the top of organisations, and I have only recently begun to fully understand why.

I have been blessed with a privileged background. I have had a good education and been fortunate to have worked with leaders who believed in me and gave me opportunities at crucial steps of my career. I had my first child while holding my first leadership role, and I was allowed to work four days a week with no change to my title, influence or salary. I was promoted to CIO seven days before I gave birth to my third child. This was despite the leaders in the organisation knowing that I was going to be on parental leave for six months. I got my first CEO position even though I did not come from a commercial background. Everybody needs support, help and a bit of luck along the way. Unfortunately, I have seen that the support and help can be scarce when you are not a White male, and the bias experienced can be overwhelming.

This is not to say that I have not experienced bias and discrimination. I most certainly have had my dose of bias being in the Danish education and business systems. These biases started with one of my math teacher's not letting a single lesson go by without cracking a "females only belong in the kitchen" joke. This extended to the workplace with the project partner giving my private phone number to the customer's male CFO without first asking me or explaining why. I only found out when I received a call from the CFO at the weekend. This is the same workplace where I had to endure an hour of "blonde jokes" at the Christmas party and these experiences influenced my decision to leave that organisation. Later in my career, a head-hunter announced that I was the first female CEO that he had ever been involved in hiring, even though he had been in the business for more than 10 years. This list goes on.

For many years, I thought things were changing on the gender front. Yes, I had experienced bias, but I had rationalised those experiences as being "just minor incidents" and simply part of the game. When I eventually stopped and looked around, I could see that very little progress had been made to increase the diversity at the top of organisations. This was not just unique to Danish companies, companies in other countries also had similar issues. What I did observe though was that those companies that were doing better on leadership diversity had a very distinct and action-oriented approach to make the change a reality. So, I decided to use my leadership to act and make an impact. I started to be vocal on the gender gap in public, supporting female leaders as a mentor, being clear on the purpose of diversity, setting targets and training leadership teams in unconscious bias. It has been, and continues to be, a tough ride.

When presented with a list of seven male names for a leadership position by my talent business partner, I recall saying: "This is not a relevant list for promotions". The talent business partner argued that: "I have tried to challenge it, but these are the best candidates from the departments". I answered: "No, it is not, and I want you to return to the leadership team and demand a list that is more diverse, more representative". This really surprised me. I found myself wondering how this could possibly happen. After all, we had implemented many different initiatives to address the gender imbalance. We reported on gender KPIs across the different layers of the business, and I had on every occasion possible been very vocal that I wanted a change. Despite all this, seven male candidates formed the set of candidates presented to me.

Habits are hard to break, and bias even more so. It is not enough as a leader to just communicate what you want. If you want cultural change, you need to live it. You need to believe it. You need to be close to the related decisions being made. You need to challenge those decisions when they are not in line with the company's strategy for diversity and inclusion. Most importantly, you need to stay firm, especially when old habits and former cultural norms reappear.

Embracing diversity requires a cultural change and I have observed that many leaders often forget that. Intentions and accompanying speeches are a good start but even when KPIs are in place and online training has been rolled out with HR being on the ball, things can go wrong.

If you want to know what can go wrong, and if you want help to succeed, then this is the book for you. Poornima and Sara have conducted research in the field of diversity, equity and inclusion and have been advising many companies for many years. They combine their rich experience in this book which enables us to both understand the kind of biases we hold and face, and how we can use our leadership to block our biases.

Bias is after all everywhere. We all have it. I also have it. And in reading this book, I have learned that my intuition bias is an area I need to work on blocking. Being constantly fed with a large amount of information, having to make numerous and often quick decisions every single day, intuition and experience often come into play. I must admit that I am not as aware as I should be of the influence of bias in these situations.

Bias can improve the efficiency of decision-making, but it can also block the value creation in your business when previously held experiences are not as relevant for the future. When untamed bias leads to an uneven playing field, it results in toxic cultures, creates inequality and threatens democracy in counties. As leaders, we have a huge responsibility to ensure that this does not happen.

Leading through bias is paramount. Through this book, you will learn that it requires you to lead with conviction, clarity, accountability, allyship and strength. It is not an easy ride. You will need to step up and even more leadership will be required of you when everybody comes with a different view. But what you stand to gain—the value you can create both in your people and in your business—is immense. This is important. For you. For your teams. For your company.

Enjoy reading and learning.

Mette Louise Kaagaard
Country General Manager/CEO
Microsoft Denmark & Iceland

Preface

Diversity, equity and inclusion (DEI)—and inclusive leadership—have become the pillars of many organisations' strategic people and culture priorities. It is hard to find an organisation today that isn't prioritising DEI, even if they do so to varying degrees. Across the world, DEI is gaining traction, and organisations are feeling the pressure to make change happen. This progress is encouraging.

Over the many years of working in this space, we have noticed the increased desire to want to do better and to make workplaces more diverse and inclusive, but we have also seen that leaders find it challenging to turn the ambition into practice. Somehow, DEI feels different from other transformation efforts and seems to face greater resistance. This is because DEI requires each one of us to address something that influences how we think, make decisions and behave. That "something" is bias.

While bias is a necessary cognitive mechanism that helps us organise the many bits of information that our brain constantly receives and thus makes us capable of efficient decision-making, bias is also one of the key barriers that organisations experience in making their workplaces more diverse and inclusive. Bias is ubiquitous and pervasive. It is everywhere—in us, in our interactions with others and in the decisions we make. Bias makes people feel excluded. Bias makes people change who they are to fit in. Bias makes people feel like they are treated unfairly. Bias makes people feel like they do not belong. Bias creates distance and separation between people and within teams. Bias weighs people down affecting their mental well-being and satisfaction at work. Bias affects team dynamics and productivity. Bias affects the organisational culture. While we cannot run away from bias, we are sure that you would agree that we should try to make sincere efforts to reduce the influence of bias to help create workplaces in which people thrive and feel included.

Many leaders, however, are still daunted by the task of blocking bias and preventing it from influencing important decisions negatively. Today, many organisations conduct bias awareness training for their employees, and there is, at the societal level, a general heightened awareness of the impact of bias. Yet, bias prevails, which raises the question: If we cannot remove bias, how can we lead through bias?

With this question in mind, we have spent the past five years developing and testing tools and strategies to block bias across dozens of global organisations including corporate, humanitarian and public sector organisations. We have worked with hundreds of leaders across organisational hierarchies and functions, in groups, in teams and in individual sessions. In this process, we looked for resources to share with the leaders, but found very little. And as Toni Morrison, Nobel Prize winner in Literature, said: "If there's a book that you want to read, but it hasn't been written yet, then you must write it". And so, we did. What we share with you in this book is our collective knowledge on what causes bias and the combined practical tools we have developed to block bias.

This book is written for individuals who have the influence and power to make changes systemically and culturally within their own *sphere of influence*. This book is written with you in mind. Being a leader is not necessarily related to a title that you hold. Leading through bias is for everyone in today's workplaces, regardless of whether you have just started your career or are a C-suite leader. Don't be put off by the word "leading" in the title of the book "leading through bias". You do not have to be a formal leader with reporting lines. As long as you have a sphere of influence (and everyone does), you are a leader with the ability to positively influence others within that sphere. Our hope is that this book will help you will feel empowered to navigate through the murkiness of bias, with the skills and tools needed to lead through bias, blocking its discriminatory impact and creating more inclusive organisations.

To clarify, this is not a book about "fixing the minority" or asking them to "lean in". This book is about stepping up to fix the system, about blocking biases where they occur, in words, processes and behaviours. "Fixing the system" can feel like it's someone else's responsibility. It isn't. Biased systems were created by humans and require humans to fix. We cannot hide behind the notion that "ignorance is bliss" or pretend that being a silent supporter is enough. In being oblivious or a bystander, we continue to allow bias and discrimination in our interactions and systems. Your organisation needs you to act inclusively. This book will help you do that. A leader who is inclusive is not just better at including others but will also move towards adopting leadership practices that are grounded in current leadership theories, which are increasingly process driven and about relationship building. The outcome for you is leadership reflexivity and flexibility, skills that are required for the 4th and 5th industrial revolution.

We would like you to view the journey of leading through bias as a marathon and not a sprint. This is not an easy journey; it will take time, and it will require you to step out of your comfort zone and into zones of discomfort that you might have avoided until now. Unlike many other transformational efforts, becoming an inclusive workplace requires all of us to do plenty of self-work to be inclusive to others.

We are both realistic optimists and firm believers that all organisations can become more inclusive. To get there, however, demands plenty of hard work from everyone. Not just some, but everyone. The best part of this journey is that when results start to show, then everyone stands to gain. Being inclusive is not just good for the underrepresented; it is good for us all.

We hope that the content in this book inspires you to take action and lead through bias, to make our workplaces more inclusive for generations to come.

Poornima Luthra
Sara Louise Muhr

Contents

1	**Introduction**	1
	1.1 Self-Reflection Exercise: My Sphere of Influence	6
2	**Leading With Conviction—Believing in the Purpose of DEI**	9
	2.1 Diversity	10
	Intersectionality	11
	Dimensions of Diversity	12
	What Is Adequate Representation?	16
	2.2 Inclusion	17
	Equity	21
	Privilege	22
	2.3 Finding Your Purpose	25
	Moving Beyond the "Business Case"	25
	What Are Quotas?	28
	Purpose of DEI	32
	Do You Have the Conviction to Convince Others?	36
	2.4 Embedding DEI Within the Strategy	36
	Self-Reflection Exercise: Ask Yourself and Your Colleagues These Questions:	37
	Self-Reflection Exercise: Identifying the Purpose of DEI—DEI's Purpose Statement	38
	Team-Activity: Articulating Your Why and Communicating It	39

3 Leading With Clarity (Part 1—Understanding the Basics of Bias and Identity Bias) — 49

- 3.1 We Are Not as Rational as We Would Like to Think We Are — 50
  - System 1 and System 2 Thinking — 51
  - Are All Biases Bad? — 53
- 3.2 Layers of Bias — 54
  - Individual, Collective, Interpersonal and Systemic Bias — 54
  - Explicit, Implicit and Unconscious Biases — 54
- 3.3 Expressions of Bias — 59
  - Prejudice, Stereotypes and Discrimination — 59
  - Overt and Subtle Biases: Microaggressions (Aka Termite Bias) — 59
  - Systemic Bias — 64
- 3.4 Identity-Related Cognitive Biases — 65
  - Surface Level Identity Bias — 68
  - Deep Level Identity Bias — 91

4 Leading With Clarity (Part 2: Situation-Related Cognitive Bias and the Impact of Bias) — 113

- 4.1 Situation-Related Cognitive Bias — 113
  - Intuition Bias — 114
  - Similarity Bias — 116
  - Focus Bias — 118
  - Expectation Bias — 119
  - Contrast Bias — 121
  - Proximity Bias — 122
  - Confirmation Bias — 122
- 4.2 The Impact of Bias on Organisations and Employees — 124
  - Employee Pay — 125
  - Employee Well-Being — 127

5 Leading With Accountability: Addressing Systemic Bias — 135

- 5.1 Moving Beyond Conviction and Clarity — 135
  - Limitations of Bias Awareness Training and the Myth of Meritocracy — 136
  - So, What Works? — 138
  - What Not To Do — 139
- 5.2 Blocking Bias in Systems and Processes Across the Entire Employee Life Cycle — 145

		Blocking Bias When Attracting Talent	146
		Blocking Bias When Recruiting and Selecting Talent	156
		Block Bias When Onboarding Talent	176
		Blocking Bias When Retaining and Developing Talent	179
		Blocking Bias When Separating	187
		Summary of Bias Blockers	188
	5.3	Blocking Bias Metrics	194
6	**Leading With Allyship: Moving Beyond Tolerance and Obligation**		**201**
	6.1	What Is Allyship?	202
	6.2	Phases of Allyship	203
		Self-Reflection: What Stage of Allyship Am I at?	204
	6.3	Moving From Passive to Active	205
	6.4	Foundations of Active Allyship	207
		Nurture Psychological Safety to Be Able to Have Honest and Open Conversations	207
		Be Aware of Your Privilege and Use It to Lift Others	209
	6.5	How Do I Become an Active Ally?	211
		Behaviours That Nurture an Inclusive Mindset	211
		Behaviours That Nurture Inclusive Interpersonal Interactions	222
		Behaviours That Nurture Inclusive Group Dynamics	231
		Behaviours That Nurture Inclusive Organisations	236
		Summary of Active Allyship Behaviours	243
	6.6	Celebrate Active Allyship	244
		Self-Reflection Exercise: My Allyship Journey Thus Far—Who Have I Been an Ally to?	245
		Self-Reflection Exercise: How Can I Be an Active Ally?	246
7	**Leading With Strength: Showing Vulnerability**		**251**
	7.1	Vulnerability, Authenticity and Strength	253
	7.2	Relational Leadership	255
		Self-Reflection Exercise: Extending My Sphere of Influence	258
	7.3	Stages of Developing Strength	259
		Identifying Fear	260
		Unlearning	262
		Learning	266
		Growth	267
	7.4	Engaging on the Tough Topics; Don't Hide From Them	276

8 Final Thoughts 281
   8.1   As an Individual, You Can: 282
   8.2   As a Team/Organisation, You Can: 283

Recommend Resources 285

Index 287

List of Figures

Image 1.1	Knowledge (K)—Attitude (A)—Behaviour (B) approach	4
Image 1.2	5 skills to lead through bias	5
Image 1.3	My sphere of influence	6
Image 2.1	15 dimensions of diversity	13
Image 2.2	My intersectional identity	18
Image 2.3	Belongingness—Uniqueness model (adapted from Shore et al., 2011)	20
Image 2.4	Understanding equity	22
Image 2.5	Sources of privilege	23
Image 2.6	Purpose of DEI from an equity lens	33
Image 3.1	System 1 and System 2 thinking	52
Image 3.2	Awareness—Control model of bias	55
Image 3.3	Prejudice—Stereotype—Discrimination	60
Image 3.4	Dimensions of diversity with corresponding biases	67
Image 3.5	The world represented in 100 people	78
Image 5.1	Employee life cycle	146
Image 6.1	15 dimensions of diversity	213
Image 7.1	Knowledge (K)—Attitude (A)—Behaviour (B) approach including vulnerability and strength	254
Image 7.2	Multi-directional leadership	257
Image 7.3	Extending my sphere of influence	259
Image 7.4	Stages of developing strength	260
Image 7.5	Bridging the gaps in my understanding	268
Image 7.6	Zones when setting objectives	271

1

Introduction

Bias is everywhere.

Bias is in us and in others; it is in our social relations, in our interactions with colleagues and in the structures, systems, policies, practices and processes of our organisations.

But what is bias?

Let's start with this basic truth: Everyone is biased. Yes, everyone. As long as you have a brain, you are biased. Bias is the brain's shortcut to thinking fast. Bias is the cognitive frames we use to help us make sense of the vast amount of information coming our way. It is the lenses through which we see and understand the world. Bias can be found in our individual thoughts, behaviours, decisions and interactions with others. Bias is embedded systemically in organisational practices and processes and in the technologies we use.

Bias is integral to thinking, but bias is also inherently discriminatory. For instance, it helps us decide between different options based on our past experiences or personal preferences, creating patterns of inclusion and exclusion. It is these patterns that have resulted in organisational cultures that are non-inclusive, leading to the inequity and discrimination that we witness and experience in our workplaces.

You may be wondering—how prevalent is bias and what is the impact of bias? According to Deloitte's 2019 state of inclusion survey of 3000 American professionals, 63% *witnessed* bias at least once a month, 61% *experienced* bias at least once a month and 83% categorise the biases they experienced in the workplace to be subtle and indirect.[1] What is important for us to bear

© The Author(s), under exclusive license to Springer Nature
Switzerland AG 2023
P. Luthra and S. L. Muhr, *Leading Through Bias*, Palgrave Executive Essentials,
https://doi.org/10.1007/978-3-031-38571-1_1

in mind is that this presence of bias can affect productivity, well-being and employee engagement: 84% of those surveyed said the biases had a negative impact on their happiness, confidence and well-being. A further 70% reported a negative impact on their engagement. We are sure that you would agree that no one should be made to feel that way at work. At the team and organisational levels, bias acts as a barrier, preventing teams and organisations from comprising of the best people, from making the best decisions, from being creative and innovative and from understanding customers' needs. All of this results in sub-optimal team and organisational performance.

To nurture inclusive workplace environments where all—let us emphasise, all—employees thrive, we need to make sincere efforts to become more aware of bias, and we must work hard to minimise the impact biases have on our organisations and the people working in them.

We need to block bias.

Now, the fact that you are reading this book tells us that you know that DEI is important to you and your organisation. A 2019 survey in the US, UK, France and Germany showed that 64% of the workers surveyed said their company was investing more in Diversity and Inclusion (D&I) than in prior years,[2] with many organisations committing to building a culture of inclusion where diverse employees thrive. When we look at the path organisations have taken to build a culture of inclusion, it often has four phases—(1) raising awareness, creating understanding and encouraging reflection, (2) developing a vision of inclusion, (3) rethinking key management concepts and principles and (4) adapting HR systems and processes.[3] While organisations today are making progress across these four phases, the journey is challenging. Why? Because there is still limited understanding of how we can minimise the influence of bias on our behaviours and decisions, as well as in systemic processes in our workplaces. Navigating—or as we like to call it, blocking—bias is not something that leaders have been taught how to do in universities, MBAs and executive training programs. This is new to many of us.

One thing is clear—*leading through bias* is key to being able to nurture equitable workplaces that are inclusive of diversity.

This book is your guide to leading through bias. It will address bias head on, recognising that we cannot eliminate bias as it is intricately woven into the way our human brain functions, but that we can make efforts to become more aware of our biases. Importantly, we can minimise the impact that our biases have on our organisations and the people working in them. By installing *bias blockers*, you become an inclusive leader, a key enabler of inclusion at work.

Where do biases show up? While there are many aspects of organisational life where bias is present, one of the key areas bias is embedded is in the employee life cycle—the journey of an employee from when they first come into contact with an organisation's job advertisement to when they leave the organisation. While it may seem like a mammoth task to block our biases and fix the system, this is what needs to be done. But how? We have both lost count of the number of times leaders have asked us exactly this.

This book will answer that question, providing you with the knowledge and tools you need to lead through bias. You will become aware of your biases and the biases around you. You will have the opportunity to reflect on your own biases and attitudes. You will be provided with concrete means of addressing systemic bias embedded throughout the employee life cycle as well as tools to address your own individual biases.

In today's business world, *inclusive leadership* is one of the newer leadership styles to join the many other leadership styles required in today's organisations—transformational, charismatic, servant, situational and humane, to name a few. Today, the societal context in which organisations are embedded is characterised by four major global mega-trends that are reshaping the environment and in turn influencing the priorities of businesses—diversity of markets, diversity of customers, diversity of ideas and diversity of talent.[4] In such a context, inclusive leadership is key. Yet, according to Korn Ferry, only 5% of all leaders are inclusive.[5]

In her book *How to Be an Inclusive Leader*,[6] Jennifer Brown notes that inclusive leaders "create a culture of belongingness where everyone can thrive in countless ways". To be able to do this, leaders need to know *how* to lead *through* bias. Addressing this and empowering leaders to lead effectively through bias are crucial to making much-needed progress in nurturing truly inclusive and equitable workplaces.

So, what does *leading through bias* entail?

Both of us have worked with hundreds of leaders and employees globally, and this book has been written based on our experience but also keeping the needs of those we have worked with in mind. In this book, we take a global human resource (HR) perspective that is grounded in the theoretical perspectives of social justice, particularly intersectionality and social identity theory, behavioural design and change, while adopting an equity lens throughout our work. Our aim? To provide you with the skills needed to nurture equitable workplaces that are inclusive for all.

Much of the literature out there focuses on addressing DEI from an American or British perspective. While the existing research, data and best practices serve an important purpose to highlight the challenges and solutions, they are focused on very narrow contexts, which means results and recommendations are often not transferrable to other settings. People of the world experience bias in different ways across different contexts. We also recognise that from a global perspective, there can be multiple realities that co-exist, and we recognise the challenge that poses to leaders today. Hence, we believe

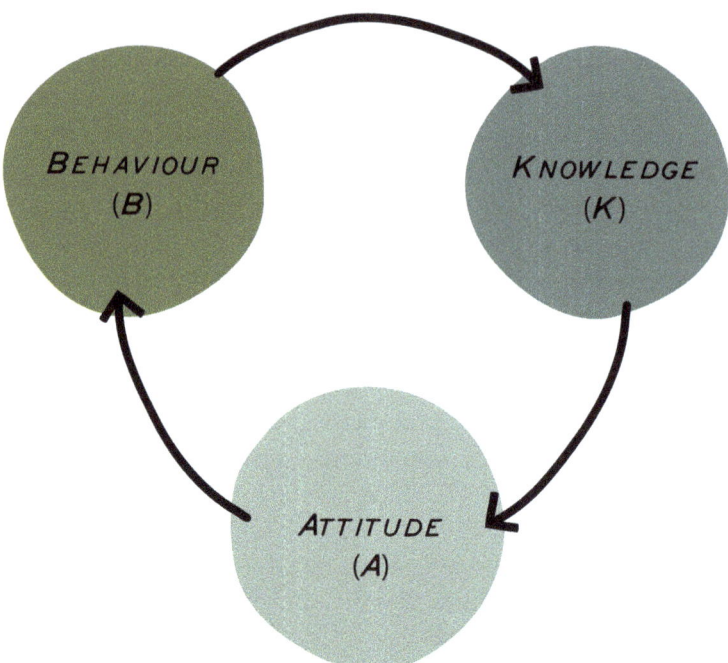

Image 1.1 Knowledge (K)—Attitude (A)—Behaviour (B) approach

that what leaders need is a practical understanding and application of DEI that considers global contexts. Our work is grounded in global research and evidence (recognising that it is sometimes hard to find credible research and data in certain contexts), while providing you with the practical skills and accompanying tools needed to lead through bias effectively, no matter where you are in the world.

With this in mind, we adopt a Knowledge-Attitude-Behaviour (KAB)[7] approach to enable the behavioural change needed to lead through bias (Image 1.1). Knowledge enables us to shift our attitudes towards others and enables us to rethink structures and systems, which in turn leads to changes in our behaviours. We believe that in order for behavioural change to happen, we need to have knowledge and the right attitude, deeply grounded in beliefs and values. With knowledge and deep reflection of our own attitudes and biases towards others, we are well prepared to act inclusively.

Leading through bias means leading with Conviction, Clarity, Accountability, Allyship and Strength (Image 1.2). Leading with conviction is about wholeheartedly believing in the purpose of diversity and inclusion, beginning from an evidence-based understanding and adopting an equity lens. Leading with clarity involves developing a deep understanding of biases while also reflecting on our own biases and the attitudes we hold towards others, learning how these impact our interactions and decisions. Leading

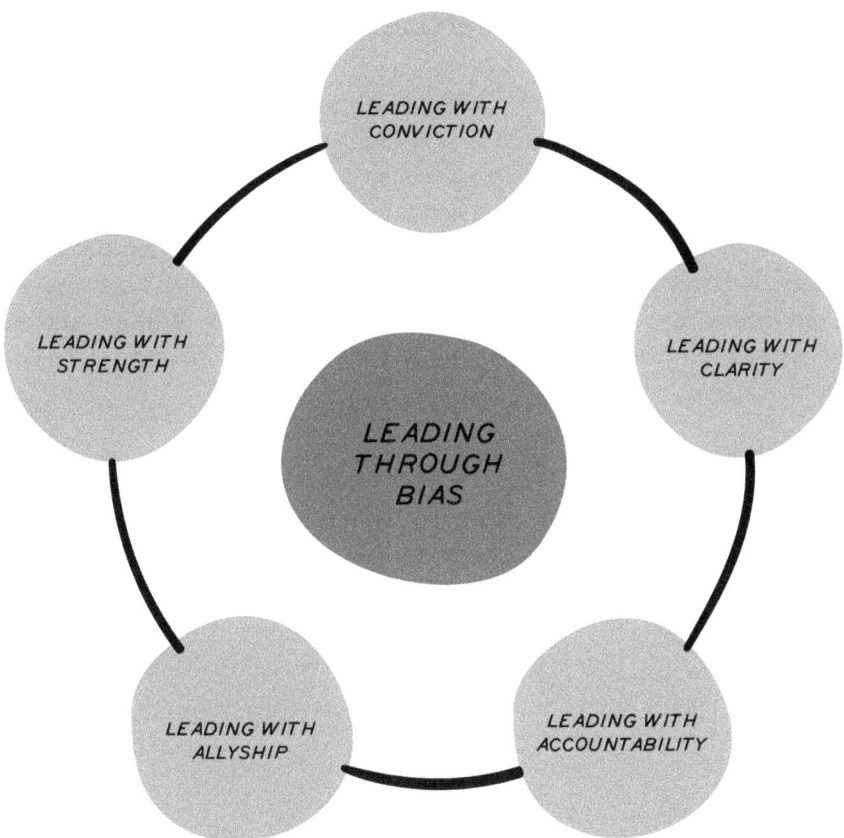

Image 1.2 5 skills to lead through bias

with accountability involves engaging in concrete bias blocking behaviours to address the bias embedded in the systems, structures, processes and policies of the organisation. Leading with allyship is about blocking bias in our behaviours as we interact with others. Finally, leading with strength is about showing vulnerability and persevering with a spirit of learning and growth. These 5 skills move from building knowledge of our attitudes/biases to learning strategies that cover all three aspects of the KAB (Knowledge-Attitude-Behaviour) model of change.

Each of these 5 skills leads to the next in a spirit of continuous improvement. In this book, we develop each of the skills, drawing on research and best practices while engaging you, the reader, in self-reflection exercises and real-life experiences to allow for reflection and even discussion in workshops and classroom settings.

So, are you ready to lead through bias? Let's begin with leading through conviction.

1.1 Self-Reflection Exercise: My Sphere of Influence

Everyone has a sphere of influence, people that we can positively influence to be inclusive. Write down all the people or groups of people within your sphere of influence at work (Image 1.3). They can be your peer-level colleagues, your managers and leaders, people who report to you, broader employees in your organisation and even stakeholders outside the organisation. Knowing who we can influence is a crucial first step to lead through bias. Without knowing who we can influence, our efforts will be unfocused, limiting their impact.

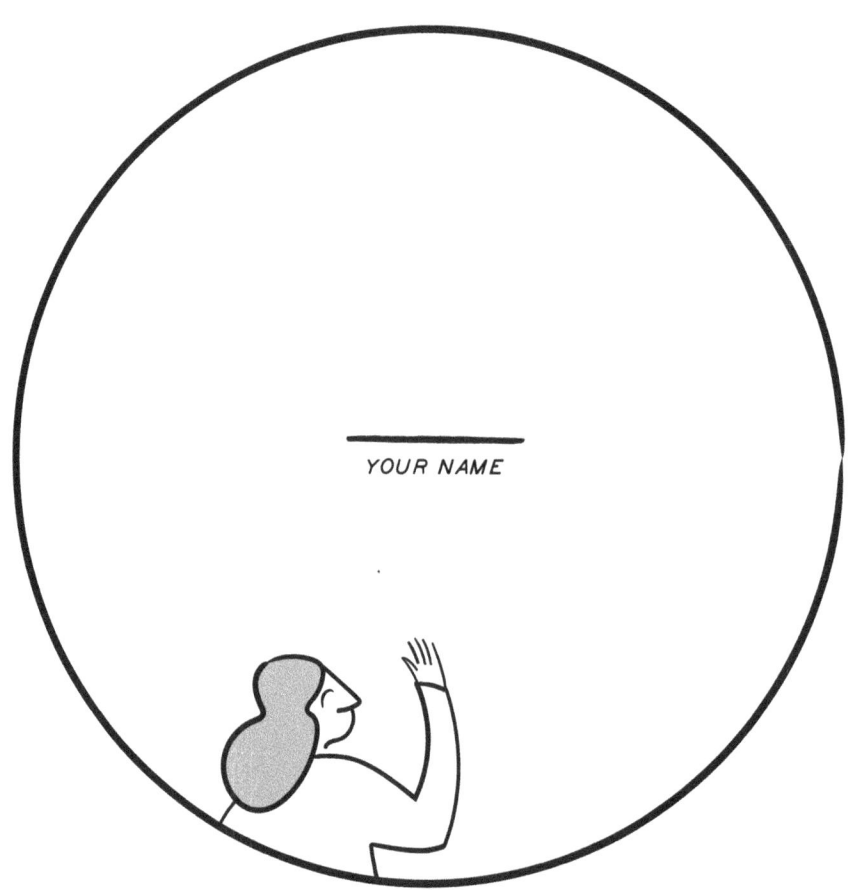

Image 1.3 My sphere of influence

Notes

1. https://www2.deloitte.com/us/en/pages/about-deloitte/articles/inclusion-insights.html.
2. https://www.glassdoor.com/research.
3. Pless, N., & Maak, T. (2004). Building an Inclusive Diversity Culture: Principles, Processes and Practice. *Journal of Business Ethics*, 54, 129–147.
4. https://www2.deloitte.com/us/en/insights/topics/talent/six-signature-traits-of-inclusive-leadership.html.
5. https://www.kornferry.com/capabilities/leadership-professional-development/leadership/inclusive-leaders.
6. Brown, J. (2019). *How to be an Inclusive Leader: Your Role in Creating Cultures of Belonging where Everyone can Thrive*. Berrett-Koehler Publishers.
7. Schrader, P. G., & Lawless, K. (2004). The Knowledge, Attitudes, & Behaviors Approach. How to Evaluate Performance and Learning in Complex Environments. *Performance Improvement,, 43*(9), 8–15.

2

Leading With Conviction—Believing in the Purpose of DEI

Leading through bias requires you to believe wholeheartedly in the purpose of Diversity, Equity and Inclusion (DEI). It requires you to lead with conviction. Leading with conviction is not about political correctness, trying to be "woke"[1] or "keeping up" with the latest business trends that everyone else is following.

Leading with conviction means being convinced that (1) inequity and inequality exist, and that they need to be addressed, (2) being more inclusive and equitable is the right thing to do, and finally, (3) your organisation will be better because of it. Do you have that conviction? If yes, great. Then, this chapter will reaffirm your conviction and provide you with the tools to convince others too. If you are not quite there yet, you may be wondering, how do I build this conviction? You know that DEI is important and adds value, but you might be wondering if that is always the case or if there are any conditions; you may need more evidence before you can wholeheartedly believe in the purpose of DEI. If this is the case, this chapter will help you build conviction through a thorough and detailed analysis of research, which demonstrates the necessity of an organisation-wide DEI strategy.

Here is the thing, to lead through conviction in a way that creates conviction in others, leaders must move beyond regarding DEI as "nice to have", viewing DEI as a separate initiative that is an "add on" to the organisation's strategy or considering DEI as something that can be deprioritised, defunded or delegated to HR in times of economic crisis. Leading through conviction is knowing that DEI is a necessary strategic action and priority. As this chapter will make clear, having a DEI strategy and being able to realise it in a way

© The Author(s), under exclusive license to Springer Nature
Switzerland AG 2023
P. Luthra and S. L. Muhr, *Leading Through Bias*, Palgrave Executive Essentials,
https://doi.org/10.1007/978-3-031-38571-1_2

that results in an inclusive and equitable culture are paramount for business success—also in times of crisis. A study of the recession of 2007 to 2009 showed that companies with inclusive workplaces outperformed companies where employees lacked inclusivity by nearly four times.[2] Furthermore, the DEI strategy should not only be permanent, it should also be pervasive, since leaders who continue to view DEI through the lens of "nice to have" will find it challenging to attract and retain both talent and customers, and retain a positive brand image.[3] All in all, DEI is important for employer branding,[4] organisational performance as well as brand image. There is a purpose to DEI—understanding it and believing in that purpose are crucial. However, before we delve further into this purpose, let us define the terms Diversity—Equity—Inclusion.

2.1 Diversity

Diversity refers to our differences and is the deliberate practice of bringing together people with a range of different identities as, for instance, stemming from their social and ethnic backgrounds. Diversity is based on the understanding that each person is unique and the recognition that people have differences across a range of intersectional or interrelated human qualities or dimensions. The meaning of diversity is often illustrated as an iceberg, comprising of surface level dimensions and deep level dimensions. Surface level dimensions of diversity are those that are usually visible and include, but are not limited to, gender, race, ethnicity, age, body size and visible disabilities. Deep level dimensions of diversity are those that are often invisible and include, but are not limited to, thinking styles, perspectives, experiences, sexual orientation, values and beliefs. It is not always easy to identify which dimensions are visible and which are invisible, and some dimensions can be both or can be considered visible in some contexts but not others.

In organisations, diversity is about embracing the differences that exist as the sum of the various identities that members bring into the organisation. Fostering diversity implies creating an environment where differences thrive, rather than expecting employees to conform to pre-established dominant norms. In organisations today, gender and ethnicity are typically the predominant focus points or, we might say, diversity dimensions. While gender and ethnicity are certainly extremely important dimensions, and we need to continue the work being done in these areas, the diversity of human beings also includes age, physical abilities, health, physical appearance and personalities, our educational backgrounds, skills, ways of working, learning and thinking, our sexual orientation, beliefs and values, socio-economic backgrounds, where we live, and the choices we make about marriage and parenthood. Gender and ethnicity don't exist in isolation, they interact with each other and with all the other dimensions of diversity. Adopting a narrow focus involves the risk of over-simplification, which means only limited progress can be made. Understanding the interactions—or intersections—of all these dimensions is necessary if we are to embrace diversity in its broadest sense. And it is crucial to our understanding of bias.

Intersectionality

The term intersectionality was coined by Professor Kimberlé Crenshaw in a 1989 academic paper[5] to describe how race, class, gender and other individual characteristics "intersect" with one another and overlap, creating multiple levels of social justice issues. The term intersectionality made it into the Oxford English Dictionary in 2015 and gained widespread attention during the 2017 Women's March. As defined by Crenshaw, intersectionality as a noun is "an analytical framework for understanding how aspects of a person's social and political identities combine to create different modes of discrimination and privilege".[6]

As a theoretical approach, intersectionality is a lens through which the construct of exclusion is studied. This theory emphasises the importance of adopting a multidimensional or intersectional view of diversity to truly understand how social inequity and inequality, oppression and discrimination interact with each other. Each one of us has an identity that is made up of multiple dimensions—gender, sexual orientation, age, physical abilities, appearances, educational background, professional or personal experiences, personality, neurodiversity, race and ethnicity, culture, beliefs, marital and parenthood choices, and socio-economic background.[7] Combined, these dimensions form our unique diversity thumbprint; who we are and are perceived to be. What is crucial to remember is that these dimensions of diversity do not exist in isolation; they intersect with each other to form the complex weave of diversity which is unique to each person. That is, we cannot just line up the various differences that people bring to organisations but must consider how each individual is shaped by their unique combination of dimensions and, crucially, the specific intersection of those dimensions. Gender bias is, for example, experienced differently by a female, White, homosexual engineer compared to a female, Southeast Asian and heterosexual HR business partner. Gender intersects with and is influenced by the other dimensions of diversity. Dimensions of diversity are not just added to each other. In embracing diversity and nurturing inclusive workplaces, we must recognise this intersectionality. We experience the workplace through our own and others' intersectional diversity thumbprints, not through any individual dimension.

This theoretical lens challenges the view that social injustice issues can be broken down into separate issues that affect individual identities. Such a "single-axis" framework creates silos in which bias and discrimination are viewed from narrow lenses such as race, age or gender, and does not provide a sufficiently deep understanding into the complexity of bias as related to intersectional diversity thumbprints.[8]

This intersectional lens enables us to understand that each person's experiences of bias are unique, arising from multiple and complex identities that interact with each other.[9] For instance, a study of gender and race among engineering students showed that the influence of gender on learning outcomes was also influenced by race.[10] In the study, Black women rated themselves significantly lower than White women on three learning outcomes of design, contextual competence and communication skills. This contrasted with White and Black men where there was no statistical difference. The study concluded that the interplay between gender and race had a significant impact on the outcome and would not have been picked out if only one identity dimension had been studied on its own.

In her pivotal 1989 piece, Crenshaw writes: "Because the intersectional experience is greater than the sum of racism and sexism, any analysis that does not take intersectionality into account cannot sufficiently address the particular manner in which Black women are subordinated".[11] While Crenshaw's work centred around Black women, the term intersectionality has had a significant impact on our understanding of the interplay between the many different dimensions that interact and impact our experiences of bias and discrimination in complex ways. The intersectionality perspective is built on the premise that bias and discrimination are never the result of a single, distinct factor. Without an appreciation and understanding of this intersectionality, DEI efforts often adopt a simplistic view that does not move us beyond specific initiatives to include certain groups. In doing so, we risk simplifying individual members of those groups to a certain identity or limited set of dimensions in an effort to include them.

Dimensions of Diversity

The visible (or surface level) and invisible (or deep level) dimensions of diversity can be divided into three categories: (1) physical and physiological, (2) cognitive and (3) social and lifestyle.[12] Our diversity thumbprint comprises the various dimensions of diversity that intersect to form our identity. We explain each of these dimensions below (Image 2.1).

Physical and Physiological Dimensions of Diversity:

- *Gender*
  Gender is a social construct referring to a person's gender identity, that is whether we identify as a man or woman or with another gender, such as non-binary, transgender, gender-fluid, agender, pangender, gender queer or third gender. Gender is different from sex (male, female and intersex[13])—the latter being biologically defined and assigned by birth.

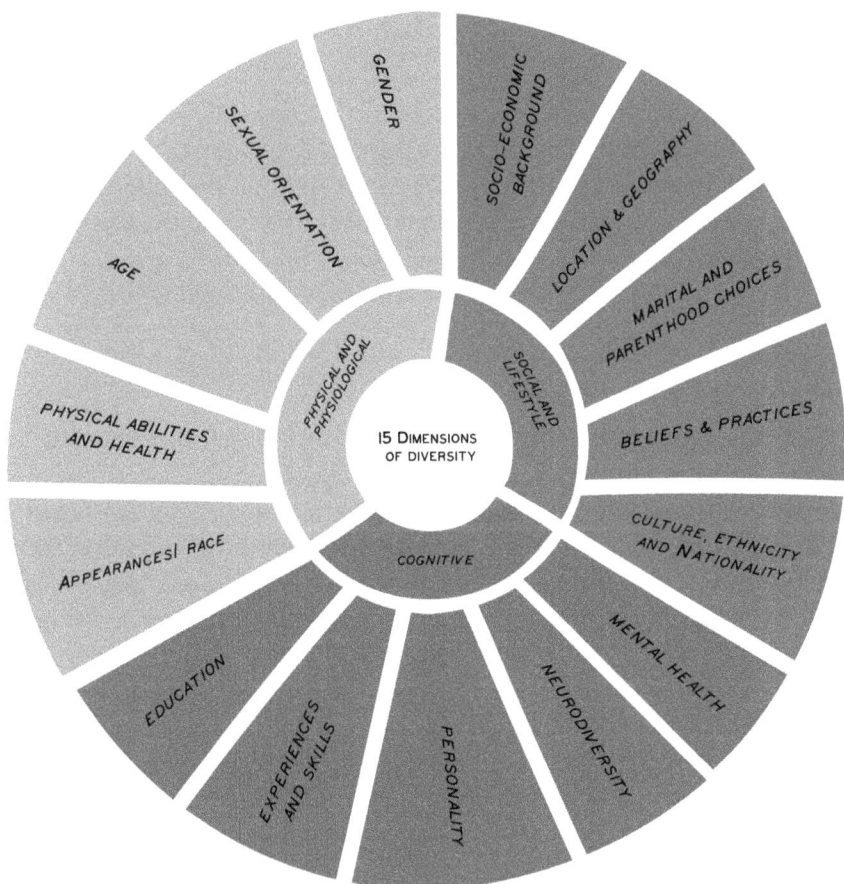

Image 2.1 15 dimensions of diversity

Our gender and sex are not always aligned, and thus, we make use of the term gender in this book, which refers to gender identity rather than the sex assigned at birth.

- *Sexual Orientation*
  Sexual orientation includes being straight, gay, lesbian, bisexual or any of the other sexual orientations. LGBTQ+ refers to Lesbian, Gay, Bisexual, Transgender/Transsexual, Queer while the plus refers to additional sexual orientations and gender identities including, among others, pansexual, intersex and asexual. Not all the letters in the acronym refer to sexual orientations—transgender is, for example, a gender identity not a sexual orientation. Still, the social movement for LGBTQ+ rights was formed by people with similar aspirations of critiquing the binary perceptions of gender, attraction, identity and presentation.

- *Age*
  Age is a dimension we all have a direct and explicit experience with. After all, we were all young once and we all age. A generation is made up of people born over a 15- to 20-year period, and our workplaces comprise multiple generations, co-existing simultaneously—currently, these include Baby Boomers, Generation X, Generation Y/Millennials and Generation Z. Each generation brings with them a set of work-related values, priorities and needs.

- *Physical Abilities and Health*
  Physical abilities and health refer to visible and invisible disabilities as well as the health challenges that people face. These health challenges can be related to (among others) fertility, pregnancy and menopause, and modern chronic diseases include (among others) cancer, heart diseases and diabetes, and hypertension. Also, 15% of the world's population—that is over a billion people—live with a disability, making this the largest "minority group".[14]

- *Appearance/Race*
  Appearance refers to how we look—our hair, weight and height—how attractive we are, how we choose to dress and, for example, if we have tattoos or piercings or not. Race is a social construct, but refers to our biological, physical traits (skin colour, facial features and even hair texture) that are deemed socially significant to categorise people.

Cognitive Dimensions of Diversity:

- *Education*
  While education may be a fundamental human right, access to and quality of education vary significantly across the world and across gender identities.

- *Experiences and Skills*
  This refers to the competencies that we each bring with us into the organisation, whether because of formal training or by way of the "school of life".

- *Personality*
  Everyone has a personality—characteristics that define how we think, feel and behave, some of which are genetic and others environmental—and our personalities are all different. No two people—even identical twins[15]—have the same personality. Our personality influences how we view and experience the world. It shapes the actions we take and affects how we interact with others.

- *Neurodiversity*
  Neurodiversity refers to the infinite variety of cognitive styles of thinking and learning that arises because each of our brains is unique. The term neurodiversity itself was only developed in 1998 and is an umbrella term that is often used to refer to people who have dyslexia, dyspraxia, autism, Asperger's and attention deficit hyperactivity disorder (ADHD). More broadly, neurodiversity refers to alternative thinking styles in which the brain may function, process and learn information in a different way from someone who is neurotypical.

- *Mental Health*
  Mental health refers to our emotional, psychological and social well-being. Mental health influences how we think, feel and act. It also helps determine how we manage stress, relate to others and make choices.

Social and Lifestyle Dimensions of Diversity:

- *Nationality, Ethnicity and Culture*
  Ethnicity, nationality and culture are terms that are very closely related to each other. Nationality is a legal construct and refers to our citizenship or relationship with the political state(s) we belong to. Ethnicity comprises

our culture, heritage, language, traditions and values. Culture is made up of artefacts, values and assumptions, and forms an integral part of ethnicity.

- *Beliefs and Practices*
  We all have beliefs, and our beliefs differ. Beliefs are the mental representations of the ways in which our brains expect things in our environment to behave and how we think things should be related to each other—the patterns that the brain expects the world to conform to. Our beliefs include religious beliefs but are not limited to these. Our beliefs in turn influence our practices—what we choose to wear, eat and drink, for example.

- *Marital and Parenthood Choices*
  We see many possibilities when it comes to relationships, marriage and parenthood. There are those who are married, others who are divorced, some who are in partnerships and yet others who are single out of choice or circumstance. Some are in heterosexual relationships while others form homosexual partnerships—married or unmarried. Some choose to have children with a partner or spouse—or on their own—while others can't have, don't have or don't want to have children. Some make use of donors to have children, and some have adopted or are planning to adopt a child.

- *Location/Geography*
  This dimension refers to where we live and have lived, and the decisions we make that are influenced by location or geography.

- *Socio-Economic background*
  Our societies are made up of people who come from different socio-economic backgrounds. Socio-economic background is influenced by, among other things, class, caste, family wealth, status, income and the neighbourhood you live in, but their meaning and importance vary across contexts. Our socio-economic background has a significant impact on the educational and career opportunities available to us.

What Is Adequate Representation?

One question we often get asked is: How do we know if we are diverse enough? This is a really tricky question to answer because adequate representation varies depending on who you ask. As much as we would like to think that it is objective and measurable, it is subjective and reflects social perceptions. In an article titled "Diversity is in the eye of the beholder", the authors found that racial minorities need to see diverse representation across hierarchical levels (i.e. people of colour at entry level, middle management, and leadership levels) before they consider an organisation to be diverse, whereas White Americans seem to think an organisation is sufficiently diverse when it has representation of racial minorities, regardless of where those people are placed within the organisational hierarchy (i.e. people of colour could be exclusively in entry-level positions and White people would still see the organisation as diverse).[16]

In another study, the findings show us that our view of whether an organisation is diverse or not depends on whether the groups we belong to are represented. In the study, Black students see a group composed of two White students and two Black students as more diverse than a group composed of two White students and two Asian students. Similarly, Asian students see a group composed of two White students and two Asian students as more diverse than a group composed of two White and two Black students.[17]

As demographics are continuously evolving, being adequately diverse is not a state to be reached but is a constant work in progress that has to be negotiated and co-constructed with organisational members. Organisations should strive to be representative of the communities in which they operate and the customers that they serve, not just across some dimensions but across multiple intersectional identities.

Self-Reflection Exercise: My Intersectional Identity

Refer back to the various dimensions of diversity we have looked at in this chapter. If you were asked the following question: Who are you as a unique individual, how would you describe yourself across as many of these fifteen dimensions as possible? Next, pick the 5 dimensions, which would best describe who you are as a unique individual. Use the illustration of a hand to guide you (Image 2.2). Write your name in the palm of the hand and the dimensions in the fingers.

2.2 Inclusion

Inclusion is a culture, an environment, where everyone is able to bring their whole unique self, feel respected and appreciated as valuable members, where their voice is heard, and where they feel a sense of belonging. Unlike diversity, inclusion is more nebulous. Still, inclusion is a critical component of a healthy organisation and goes beyond being compliant with non-discrimination legislation and organisation policy. This compliance is necessary and lays the foundation, but inclusion is so much more.

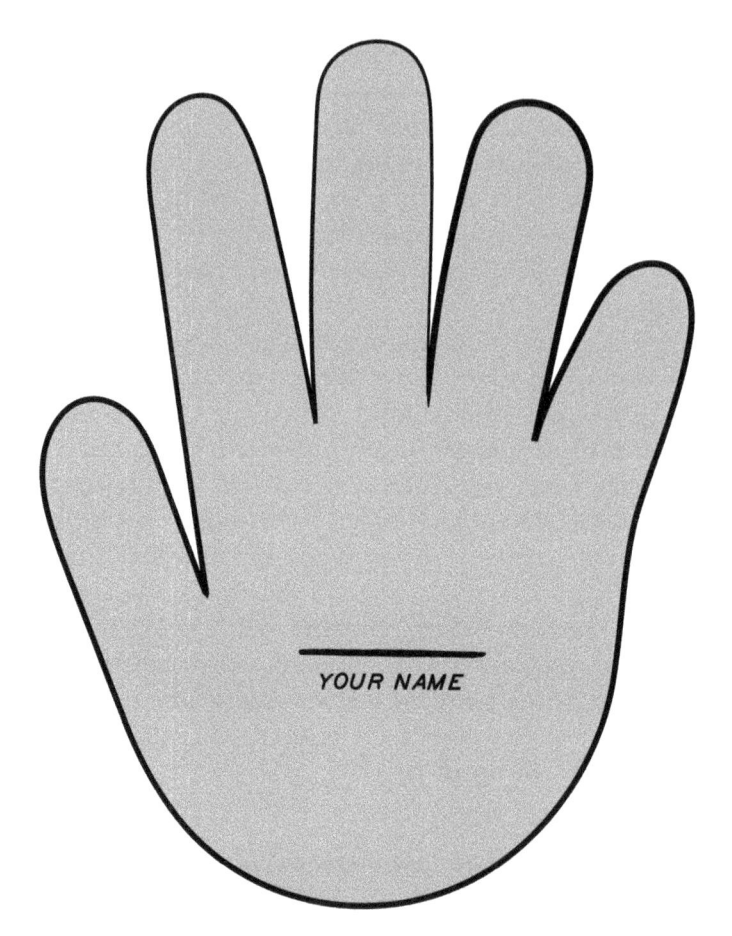

Image 2.2 My intersectional identity

Here is the thing, diversity alone is insufficient to gaining positive outcomes for employees, teams or the organisation. In fact, diversity can result in social divisions and intra-group conflict that can reduce group performance.[18] Simply bringing together a group of individuals with diverse identities is not enough. In such an environment, absenteeism, turnover, stress and emotional exhaustion can be elevated.[19] According to Mor Barak,[20] who has developed the Conceptual Model for Climate of Inclusion Multiculturalism, a climate of inclusion moderates the effect of diversity characteristics (both visible and invisible diversity) on whether the outcomes are beneficial or detrimental to the organisation and society. So, it is the culture of inclusion in the team or organisation that makes all the difference. Organisations with a climate of inclusion, accompanied by multicultural and diversity management policies, benefit from improved job satisfaction, satisfaction with co-workers, organisational commitment and retention. At the same time, society benefits from increased engagement in civic activities, economic and social involvement, and contribution to the wider society.

Inclusion is made up of emotions and feelings from our lived experiences when interacting with others. We feel inclusion, and our interactions with others are the vehicle through which we experience inclusion. Our answers to questions in employee engagement surveys like "Do you feel included?" or "Do you feel like you belong?" are highly subjective. The very same environment can be experienced very differently by two different people. Our perceptions of inclusion are influenced by the lens through which we experience it. This lens comprises who we are, our life experiences and the social conditioning we have had. So, while diversity comprises facts, inclusion comprises feelings and while diversity targets can be set, inclusion requires a cultural transformation towards an environment where everyone feels like they belong, are respected and valued. Being inclusive is a choice that organisations and individuals need to actively make.

Inclusion is, however, not "real" without diversity. Put differently, it is very easy to foster a culture of inclusion among people who are all alike. This is one of the greatest pitfalls of inclusion that we encounter in our work with organisations—leaders, who think they are inclusive, but then realise that they are only inclusive to people who are like themselves.

This has been brilliantly captured by Lynn M. Shore and her colleagues from San Diego State University.[21] In the model (Image 2.3), which is inspired by their work, they operate with two axes: feeling of belongingness and value of uniqueness. When an organisation doesn't value uniqueness and individuals don't feel belongingness, there is exclusion. We can probably very quickly agree on the fact that this is not where organisations should be.

However, many leaders think they are practising inclusion in the next two scenarios: assimilation and differentiation. The most tricky one is when feeling of belongingness is high and value of uniqueness is low. This state might mislead us to think that the organisation is inclusive. But this is assimilation, where people who can adapt and hide their uniqueness in order to conform to dominant norms end up belonging to the culture. On the other hand, people who are different from the dominant groups are not valued for their uniqueness and don't "fit" in. They either leave or their employment is terminated. Assimilation is not inclusion, but a sort of pseudo-inclusion, which often happens in situations where inclusion is not a strategic priority. In such situations, only those who fit in or are able to adjust thrive. In such pseudo-inclusion environments, the organisation does not enjoy the benefits of diversity.

	HIGH VALUE OF UNIQUENESS	LOW VALUE OF UNIQUENESS
LOW BELONGINGNESS	DIFFERENTIATION	EXCLUSION
HIGH BELONGINGNESS	INCLUSION	ASSIMILATION

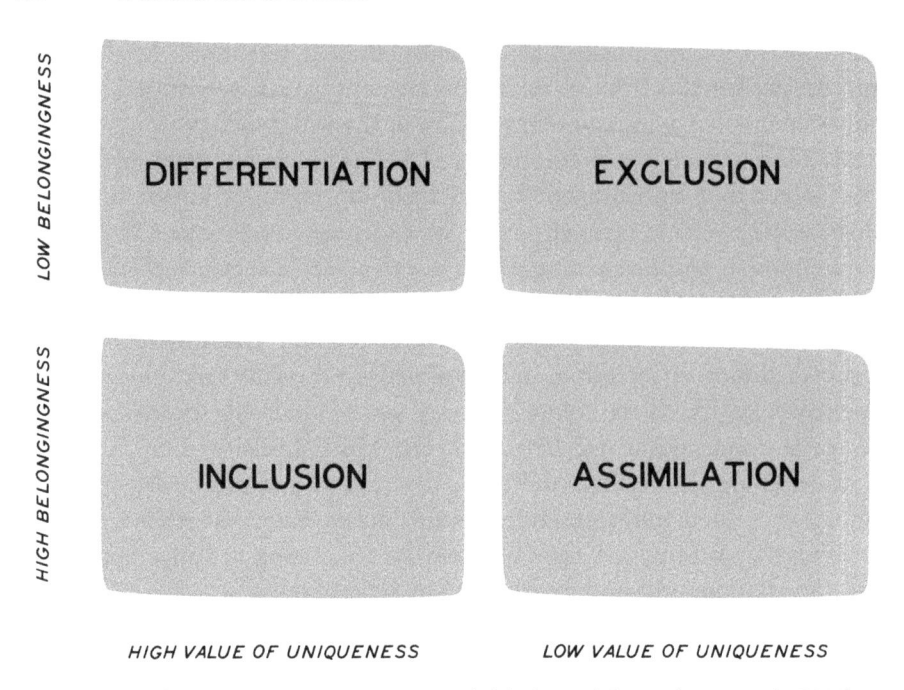

Image 2.3 Belongingness—Uniqueness model (adapted from Shore et al., 2011)

The other scenario is differentiation. This is seen in organisations with explicit diversity policies, but where there is little effort on inclusion. This is where leaders might be good at hiring diverse employees but are not good at making the diverse mix work well together. In such situations, people might feel valued for their uniqueness, but they don't feel a sense of belonging to the wider organisational culture, and therefore, subcultures are formed. This can be seen in the way that both work groups stick to themselves and how people segregate during lunch, at meetings or at organisational gatherings. Again, this is an instance of pseudo-inclusion, where many leaders might think that they excel in diversity and inclusion, but what they in fact have managed to produce is a lot of different sub-groups, who might feel belongingness to their own groups, but not across the sub-groups or as an organisation.

Real inclusion happens when you manage to create a feeling of belongingness across different groups, so that people can feel valued for their uniqueness while belonging to a whole—your organisation. This underpins this book. It is the essence of creating value from your DEI strategy—creating a sense of belonging as well as valuing uniqueness. We have on purpose placed inclusion in the lower left corner. Inclusion should not be thought of as a higher or evolved stage reached by progressive thinking, but rather a stage of blocking and unlearning our biased practices that we have learned and normalised through years of socialisation. This should make us question what we consider to be "normal" and "natural". If we are to unlearn practices and block biases to nurture inclusion, we have to understand that certain dynamics and characteristics that we might have seen as "natural" (such as women's assumed "natural" nurturing competencies or men's "natural" leadership abilities) are in fact not natural, but rather things that we have been socially conditioned to see as "normal". We must question such normalisation and unlearn to become more inclusive.

Equity

Now, what about the E that we find between D and I? E stands for equity. When working with and for equity, the starting point is recognition of the existence of individual, collective and systemic bias in society and in our workplaces. That is, we do not have equity, as organisational environments favour some groups and not others, but that is why we should make efforts to block such favouritism and fight discriminatory biases by providing tools, opportunities and support to employees from underrepresented, marginalised and disfavoured groups. The aim is to level the playing field. The world around us—even at work—is not experienced in the same way by everyone. Sometimes, equity appears to be "taking away" from the well-represented to give to the underrepresented, but if DEI is done right, there will be space for everyone—in a more equitable way. After all, we are not talking about a pizza or a pie, where giving one person a slice means less for others.

Equity is sometimes confused with equality. Both equity and equality are enablers of fairness. But even though they sound similar and operate in the same space, they are different. Equality focuses on providing everyone with the same tools, opportunities and support, and does not take into account individual, collective and systemic bias that results in different life and workplace experiences. Equity, then, is about fairness in outcomes as well as in starting points.

What about justice? Justice reflects a world free from bias where everyone would have fair and equal experiences, and therefore equal access to tools, opportunities and support. We don't live in a just world, just yet. Based on the reports from the World Economic Forum and UN, it is likely going to be a while—132 to 300 years from now—before we even achieve gender parity, let alone a just world. So, for now, a realistic goal is to address the organisational inequity, hoping to create more just workplaces (Image 2.4).

Image 2.4 Understanding equity

Privilege

A section on equity would not be complete without talking about privilege. Hearing the word "privilege" is enough to make many feel uncomfortable. Recognising one's privilege can be painful, as it is about recognising (dis)advantages we have because of who we are, what we have and our life experiences. But what is privilege? When recognising organisational inequity, we also recognise that some people have more advantages than others. These advantages constitute our privilege. Privilege comes from all the things we don't need to worry about or consider when making choices or decisions. When we are privileged, we might assume that something isn't a problem or an issue because it isn't a problem for us. Privilege exists when we benefit from structures and systems that we may not have built ourselves, but that favour us and not others. Thus, privilege comes from many different places and is also about that which we have (or don't have) through no effort (or fault) of our own. Having privilege is, therefore, not always our making, as such, and should, therefore, not be connected to guilt and shame. Quite the contrary, realising one's privilege and how to use it to lift others can be an extremely powerful DEI action (which we will return to in Chapter 6). Instead of feeling

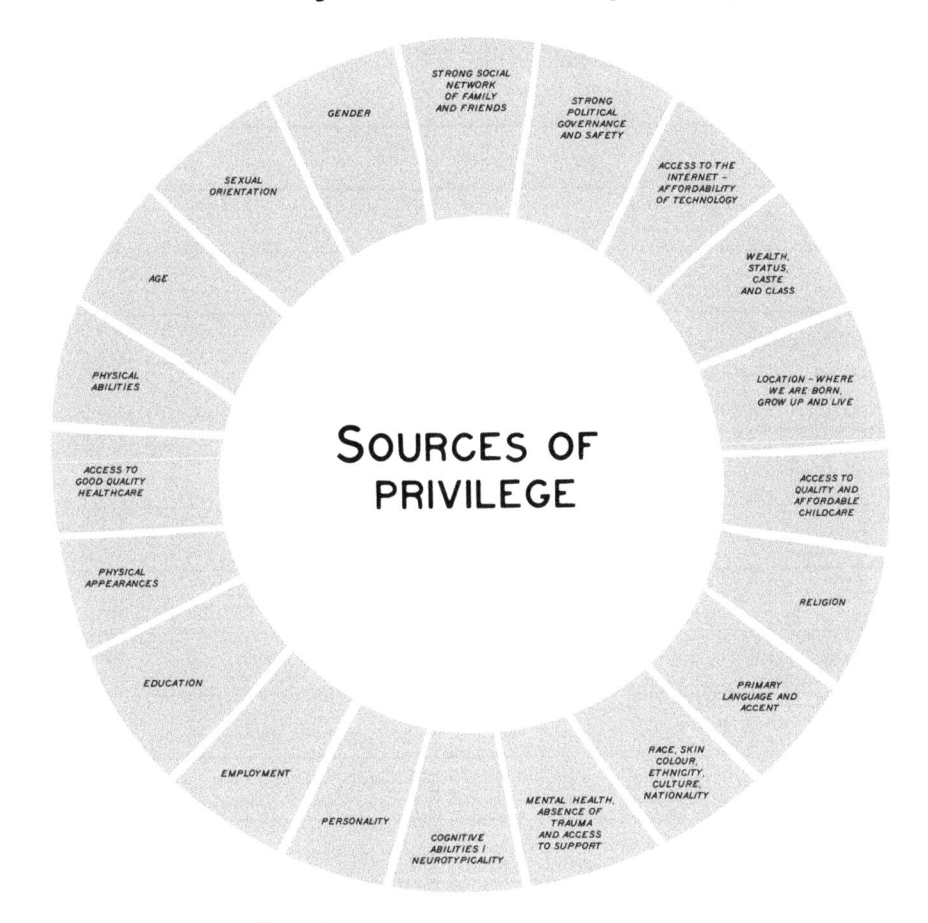

Image 2.5 Sources of privilege

shameful about your privilege, try to identify how you can use it to further inclusion for others (Image 2.5).

Self-Reflection Exercise: Where Does My Privilege Lie?

With reference to the image on the sources of privilege, reflect on where your privilege lies. Select 5 of the main sources of your privilege—what are those aspects from the image that you have had little to do with but that have given you an advantage. Ask yourself where this privilege comes from—it could be because of the opportunities you have had, your family, environment, structures and systems that favour you, and so on. Reflect deeply. Then think about how you can harness your privilege and list 3 concrete ways in which you can lift others at work who are less privileged than you.

The 5 main sources of privilege for me are:

1._____

2._____

3._____

4._____

5._____

Where does my privilege come from?

_____

_____

_____

_____

_____

_____

_____

_____

3 concrete ways in which I can lift others who are less privileged that I am:

1._____

2._____

3._____

2.3 Finding Your Purpose

Moving Beyond the "Business Case"

The "business case" for DEI has been well researched and well established. There are plenty of studies that show us that there is a positive impact on business performance of engaging in DEI. In fact, according to Korn Ferry, 87% of the most admired companies see a positive impact of diversity and inclusion on their business performance,[22] with diverse and inclusive organisations being 70% more likely to capture new markets.[23] A 2020 global McKinsey study of more than 1,000 companies in 15 countries found that organisations in the top quartile of gender diversity were 25% more likely to perform better than average on profitability (measured through average EBIT margins) if they had gender-diverse executive teams. The percentage rose to 28% if the organisation had gender-diverse boards. Organisations in the top quartile for ethnic/cultural diversity among executives were 36% more likely to achieve above-average profitability. At the other end of the spectrum, companies in the bottom quartile for both gender and ethnic/cultural diversity were 27% *less* likely to experience profitability above the industry average.[23]

Similarly, a Boston Consulting Group (BCG) study shows that companies with more diverse management teams have 19% higher revenues due to innovation.[25] Another study conducted by BCG in 2017[26] found that diversity among leaders in terms of gender, nationality, career path and industry background is closely linked to innovation. This report also showed that over a three-year period, companies with more diversity in management earned on average 38% more from their innovative products and service than companies with lowest diversity. Credit Suisse Research Institute found that companies in which women held 20% or more of management roles generated 2.04% higher cash flow returns on investment than companies with 15% or less women in management roles.[27] Bloomberg reports that companies with gender-balanced teams have a higher return on equity, and large UK firms whose executive boards were one-third female were 10 times more profitable on average than companies with all-male boards.[28] Many other studies show similar benefits from having diverse talent, improved financial performance in gross and net margins, internal rate of return, investment performance, market value, operating profit margin, Return on Assets (ROA), Return on Equity (ROE), Return on Sales (ROS) and sales performance.[29]

Organisations that embrace DEI are also better able to meet their Environment, Social and Governance (ESG) requirements. Women board directors are also more likely than men to identify social issues like human rights, climate change and income inequality as critical to corporate strategy.[30] At the same time, having women on boards has been shown to result in fewer financial reporting mistakes,[31] and it reduces controversial business practices such as fraud and earnings manipulation[32] and leads to fewer operations-related lawsuits.[33] Gender-diverse boards are also seen to adopt more progressive organisational management practices, such as work-life support programs, and to increase employee satisfaction.[34] Adding women to a board is also seen to improve investment efficiency and prevent risky over-investment decisions[35] as well as to reduce the over-confidence of male CEOs.[36]

The research to date has been focused on assessing the financial impact of gender and (to some extent) ethnic diversity—dimensions that can easily be tracked and measured. However, many other dimensions of diversity are also linked to improved financial performance. A Credit Suisse study from 2016 found that LGBT-led companies had outperformed the other index companies by 3% annually since 2010,[37] and a 2018 study by Accenture found that businesses that actively seek to employ people with disabilities had revenues that were 28% higher, their net income was two times more and profit margins were 30% higher than those that do not.[38] Similarly, research suggests that some groups of neurodivergent employees are 90% to 140% more productive than their neurotypical colleagues because of their increased ability to focus on certain tasks and their ability to concentrate for an extended period of time.[39] Companies across various industries in India have seen that employing people with disabilities makes sound business sense given the lower attrition rates, higher productivity in addition to lower absenteeism that stems from the loyalty that people with disabilities have towards organisations that give them opportunities for employment that are otherwise difficult to find.[40]

Sidestepping all these numbers, the claim has been made that companies do not need a "business case" for DEI—it is, after all, the right thing to do, and doing the right thing should not depend on a business case. Also, if the business case was indeed, so compelling, it is surprising that so many companies reduce or eliminate DEI efforts during difficult times. So, where does the problem with the business case lie?

To date, the emphasis on the business case, stemming from studies like those cited above, has resulted in an increased focus on the diversity or differences in employees, with the assumption that someone "diverse" can bring something specifically different to add to the business. There is, however, a risk in focusing on difference, as it tends to marginalise minorities and reinforce stereotypes. Some of the research we have looked at here on the positive financial impact of hiring women, people of colour, or other underrepresented groups make it sound like companies are "exploiting" people with certain dimensions of diversity to gain those positive business outcomes. It pushes organisations towards the differentiation square in Shore and colleagues' inclusion model (see Image 2.3).

To supplement the business case and address its shortcomings, we need an *equity lens* on DEI, and a focus on removing the barriers for increased representation across the dimensions of diversity. If barriers are removed, rather than the numbers of employees from specific target groups increased, there is basis for real inclusion and not assimilation and differentiation. Addressing inequity and inequality to make workplaces more equitable and equal for all should be motivation enough. According to Oriane Georgeac, Professor at Yale School of Management, and Aneeta Rattan, Professor at London Business School, "most organisations don't feel the need to explain why they care about core values such as innovation, resilience, or integrity. And yet when it comes to diversity, lengthy justifications of the value of hiring a diverse workforce have become the norm in corporate America and beyond".[41] The authors analysed all Fortune 500 companies' websites, diversity reports and blogs using a machine learning algorithm to classify the data into one of two categories: the "business case" for diversity (a rhetoric that justifies diversity in the workplace on the grounds that it benefits companies' bottom line) and the "fairness case" for diversity (a rhetoric that justifies diversity on moral grounds of fairness and equal opportunity). What they found is very interesting: 404 of the 500 companies—that is approximately 80% of the organisations—used the business case to justify the importance of diversity, whereas less than 5% used the fairness case. What about the remainder? These companies did not list diversity as a value or did so without providing any justification for why it mattered to the organisation.

Georgeac and Rattan's research also shows that while many leaders hope that the business case resonates with underrepresented employees, the reality is very different. They conducted a series of five studies during which they asked more than 2,500 individuals—including LGBTQ+ professionals, women in STEM fields and Black American college students—to read messages from a prospective employer's webpage, which either made the business case and the fairness case or offered no justification for valuing diversity. Those that read the business case for diversity reported that they were 11% less likely to feel a sense of belonging to the company, while they were 16% more concerned that they would be stereotyped at the company as well as 10% more concerned that the company would view them as interchangeable with other members of their identity group. As a result, the underrepresented groups were less likely to say they wanted to join the company which used the business case.[42]

While we would love for all companies and leaders to embrace DEI because it is the right thing to do, we also recognise that companies are at different stages and that maturity levels across countries and societies are different. In countries and companies where DEI is in its infancy, a business case may seem like the perfect lever to help propel things forward. Our hope is that as DEI matures globally, we will collectively move to the stage of not needing this lever. DEI will be the right thing to do—the equitable thing to do—for societies, organisations, teams and individuals.

While a business case may not be needed and may, in fact, do more harm than good, what is needed is for leaders to have absolute conviction in the purpose of DEI to ensure that DEI efforts are driven by purpose, a purpose that goes beyond needing to fulfil compliance and legal requirements. Today, most employees want to work for organisations that are driven by purpose, rather than profit. When it comes to DEI, it is the purpose motivators that will enable us to influence others to be more inclusive and equitable.

One can't talk about the business case for DEI without the topic of quotas and targets (both these terms are used interchangeably) coming up. But what are quotas?

What Are Quotas?

Quotas are targets that are set by organisations and teams to ensure that there is adequate representation of underrepresented, marginalised and discriminated groups in an effort to address systemic inequity—internally in and externally to the organisation. Quotas can be set at various levels of the organisation—senior leadership levels and/or at entry-level positions, and every level in between. To meet these quotas, companies hire and promote a specific number of people from an underrepresented group, thereby contributing to the practice of affirmative action—also, known as positive discrimination. Positive discrimination is the process of increasing the number of employees from underrepresented groups—such as ethnic minorities, women or disabled people—in workplaces from which they have been excluded, by preferentially selecting recruits with those characteristics.

Gender quotas are the most widely used—and debated—form of affirmative action, which have not only made it into organisational practice but also legal frameworks. One of the earliest legislative efforts in this area was in Norway, which has passed a quota-law requiring that women make up a minimum of 40% of corporate boards. The law was first adopted in 2003, and after an initial grace period of two years for existing companies, a failure to achieve the 40% quota led to the delisting of the company. As a result of this law, the ratio of women board members increased from 5% in 2001 to 40% in 2008. The legislation meant that organisations in Norway had to force themselves to actively seek out women who could take on board membership. It also had a knock-on effect, as companies not required to do so by law also began to recruit and hire more women. While there were certainly positive effects in the boardroom, these did not trickle down to managerial levels, and underrepresentation persisted there.[43] In addition, the quotas did not necessarily address the underlying causes of discrimination and bias. Thus, quotas are not the solution per se, but it is part of it. Specifically, the Norwegian legislation solved the problem of underrepresentation of women in boards, which persists in countries that do not have quotas. For instance, there are 24.5% women on boards in Britain, 24.9% in Sweden and 28.6% in the US.[44] Quotas can be a necessary means to solving the persistent numerical unbalance, but they do not in themselves solve underlying problems of systemic discrimination nor do they guarantee positive organisational outcomes.

What about ethnic quotas? One of the world's oldest positive discrimination policies is found in India, where it is known as the "reservation" policy. Put into place in 1950, it was designed to address the prejudices of India's caste system, setting quotas in education, the workplace and positions of governance for those considered to be part of the lower castes. The quotas, which vary across India, have been partly successful. In 1965, Dalits, who formed the lowest rung of the Hindu caste system, occupied 1.6% of the most senior positions in the civil service. By 2011, that had risen to almost 12%, just 4% lower than their 16% populational representation.

In the US, a scandal that evolved around the firing of two African-American football head coaches led to the establishment of the "Rooney Rule" in 2003, requiring National Football League teams to interview at least one underrepresented candidate for all head coach and general manager roles.[45] In education, we see quotas being used in Brazil and France to provide opportunities for indigenous, underrepresented or disadvantaged students. Race quotas have also been woven into Malaysian society since 1971, when Chinese and Indians dominated the upper classes: a legacy of British colonisation. Sweeping changes were introduced under the Bumiputera (indigenous Malay communities) policy, designed to ensure that the majority group of Malays would no longer be discriminated against. These quotas still persist across the public sector, in NGOs and elements of the business sector, but have become contentious.

While positive discrimination is practised in many countries, including the US, it is illegal in the UK under the Equality Act of 2010.[46] Instead, *positive action* became legal in the UK in April 2011 to ensure measures are taken to support the recruitment and promotion of underrepresented minorities, without the risk of hiring candidates who are not qualified for the job, resulting in qualified candidates missing out on jobs.

Positive Discrimination, Affirmative Action and Positive Action: What's the Difference?

You may be wondering: What is the difference between positive action and positive discrimination? The terms are often used interchangeably, though they are different. The subtle difference lies in the fact that *positive discrimination*—also known as *affirmative action*—involves hiring an individual purely based on their protected characteristic, despite the person being less capable or less qualified. Protected characteristics can include race, gender, age, disability, religion and sexual orientation. *Positive action* occurs when an organisation that is deciding who to hire or promote has to make a choice between two equally qualified candidates, and positive action would involve hiring/promoting the candidate who pertains to the most underrepresented group.

The challenges of positive discrimination lie in the legal, moral and economic questions that arise from the preferential treatment of certain groups of people in society. Underlying the debate about what forms of positive discrimination/action might be appropriate are various concerns about the notion of reverse discrimination, or the unfair disadvantage to individuals who bear no responsibility for past or present discrimination practised by others. While that may, indeed, be the case, those from well-represented groups have indirectly or directly benefited from—been privileged or advantaged by—the structures, systems and practices that favour them over others. Positive discrimination/action addresses this inequity with a focus on ensuring that the structures, systems and practices are equitable.

Challenging Quotas

While quotas may increase the numbers of organisational members from underrepresented groups, there is also the risk of it being seen as tokenism or nothing more than a symbolic effort. *Tokenism* involves hiring a person who belongs to an underrepresented group only to prevent criticism and give the appearance of diversity. Quotas do a disservice to underrepresented groups by perpetuating the bias that the person "only got the job because they are a minority" and not because of their skills, competencies and behaviours. In turn, quotas cause resentment among those who are not part of the underrepresented group, making hampering the creation of nurturing an inclusive environment. In Norway, the initial small group of women who were appointed to several boards at once were nicknamed the "golden skirts", implying that they were there only to fulfil the government requirement rather than to harness their competencies and add value to the boards. We have met numerous women in senior leadership roles who faced casual comments that their presence was part of the hiring manager's "diversity quota for the year". It isn't just women who experience this. Minority ethnic groups and the disabled have also long experienced the resentment of members of majority groups who feel entitled to suggest that minorities were only hired or promoted because of positive discrimination.

Here is an important thing to keep in mind. Quotas and targets focus on equality from the standpoint of "outcomes". In this book, we advocate a focus on equity—to unpack and block the bias that is embedded within our systems, structures, processes and policies. In doing so, we work towards creating more equitable and eventually equal opportunities for all through the processes in our organisations, rather than a focus on the equality of the outcomes.

Also, quotas can only be used with dimensions of diversity whose representation can be measured. This limits its use and is one of the reasons why gender quotas are among the only quotas that have been used with reasonable success. The risk with targets and quotas is that the only dimension of focus becomes gender—and usually a binary definition of gender—because that is what we can measure, and so we risk getting stuck in only addressing gender diversity, never moving on to inclusion or equity across intersectional identities. Quotas are often the first measure and are a quick fix approach to increasing the diversity in organisations. What is needed to see sustainable change is sincere efforts to block bias in structures, systems, policies and practices.

Should you as a leader decide to use quotas, this will need to be communicated very carefully to your colleagues across the organisation. Your communication should emphasise that quotas are used in response to the persistence of bias to ensure that unrecognised talent is seen, rather than merely hiring members of an underrepresented group. It is in other words, to reverse ongoing bias and discrimination that has resulted in missing out on talent, rather than to be "fair" to an underrepresented group. It should be communicated as an effort to level the playing field and balance the power or unfair advantage that some groups have enjoyed. That is the only way to counter the negative quota narrative. Also, ensure that quotas have an expiry date and, in the meantime, make conscious efforts to block the bias that exists in people, structures, systems, policies and practices.

Our hope is that in leading with the five principles laid out in this book, the need for quotas will become unnecessary. Leading with conviction, clarity, accountability, allyship and strength will lead to long-term and sustainable change towards inclusion. So, if you are looking for an alternative to quotas, this is the book for you.

Purpose of DEI

In this book, we view the purpose of DEI through the lens of equity with the main goal to make our workplaces more equitable and fairer for all—to level the playing field and rebalance the power and privilege away from historically advantaged individuals and groups. From this perspective, the purpose of DEI is fourfold: (1) to mirror the demographics of society, (2) to ensure employee well-being, (3) to be a customer-centric organisation and (4) finally, to foster creativity and innovation (Image 2.6).

To Mirror the Demographics of Society by Attracting and Retaining Talent

To be equitable and to have adequate representation of the viewpoints of society, organisations need to be representative of the societies in which they operate, at all levels of the organisation. To do this, organisations need to focus on being able to both attract and retain talent, which is what organisations that focus on equity can do. Studies show that women are more likely to apply for a job in an organisation if women are already well represented in senior management positions.[47] At the same time, it has been shown that companies with higher levels of gender diversity, accompanied by supporting HR policies, have lower levels of employee turnover.[48]

Increasingly, companies are also finding that having a diverse organisation and inclusive workplaces is a key factor in attracting younger talent. A 2016 survey by Weber Shandwick, one of the world's leading global public relations firms, shows that 47% of Millennials are actively looking for diversity and inclusion when sizing up potential employers.[49] The 2020

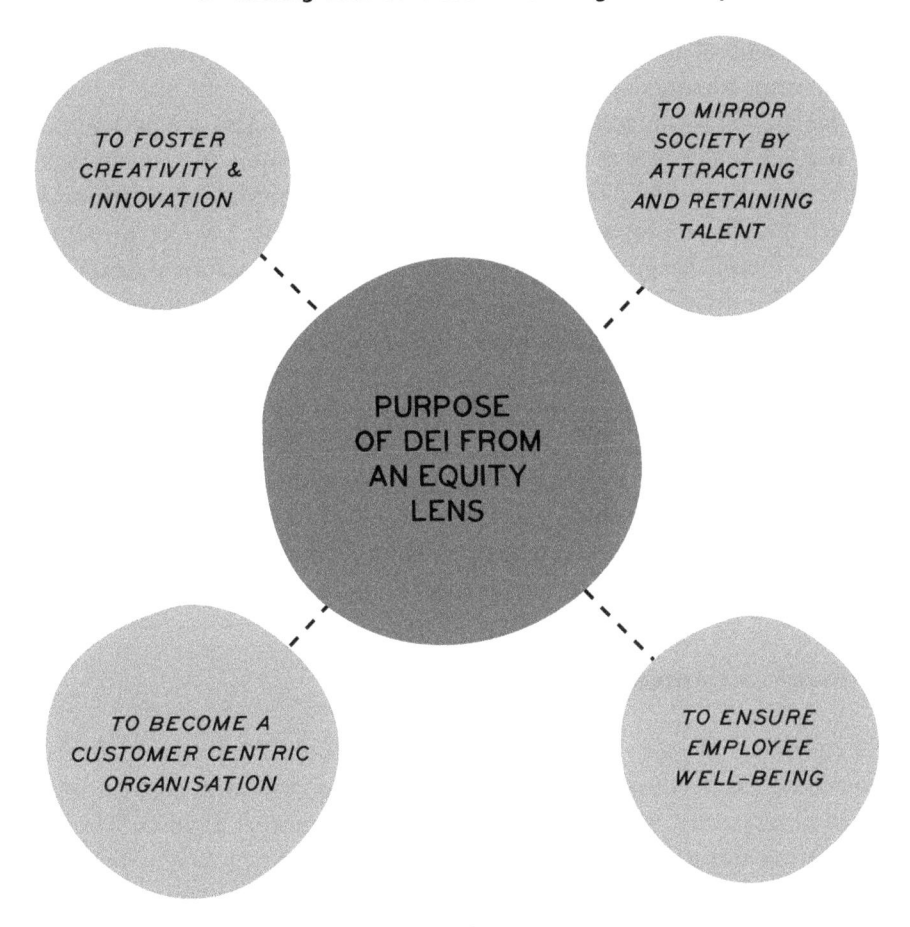

Image 2.6 Purpose of DEI from an equity lens

Deloitte Millennial Survey shows that Millennials and Gen Z expect leaders to ensure "diversity and inclusion across the organisation"[50] and that diversity/inclusion is seen as being essential to keep these generations "happy" at work.[51] In a Danish context, managers have shared with us that the number one question Millennials and Gen Z ask a potential employer at a job interview is what their diversity and sustainability policies are.

To Ensure Employee Well-Being

Organisations with inclusive work cultures have reduced incidents of interpersonal aggression and discrimination, with women experiencing less discrimination and fewer episodes of sexual harassment,[52] thereby improving employee well-being. What is really interesting is that as little as 10% increase in perceptions of inclusion reduces absenteeism, adding nearly one day a year in work attendance per employee.[53] A 2016 report by the European commission draws on studies that show that having LGBT-supportive policies reduces incidences of discrimination, thereby improving psychological health and increasing job satisfaction, while also improving relationships between LGBT employees and their colleagues.[54] The US Department of Labour[55] found that employers who addressed the organisational inequity of people with a disability—through conscious efforts to hire talent with disabilities, engaging in awareness building through disability education programs for all employees as well as offering mentor and mentee opportunities, implementing skill-building programs and making space for diverse talent to hold roles at all levels—saw a 90% increase in employee retention.[56] While diverse organisations certainly attract more diverse talent through their doors, it is also worth noting that employees' experiences of inclusion play a key role in improved job satisfaction and commitment to their employer[57] as well as greater trust,[58] employee engagement and retention.[59]

To Become a Customer-Centric Organisation

The customers of many organisations today are global and diverse. To truly understand the needs of these diverse markets and customers requires representation internally. At a speech at New York University's Tandon School of Engineering and the Stern School of Business in February 2017, Microsoft's CEO Satya Nadella shared that, "an aspect we are focused a ton on is we say we want to empower the world, everyone and every organisation. That means we have got to look like everyone and every organisation in the world".

Diversity at all levels in the organisation increases the likelihood of representing diverse perspectives and diverse experiences that match a broader and more diverse customer base. This of course does not mean that an employee with certain diversity dimensions will know the exact needs and preferences of a potential customer with the same dimensions—because all diversity thumbprints are unique, and everyone experiences the world differently. It is these unique experiences of the world that form our preferences. However, since homogeneous work teams will be less likely to be aware of the needs and preferences of a more diverse customer base, bringing onboard talent and leadership, which represents the diversity of the customers, increases the likelihood of creating products and services, which meet the diverse needs and preferences of their customers in the various markets the organisation operates or is seeking to operate in, and to create inclusive marketing and advertising campaigns, which resonate better with their customers. The result is improved customer satisfaction.[60]

To Foster Creativity and Innovation

Innovation flourishes when there is an inclusive culture. Research by Catalyst.org shows us that companies with an inclusive culture and accompanying DEI policies are shown to have a 59.1% increase in creativity, innovation and openness,[61] with diverse and inclusive teams making better decisions 87% of the time.[62] A 2011 study of top management teams showed that teams with heterogeneity in educational, functional, industry and organisational background had a strong positive effect on the organisation's innovation orientation and in turn produced more innovative products.[63] Diverse and inclusive teams are 76% more likely to see ideas become reality.[64] Also worth noting is that employees' overall experiences of inclusion may help explain 49% of problem-solving in teams and 18% of employee innovation.[65] What was common in the companies who participated in the Catalyst study were six core behaviours of accountability, ownership, allyship, curiosity, humility and courage. These core behaviours then help nurture an inclusive workplace where employees are valued, trusted, authentic and experience psychological safety.[66]

Compared to homogeneous teams where people see, think and do things in similar ways to each other,[67] the magic of diversity lies in having colleagues who see things we don't see, who approach things in different ways and who do things differently. Homogeneous teams are more likely to design and solve problems in a way that is most helpful to users and customers who sound and behave like them. This might mean a potential loss in market shares, but it often feels like it brings a better working environment, as people who readily understand each other seem to collaborate smoothly. But beware of this smoothness; homogeneous teams may feel easier, but it is exactly this ease and comfort that is bad for performance.[68] And conversely, even though it is harder to work in heterogeneous teams, the lack of comfort is what produces better outcomes. Teams with diversity who leverage the variety of perspectives and experiences—and don't hide their differences—consider information more thoroughly and accurately,[69] resulting in faster problem-solving[70] as well as decisions and intellectual output of higher quality.[71] Of course, there are times when the conflict in teams can be corrosive, but in those situations it is quite likely that the team members are bringing different values rather than different ideas.[72] In a culture of inclusion, overall heterogeneous teams do, indeed, perform better than homogeneous teams.

Do You Have the Conviction to Convince Others?

The evidence supporting the need for DEI is indisputable. Removing barriers to hiring and promoting talent equitably in a culture of inclusion is the right thing to do. Leading with conviction requires you to not only deeply understand the intrinsic purpose of diversity—well and truly beyond the business case—but also to be able to convince others through evidence and clear, frequent and consistent communication. Your team, your colleagues and your employees need you to share why you believe DEI is necessary for the organisation. This communication is crucial to leading with conviction.

Ruchika Tulshyan, author of the book *Inclusion on Purpose*, explains: "The problem is, much of these benefits aren't communicated well by company leaders, so many employees think steps to create greater DEI are check-the-box. Too many leaders implicitly frame their solutions as: We're doing this because we are forced to. We're downgrading our processes to accommodate. This is a side project or charity, it's not related to our company's core strategic priorities or mission. It is possible to do better".[73] Tulshyan highlights that leaders need to communicate on DEI efforts by explicitly sharing the reasoning behind it, making clear the historical inequalities and inequities that these DEI efforts are addressing. To do this, you as a leader need to have deep conviction.

2.4 Embedding DEI Within the Strategy

With a clear purpose identified, leading with conviction also means ensuring that:

- DEI is embedded into the organisation's strategy, values and purpose. Empower the business to prioritise DEI alongside other business KPIs and objectives.
- Ensure that you look at DEI through an intersectional lens. Addressing inequity and inequality for some and not others isn't enough. Until and unless we adopt an intersectional lens and truly see how we can lift others across intersectional identities, we won't see progress. Why? Because we would be continuing to do what we have done in the past, favouring some and not others. This isn't easy but it must be done. We often hear that we need to start somewhere. That usually means starting with identities within our comfort zone and leads to limited progress. To make your efforts

matter, you must do the hard work and enact an intersectional approach to diversity.
- Make a shared commitment as leaders to role-model purposeful, authentic and inclusive leadership for the rest of the organisation.
- Ensure that the organisation's board and executive leadership team are diverse, including women, minorities and diverse points of view. Also, engage in creative efforts to diversify the talent pipeline.
- Create an inclusive culture that fully harnesses the benefits of a diverse talent pool and encourages all employees to contribute and constructively challenge ingrained assumptions and perspectives.
- Set the tone that DEI is important to the organisation by keeping it on the leadership agenda, asking the right questions and monitoring the relevant data.

Self-Reflection Exercise: Ask Yourself and Your Colleagues These Questions:

- What is the purpose of DEI for yourself, your colleagues, your team and your organisation?
- Do you think the purpose of DEI is adequately communicated across the organisation?

Use the space below to identify key themes expressed.

Self-Reflection Exercise: Identifying the Purpose of DEI—DEI's Purpose Statement

What is the purpose of DEI for your organisation? List what the purpose of DEI is for your employees, team and organisation. Be as specific as possible. It would be helpful to speak to colleagues who have diverse perspectives and experiences across the organisation to understand what they believe the purpose of DEI is for themselves, their team and the organisation. Is your list focused on removing barriers and increasing equity?

What about DEI being the right thing or the equitable thing to do? How would you incorporate that into your purpose statement for DEI?

_____

_____

_____

_____

Team-Activity: Articulating Your Why and Communicating It

This activity can be done with your leadership team and/or relevant members with diverse perspectives and experiences from your organisation. Bring in everyone who can help answer the question: What is the purpose of DEI for our organisation?

Step 1: Ask each participant to take a few minutes to write down what they believe is the purpose of DEI for your organisation. How will DEI enable you to reduce entry barriers for underrepresented groups and increase equity? Write each idea on a single post-it.

Step 2: Have each participant share their ideas and group them and identify the themes as you do so. The themes could be the "right thing to do", employee well-being, attract and retain talent, creativity and innovation and customer-centric approach.

Step 3. Once the themes have been identified, write down your WHY:

At [organisation name], we believe/are convinced* that an inclusive and equitable workplace/culture* enables us to (add in your themes).

*select the word(s) you prefer

Once you have clearly articulated the purpose, create a communication plan with your team that is clear, frequent and consistent in the messaging.

_____

_____

What Can You Do Differently From Today? Leading With Conviction Means:
- Asking yourself if you wholeheartedly believe in the purpose of DEI and being honest with yourself.
- Recognising the need to make an effort to understand and believe in the purpose of DEI.
- Engaging with colleagues with diverse perspectives across the organisation to understand what they believe the purpose of DEI is for themselves, their team and the organisation.
- Defining the purpose of DEI for your organisation, team and individual employees. Be as specific as you can be and keep focused on removing barriers and increasing equity. Embed DEI within your company strategy.
- Clearly, frequently and consistently communicating the purpose of DEI to your employees.

Notes

1. Woke: Being aware of and actively attentive to important societal facts and issues, particularly issues of racial and social justice.
2. https://www.forbes.com/sites/forbesbusinesscouncil/2022/12/30/four-reasons-to-prioritize-dei-during-a-recession/?sh=566b847c4b13.
3. https://www.forbes.com/sites/forbesbusinesscouncil/2022/12/30/four-reasons-to-prioritize-dei-during-a-recession/?sh=566b847c4b13.
4. Employer branding is the branding efforts that are meant to give current and potential employees a positive image of the organisation, thereby assisting in retaining current employees and attracting new ones.
5. Crenshaw, K. (1989). Demarginalizing the Intersection of Race and Sex: A Black Feminist Critique of Antidiscrimination Doctrine, Feminist Theory and Antiracist Politics. *University of Chicago Legal Forum, 1989(1)*, Article 8.
6. Crenshaw, K. (1989). Demarginalizing the Intersection of Race and Sex: A Black Feminist Critique of Antidiscrimination Doctrine, Feminist Theory and Antiracist Politics. *University of Chicago Legal Forum, 1989(1)*, Article 8.
7. Luthra, P. (2021). Diversifying Diversity. København: TalentED.
8. Cho, S., Crenshaw, K., & McCall, L. (2013). Toward a Field of Intersectionality Studies: Theory, Applications, and Praxis. *Signs*, 38, 785–810; Crenshaw, K. (1989). Demarginalizing the Intersection of Race and Sex: A Black Feminist Critique of Antidiscrimination Doctrine, Feminist Theory and Antiracist Politics. *University of Chicago Legal Forum, 1989(1)*, Article

8; Wells, C., Gill, R., & McDonald, J. (2015). "Us Foreigners": Intersectionality in a Scientific Organisation. *Equality, Diversity and Inclusion: An International Journal*, 34, 539–553.
9. Crenshaw, K. (1989). Demarginalizing the Intersection of Race and Sex: A Black Feminist Critique of Antidiscrimination Doctrine, Feminist Theory and Antiracist Politics. *University of Chicago Legal Forum, 1989(1)*, Article 8; McBride, A., Hebson, G., & Holgate, J. (2015). Intersectionality: Are We Taking Enough Notice in the Field of Work and Employment Relations? *Work, Employment and Society*, 29(2), 331–341.
10. Ro, H., & Loya, K. (2015). The Effect of Gender and Race Intersectionality on Student Learning Outcomes In Engineering. *The Review of Higher Education*, 38, 359–396.
11. Crenshaw, K. (1989). "Demarginalizing the Intersection of Race and Sex: A Black Feminist Critique of Antidiscrimination Doctrine, Feminist Theory and Antiracist Politics," *University of Chicago Legal Forum, 1989*, Article 8.
12. Luthra, P. (2021). *Diversifying Diversity*. København: TalentED.
13. https://www.who.int/en/news-room/fact-sheets/detail/disability-and-health.
14. Intersex: A variety of conditions in which a person is born with a reproductive or sexual anatomy that does not seem to fit the typical definitions of male or female.
15. https://www.discovermagazine.com/the-sciences/how-identical-twins-develop-different-personalities.
16. Unzueta, M. M., & Binning, K. R. (2012). Diversity Is in the Eye of the Beholder: How Concern for the In-Group Affects Perceptions of Racial Diversity. *Personality and Social Psychology Bulletin*, 38(1), 26–38.
17. Bauman, C. W., Trawalter, S., & Unzueta, M. M. (2014). Diverse According to Whom? Racial Group Membership and Concerns about Discrimination Shape Diversity Judgments. *Personality and Social Psychology Bulletin*, 40(10), 1354–1372.
18. Mannix, E. A., & Neale, M. A. (2005). What Differences Make a Difference? The Promise and Reality of Diverse Teams in Organisations. *Psychological Science in the Public Interest*, 6(2), 31–55.
19. Mannix, E. A., & Neale, M. A. (2005). What Differences Make a Difference? The Promise and Reality of Diverse Teams in Organisations. *Psychological Science in the Public Interest*, 6(2), 31–55.
20. Mor Barak, M. (2013). *The Paradox of Multiculturalism "Failure" and Diversity Management "Success": An Overview and Conceptual Model*. Conference Organizing Concept paper. Chateau de la Bretesche Colloquium, France.
21. Shore, L., Randel, A., Chung, B., Dean, M., Ehrhart, K., & Singh, G. (2011). Inclusion and Diversity in Work Groups: A Review and Model for Future Research. *Journal of Management*, 37(4), 1262–1289.
22. https://www.kornferry.com/insights/featured-topics/diversity-equity-inclusion/guide-to-dei-in-the-workplace.

23. https://www.kornferry.com/insights/featured-topics/diversity-equity-inclusion/guide-to-dei-in-the-workplace.
24. *Diversity Wins: How Inclusion Matters.* McKinsey & Company. May 19, 2020. https://www.mckinsey.com/~/media/mckinsey/featured%20insights/diversity%20and%20inclusion/diversity%20wins%20how%20inclusion%20matters/diversity-wins-how-inclusion-matters-vf.pdf.
25. https://www.bcg.com/en-us/publications/2018/how-diverse-leadership-teams-boost-innovation.aspx.
26. Lorenzo, R., Voigt, N., Schetelig, K., Zawadzki, A., Welpe, I. M., & Brosi, P. (2017). *The Mix That Matters: Innovation Through Diversity.* The Boston Consulting Group, https://www.bcg.com/publications/2017/people-organization-leadership-talent-innovation-through-diversity-mix-that-matters.
27. The CS Gender 3000 in 2019: The Changing Face of Companies. Credit Suisse Research Institute. October 10, 2019. https://www.credit-suisse.com/about-us-news/en/articles/media-releases/cs-gender-3000-report-shows-one-fifth-of-board-positions-globall-201910.html.
28. https://www.bloomberg.com/news/articles/2020-07-27/u-k-firms-with-more-women-on-exec-boards-outperform-on-profits.
29. https://www.catalyst.org/research/why-diversity-and-inclusion-matter-financial-performance/.
30. Loop, P., & DeNicola, P. (2019, February 18). You've Committed to Increasing Gender Diversity on Your Board. Here's How to Make It Happen. *Harvard Business Review.*
31. Chen, J., Leung, W. S., Song, W., & Goergen, M. (2019, September 12). When Women Are on Boards, Male CEOs Are Less Overconfident. *Harvard Business Review*; Chen, J., Leung, W. S., Song, W., & Goergen, M. (2019). Why Female Board Representation Matters: The Role of Female Directors in Reducing Male CEO Overconfidence. *Journal of Empirical Finance*, 52, 70–90.
32. Fan, Y., Jiang, Y., Zhang, X., & Zhou, Y. (2019). Women on Boards and Bank Earnings Management: From Zero to Hero. *Journal of Banking & Finance*, 107(4), 1–21.
33. Adhikari, B. K., Agrawal, A., & Malm, J. (2019). Do Women Managers Keep Firms Out of Trouble? Evidence from Corporate Litigation and Policies. *Journal of Accounting and Economics*, 67(1), 202–225.
34. Creek, S. A., Kuhn, K. M., & Sahaym, A. (2017). Board Diversity and Employee Satisfaction: The Mediating Role of Progressive Programs. *Group & Organisation Management*, 44(3), 521–548.
35. Creek, S. A., Kuhn, K. M., & Sahaym, A. (2017). Board Diversity and Employee Satisfaction: The Mediating Role of Progressive Programs. *Group & Organisation Management*, 44(3), 521–548.
36. Chen, J., Leung, W. S., Song, W., & Goergen, M. (2019, September 12). When Women Are on Boards, Male CEOs Are Less Overconfident. *Harvard Business Review*; Chen, J., Leung, W. S., Song, W., & Goergen, M. (2019).

Why Female Board Representation Matters: The Role of Female Directors in Reducing Male CEO Overconfidence. *Journal of Empirical Finance*, 52, 70–90.
37. https://www.cnbc.com/2016/04/17/lgbt-companies-are-beating-the-stock-market.html.
38. Companies Leading in Disability Inclusion Have Outperformed Peers, Accenture Research Finds. Accenture: https://newsroom.accenture.com/news/2018/companies-leading-in-disability-inclusion-have-outperformed-peers-accenture-research-finds.
39. Companies that embrace neurodiversity can gain competitive advantage in many areas—productivity, innovation, culture and talent retention. Ernst & Young: https://www.ey.com/en_kz/forensic-integrity-services/how-to-get-the-benefits-of-a-neurodiverse-workforce.
40. What companies and government are doing to empower persons with disabilities. The Economic Times: https://economictimes.indiatimes.com/news/company/corporate-trends/what-companies-and-government-are-doing-to-empower-persons-with-disabilities/articleshow/65254315.cms?from=mdr.
41. https://hbr.org/2022/06/stop-making-the-business-case-for-diversity.
42. Georgeac, O. A. M., & Rattan, A. (2023). The Business Case for Diversity Backfires: Detrimental Effects of Organisations' Instrumental Diversity Rhetoric for Underrepresented Group Members' Sense of Belonging. *Journal of Personality and Social Psychology*, 124(1), 69–108; https://hbr.org/2022/06/stop-making-the-business-case-for-diversity; https://www.forbes.com/sites/kimelsesser/2022/06/20/the-business-case-for-diversity-is-backfiring/?sh=7158b953351d
43. Bertrand, M., Black, S. E., Jensen, S., & Lleras-Muney, A. (2014). *Breaking the Glass Ceiling? The Effect of Board Quotas on Female Labour Market Outcomes in Norway. The Review of Economic Studies.* 86(1), 191–239.
44. https://edition.cnn.com/2020/11/23/business/germany-quotas-women-boards/index.html.
45. https://operations.nfl.com/inside-football-ops/inclusion/the-rooney-rule/.
46. https://www.gov.uk/discrimination-your-rights.
47. Madera, J. M., Ng, L., Sundermann, J. M., & Hebl, M. (2019). Top Management Gender Diversity and Organisational Attraction: When and Why It Matters. *Archives of Scientific Psychology*, 7(1), 90–101.
48. Maurer, C. C., & Qureshi, I. (2019). Not Just Good for Her: A Temporal Analysis of the Dynamic Relationship Between Representation of Women and Collective Employee Turnover. *Organisation Studies.*, 42(1), 85–107.
49. https://www.webershandwick.com/news/millennials-at-work-perspectives-on-diversity-inclusion/.
50. https://www2.deloitte.com/global/en/pages/about-deloitte/articles/millennialsurvey.html Deloitte Millennial Survey 2020: file:///C:/Users/User/Downloads/deloitte-2020-millennial-survey.pdf.

51. Deloitte Millennial Survey 2018: https://www2.deloitte.com/content/dam/Deloitte/global/Documents/About-Deloitte/gx-2018-millennial-survey-report.pdf.
52. Yu, H., & Lee, D. (2020). Gender and Public Organization: A Quasi-Experimental Examination of Inclusion on Experiencing and Reporting Wrongful Behavior in the Workplace. *Public Personnel Management*, 49(1), 3–28.
53. Bourke, J., & Espedido, A. (2019, March 29). Why Inclusive Leaders Are Good for Organisations, and How to Become One. *Harvard Business Review*.
54. *The Business Case for Diversity in the Workplace: Sexual Orientation and Gender Identity*. Report on Good Practices, European Commission: https://www.raznolikost.eu/wp-content/uploads/The-buisiness-case-for-diversity.pdf.
55. https://www.dol.gov/.
56. https://www.business.com/articles/hire-disabled-people/.
57. McCallaghan, S., Jackson, L. T. B., & Heyns, M. M. (2019). Examining the Mediating Effect of Diversity Climate on the Relationship between Destructive Leadership and Employee Attitudes. *Journal of Psychology in Africa*, 29(6), 563–569; Perry, E. L., & Li, A. (2020). *Diversity Climate in Organisations, in Oxford Research Encyclopedia of Business and Management*. Oxford University Press.
58. Tuan, L. T., Rowley, C., & Thao, V. T. (2019). Addressing Employee Diversity to Foster Their Work Engagement. *Journal of Business Research*, 95, 303–315.
59. Travis, D. J., Shaffer, E., & Thorpe-Moscon, J. (2019). *Getting Real About Inclusive Leadership: Why Change Starts With You*. Catalyst: https://www.catalyst.org/wp-content/uploads/2020/03/Getting-Real-About-Inclusive-Leadership-Report-2020update.pdf.
60. McKay, P. F., Avery, D. R., Liao, H., & Morris, M. A. (2011). Does Diversity Climate Lead to Customer Satisfaction? It Depends on the Service Climate and Business Unit Demography. *Organisation Science*, 22(3), 788–803.
61. *Women in Business and Management: The Business Case for Change*. International Labour Office. - Geneva:ILO, 2019: https://www.ilo.org/wcmsp5/groups/public/---dgreports/---dcomm/---publ/documents/publication/wcms_700953.pdf.
62. https://www.kornferry.com/insights/featured-topics/diversity-equity-inclusion/guide-to-dei-in-the-workplace.
63. Kock, A. (2012). Top Management Team Diversity and Strategic Innovation Orientation: The Relationship and Consequences for Innovativeness and Performance. *Strategic Direction*, 28(4), 819–833.
64. https://www.kornferry.com/insights/featured-topics/diversity-equity-inclusion/guide-to-dei-in-the-workplace.

65. Travis, D. J., Shaffer, E., & Thorpe-Moscon, J. (2019). *Getting Real About Inclusive Leadership: Why Change Starts with You.* Catalyst: https://www.catalyst.org/wp-content/uploads/2020/03/Getting-Real-About-Inclusive-Leadership-Report-2020update.pdf.
66. Travis, D. J., Shaffer, E., & Thorpe-Moscon, J. (2019). *Getting Real About Inclusive Leadership: Why Change Starts with You.* Catalyst: https://www.catalyst.org/wp-content/uploads/2020/03/Getting-Real-About-Inclusive-Leadership-Report-2020update.pdf.
67. https://www.forbes.com/sites/forbesinsights/2020/01/15/diversity-confirmed-to-boost-innovation-and-financial-results/.
68. https://hbr.org/2016/09/diverse-teams-feel-less-comfortable-and-thats-why-they-perform-better?utm_medium=social&utm_campaign=hbr&utm_source=LinkedIn&tpcc=orgsocial_edit.
69. Homan, A. (2019). Dealing with Diversity in Workgroups: Preventing Problems and Promoting Potential. *Social and Personality Psychology Compass*, 13(5), 1-15.
70. Reynolds, A., & Lewis, D. (2017, March 30). Teams Solve Problems Faster When They're More Cognitively Diverse. *Harvard Business Review.*
71. Corritore, M., Goldberg, A., & Srivastava, S. B. (2020, January–February). The New Analytics of Culture. *Harvard Business Review.*
72. https://hbr.org/2016/09/diverse-teams-feel-less-comfortable-and-thats-why-they-perform-better?utm_medium=social&utm_campaign=hbr&utm_source=LinkedIn&tpcc=orgsocial_edit.
73. Tulshyan, R. (2020). Do Your Employees Know Why You Believe in Diversity?: https://hbr.org/2020/06/do-your-employees-know-why-you-believe-in-diversity.

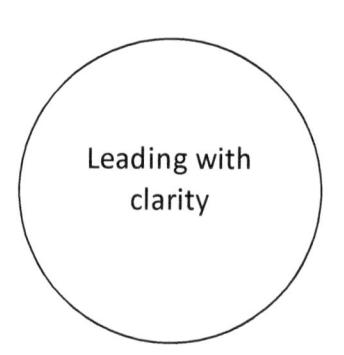

Leading with clarity

3

Leading With Clarity (Part 1—Understanding the Basics of Bias and Identity Bias)

Having developed a deep conviction in DEI, you are now ready to explore what leading with clarity entails. Being aware of and clear about bias is particularly important for leaders whose interactions and decisions influence other people and impact organisations. Bias comprises of the mental shortcuts that we take to help us make sense of the vast amount of information coming our way. As such, bias is unavoidable and leading with clarity does not imply leading with complete information or perfect rationality; it involves leading with the knowledge that we never have full knowledge. Clarity is an analytical ability rather than a state of mind. As the Greek Philosopher Socrates is often cited for saying, "true knowledge exists in knowing that you know nothing", and this requires us to unlearn some of the myths and illusions that make us think we know more than we do.

Leading with clarity is a complex and challenging task, which is why it takes up two chapters in this book. In the present chapter, we develop an understanding of the fundamentals of bias and explore identity-related cognitive biases. In the next chapter, we look at situation-related cognitive biases. Through these two chapters, we will provide you with a solid research-based understanding of how bias influences you and those around you.

Before we delve deeper into bias, we want to clarify that in this book we refer to the term "bias" as a general category and "biases" as its more specific manifestations.

3.1 We Are Not as Rational as We Would Like to Think We Are

It is an accepted fact that human cognition is flawed. Our human brain receives an extraordinary amount of information—about 11 million bits of information every, single second.[1] We consciously process about 40 bits of information per second, not 4 million; not 40,000; not 400; just 40. This means the remaining 99.9996% of information is covered by our unconscious mind. Since we cannot process all available information all the time and all at once, our brains often rely on shortcuts, especially when we need to act fast, based on quick assessments and hurried decisions.[2]

This means that most (if not all!) of our decisions are made under suboptimal conditions. There is no time for the human mind to rationally compute all the impressions it must process in order to make a decision. To the contrary, individual knowledge is extremely shallow and only scratches the surface of the complexity of the world.[3] What this means is that the human mind does not have the capacity that we would like to think it does. On the contrary, seemingly rational people constantly make totally irrational decisions. This is particularly true in business and leadership contexts, where there is rarely time for lengthy analyses, and where good leaders must react fast, "based on their experience" or their "gut feeling". Does this sound familiar?

And yet, we have somehow convinced ourselves that experience forms a rational basis for decision-making. Maybe this is just human arrogance; we like to think of ourselves as distinct from other animals. Being the smartest species on the planet, we must be the best decision-makers, right? Be that as it may, the human mind is far from capable of consciously and rationally processing the vast amount of information that surrounds every single decision.

This is where the shortcuts come in, as they enable quick information processing, simplifying the complex world we live in and helping us make decisions. Without this help, we would freeze and become unable to function effectively in the world. The downside of these shortcuts that aim to "help" us to make fast decisions is that these very shortcuts are very likely to be biased[4] as they are formed through heuristics and algorithms that we have developed through our life experiences and social conditioning.[5] This is best explained by Daniel Kahneman's theory of System 1 and System 2 thinking.

System 1 and System 2 Thinking

Bias research is often based on the decision-making theories developed by Daniel Kahneman and Amos Tversky. In 2002, 6 years after Tversky died, Kahneman won the Nobel Prize in economic sciences for the work he had done together with Tversky. The prize was ground-breaking, as no psychologist had ever won the Nobel Prize in economics. Kahneman and Tversky changed our understanding of decision-making processes by combining cognitive psychology with economic thinking, as their research showed that we humans are more context- and habit-driven in our decision-making processes than we realise. In the bestseller *Thinking, Fast and Slow*, Kahneman succeeded in communicating his and Tversky's theory of the difference between rational and intuitive thinking to a wider audience through the concepts of System 1 and System 2 thinking.[6]

The intuitive System 1 runs on routines and habits that we have learned throughout our lives. For example, it allows us to avoid obstacles on a walk, all the while concentrating on a conversation with another person. It helps us brush our teeth or ride a bike. We don't have to think rationally about how these things happen anymore; our brain and body know what to do. Besides helping our body move physically through the world, it also helps us have casual conversations, understand a joke or decode body language and the tone of voice of our boss at a meeting. Whether the decision results in a body movement or an interaction with a colleague, System 1 thinking occurs when we don't focus on what and how we do something. We just do it. Conversely, the rational System 2 requires both focus and energy, like when filling out a tax return form, learning how to drive a car or analysing figures for the annual report.

We have tried to capture System 1 and System 2 thinking in Image 3.1. System 1 thinking is made possible through the ways in which we have experienced the world and how this experience forms our opinions and perceptions. First of all, such experience is formed by the text and symbols that we are presented with in the material world. These include the books we read as a child, the movies we have watched, the buildings we live and work in, as well as street names and bathroom signs, just to mention a few. The next level is how all these experiences have gradually produced norms and values and led us to identify with these social constructs. Norms and values are context dependent and thus differ from country to country, from city to city, from generation to generation, from organisation to organisation and from team to team. But norms and values are what we have learned to perceive as "normal". Meaning, they are not normal, objectively speaking, but perceived to be normal, normalised through the repetition of them.[7] Finally, System 1 is also activated through the ways in which we are represented by language and how we use language. The words we use about people are often not necessarily reflexive but are words we have learned to use in specific situations. System 1 is, therefore, driven by associations among sensory input, the memory of our own experiences and the cultural knowledge we have grown up with. System 1 makes up around 95% of our thinking.

System 2 represents our rational and analytical thinking. This is where our thinking slows down and we are able to be reflexive—we are able to examine our own feelings, reactions and motives as well as how these influence what we do or think in a situation. System 2, we might say, is a meta-mode, where we perceive a problem from several angles, receive inputs and actively seek new knowledge—and are open to its influence—to inform our decision.

We can think of both systems as constantly active in the brain, but we make the most use of System 2 when we encounter something that puzzles us or when we sit down with a problem that we have to solve analytically. This applies to things that are out of context, something that is new or something that seems like a mistake. Puzzlement most often occurs because the situation we are facing or dealing with doesn't fit into our current cognitive

SYSTEM 2
SLOW AND CRITICAL THINKING

META

SYSTEM 1
FAST AND EFFICIENT THINKING

LANGUAGE

NORMS AND VALUES

TEXT AND SYMBOLS

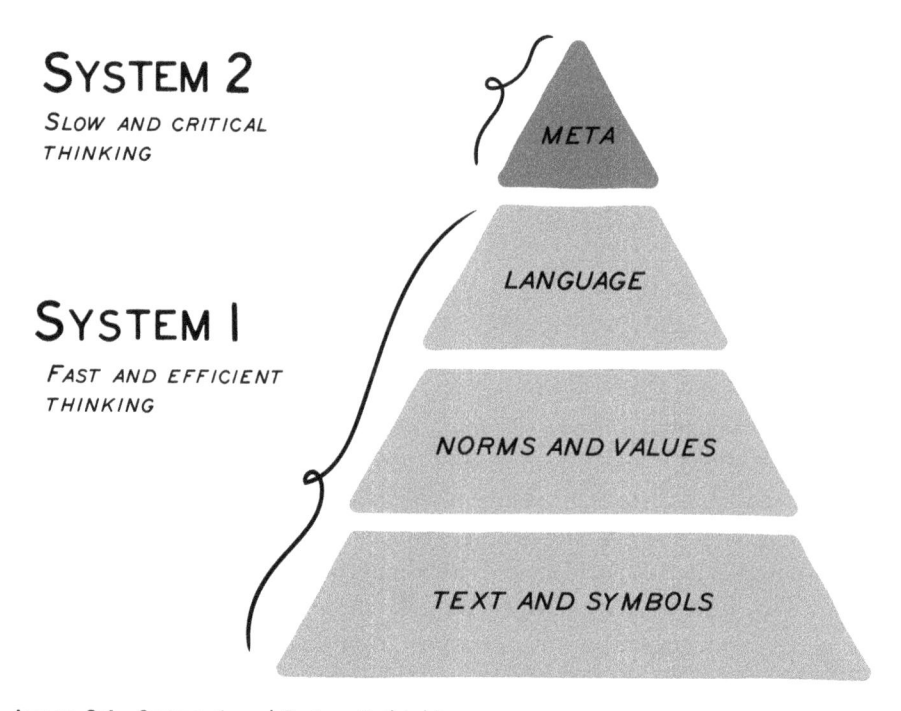

Image 3.1 System 1 and System 2 thinking

schemas. But most of the time, we let the habit-based System 1 control our thoughts and actions because life would be too energy consuming otherwise. System 1 synthesises the various elements so that we always have a coherent interpretation of what is happening around us. But the synthesis is always context dependent. And as we are rarely aware of the historical and cultural context of our own thinking, System 1 is likely to be biased and can lead us astray.

Are All Biases Bad?

Bias can be either good or bad. Bias is the brain's shortcut to thinking fast and efficiently managing the vast amount of information coming its way, without which we would be cognitively overwhelmed. It is the lens through which we see and understand the world. The biased System 1 makes decision-making easier, helps us ease feelings of uncertainty, and supports social status by confirming our beliefs and making decisions for us.

Regardless of whether bias is good or bad, all biases prevent us from being rational and objective, as it activates automated decision-making. Bias—or rather the discriminatory effects of bias—can be found and measured both in individual thoughts and actions, in interpersonal relationships and embedded systemically in organisational practices and processes or in technologies. However, regardless of where they manifest, they originate, as described above, from human cognition. This means that wherever humans are—or have been—involved, there is (potential) bias. Or as we say when we give public lectures about bias: "If you have a brain, you're biased". Bias is present regardless of whether you are in a meeting, joining a lunch-time interaction between two colleagues, designing an interview process, writing a job advertisement or updating your organisation's recruitment database.

Because of its necessity, bias is not in itself problematic; without biases and the shortcuts they produce, we wouldn't be able to make decisions. What is potentially problematic, however, is not having knowledge and awareness of bias and how they influence the judgements that we make and decisions we take. Steven Slowman and Philip Fernback call this the human knowledge illusion.[8] Because we think we are smarter than we are, we end up making decisions that are worse than we otherwise could. So, rather than thinking that we can eliminate bias (which we can't), we need to get better at understanding how our decisions are shaped by the shortcuts we take. Referring to Kahneman's terminology above, leading with clarity is not about constantly being in the meta-mode of System 2, but it is about knowing which decisions are likely to be influenced negatively by bias and finding ways to slow down our thinking in those instances or, as we will discuss in Chapter 5, it is about being able to block biases.

To summarise, the point is not that we should learn to make decisions without shortcuts. After all, the shortcuts are impossible to avoid, and if we aim to be more rational in all decisions, we would just be delusional. A more realistic approach is to become aware of the shortcuts we take. That is, we need a better understanding of bias, and of how they influence us and our decisions. We also need to learn how to block them. When we know which biases shape our fast decisions, we can begin slowing our decisions down by blocking the bias that would otherwise guide our decision-making. We can outsmart the brain to stop its gut reactions.

3.2 Layers of Bias

Individual, Collective, Interpersonal and Systemic Bias

We hold bias in us as individuals, in the collective groups we belong to and in systems, structures, processes, policies and technologies. We are all biased and we hold biases about others and ourselves, the latter being known as self-directed bias. We also hold biases as collective groups (groups that are based on social identity categories or functions/teams in the workplace) about individuals and/or other groups. These individual and collective biases express as interpersonal bias in the interactions we have with other people—individuals interacting with other individuals and individuals interacting with groups of people and/or between groups. Finally, we have systemic or institutional biases that are embedded by people into workplace systems, structures, processes and policies.

Explicit, Implicit and Unconscious Biases

These individual, collective and systemic biases can be explicit, implicit or unconscious. While some forms of bias are audible, observable or explicit, most of the biases that influence decisions are much more difficult to detect, suggesting that many biases also impact social and organisational contexts in ways that are not easily observable yet insidious and deep-rooted.[9] In describing the phenomenon, the literature on bias is not consistent in its terminology, and you may have heard both the term implicit bias and unconscious bias in reference to these more subtle and less explicit biases. We have, however, through our extensive work with organisations and leaders found it

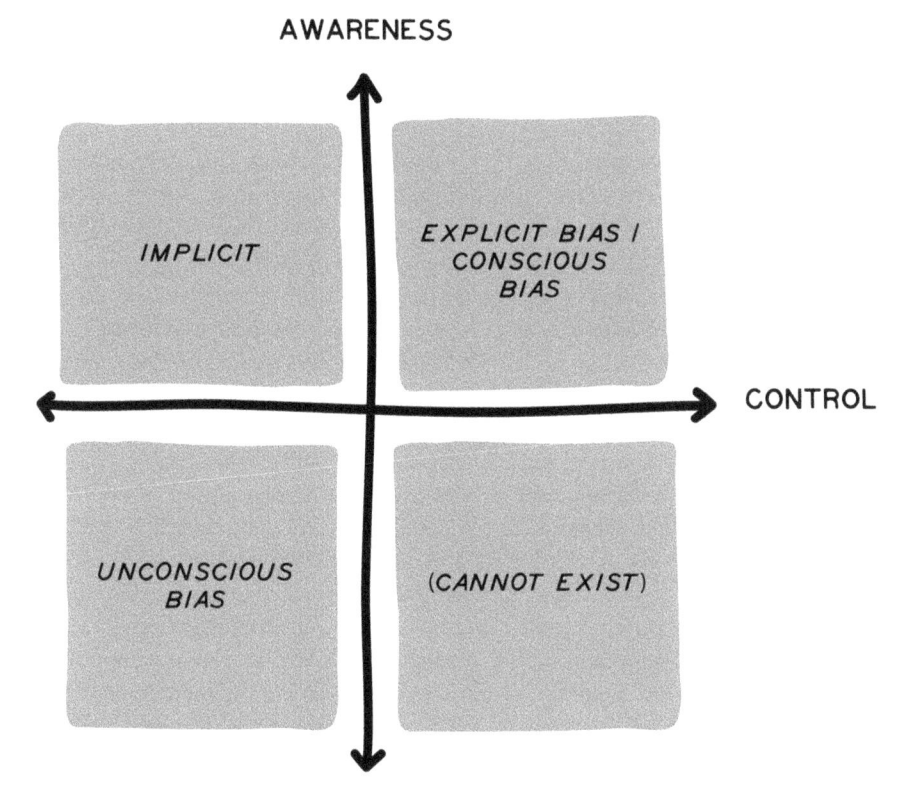

```
                    AWARENESS
                        ▲
                        │
    ┌─────────────┐     │    ┌─────────────┐
    │             │     │    │ EXPLICIT BIAS /│
    │  IMPLICIT   │     │    │  CONSCIOUS   │
    │             │     │    │    BIAS      │
    └─────────────┘     │    └─────────────┘
                        │
◄───────────────────────┼──────────────────────► CONTROL
                        │
    ┌─────────────┐     │    ┌─────────────┐
    │ UNCONSCIOUS │     │    │(CANNOT EXIST)│
    │    BIAS     │     │    │              │
    │             │     │    │              │
    └─────────────┘     │    └─────────────┘
                        │
                        ▼
```

Image 3.2 Awareness—Control model of bias

helpful to operationalise a distinction between unconscious and implicit bias, and we will therefore in this book operate with the following three forms of bias: explicit, implicit and unconscious (Image 3.2).

Explicit Bias

Explicit biases are those views and opinions that we are aware of, making them relatively easy to monitor and self-regulate. We are, in other words, to a large degree able to decide whether we want to express an opinion and to whom we want to express it. This is also why explicit bias can be measured in a survey. As a result, it is possible to map the explicit biases of an organisation, and these are also easier to change than implicit biases, as they can be discussed rationally. In other words, if we identify that explicit biases are forming our System 1 thinking, we can through rational System 2 thinking change this pattern of thinking. As explicit bias can be articulated and explained, rational arguments and education can effectively change them.

> *Making Connections: Poornima & Sara's Experiences*
>
> Sara was recently hired as an expert advisor in an organisation where it was a widely held belief that women had less interest in top leadership positions than men, which was why more men participated in leadership development or talent management programs. To address this explicit bias, she and her collaborators conducted a study in the organisation and asked all employees to answer two sets of questions: First, employees were asked what they thought were the reasons for the lack of women in leadership positions. Second, they were asked to what degree they wanted to advance to the next leadership level and what held them back. The first set of questions was directed at the general perception in the organisation and the second concerned the individual career aspirations of the organisational members. This approach enabled the team to expose explicit bias and find the evidence that contradicts the bias.
>
> To the first question, the most frequent answer (by men as well as women) was that women themselves chose to prioritize family over career. However, it is the answers to the second set of questions which makes this study really interesting. Here, significantly more women than men answered that they aspired to a higher tier of leadership. What was even more interesting was that this was most significant at the second highest level of the organisation's hierarchy. In addition, significantly more women than men answered that they wanted to advance now, not in five years' time, both of which were possible options that the respondent could choose from. The results from the survey both documented and countered the explicit bias that shaped the organisation's actions in relation to women's leadership potential and prospects. The documentation of the bias made it possible to change it. Presented with the data, people changed their minds and previously held beliefs.

Explicit bias is much easier to manage compared to implicit and unconscious bias, particularly if you hold a managerial position or have the power to educate your team members on the topic of bias. If you encounter such explicit bias in your organisation, first make sure you get the data to educate your colleagues about the fact that it is, indeed, a bias that is generalised from personal experiences and/or unbacked stereotypes. Second, find the data to prove the bias wrong. Third, make sure you never generalise from one to many—or from many to one. Instead of assuming that your female employee probably wants children and that this will lead her to prioritise work-life balance, ask her what her vision for her career is. Similarly, instead of assuming that your 55+-year-old employee is not interested in career development plans, ask them what their aspirations are.

Implicit and Unconscious Biases

In contrast to the observability of explicit bias, implicit and unconscious biases produce those views and opinions that are automatically triggered when we encounter new people or new situations. We have no control over these biases; the thought is in our head before we get a chance to think, so to speak. As we have already mentioned in the section on System 1 and System 2 thinking, studies show that over 99% of our brain's activity is unconscious, meaning that the majority of the decisions we make, the actions we take, our emotions and behaviours depend on the majority of brain activity that lies beyond conscious awareness. In fact, our unconscious thought processes engage 200–280 milliseconds before our conscious thoughts do.[10]

Implicit and unconscious biases are the gut feelings that you get before you rationally analyse a situation. The difference between them is small, but significant. Implicit biases are biases you are aware of, but still unable to control; unconscious biases are biases you don't even know you have. In both cases, they influence you and your decisions in ways that cannot easily be identified or articulated, let alone explained—and thus can't be countered with rational arguments, unlike explicit bias.

Implicit bias stems from automatic associations that are pre-reflexive and therefore might not always be noticed when they happen—or have already happened before we have had time to stop ourselves. Implicit bias often takes over when we're busy or tired, but still, we are not completely unconscious of them. We are not in control of neither implicit nor unconscious bias, but if we are in the reflexive System 2 mode of thinking, we can stop ourselves from acting on our implicit bias. In contrast, when it comes to unconscious bias, we cannot access them willingly, as we don't know we have them. It takes an external event—or another person—to make us aware of them.

At many of the workshops we facilitate in organisations, we often hear participants expressing how they "feel a bias creeping in". Paying attention to this feeling is an example of increased bias awareness. We will discuss the advantages of bias awareness training and, particularly, its limits in Chapter 5, but for now it is important to note that this is exactly the point of bias awareness training—becoming conscious about our former unconscious bias. However, even though we might become aware of some of our unconscious bias, much bias remains implicit, triggered automatically and beyond our will. It happens as an involuntarily activated response that we are often unable to explain.[11] Unconscious bias is, therefore, relatively difficult to monitor and self-regulate[12]—even if we can become aware of it and make it implicit.

This is also why implicit bias has nothing to do with your level of education or your morals. You can—as we have—read an endless number of books and articles about bias, not be in doubt about the wrong assumptions behind bias, in principle know what to do about it and still experience that it is triggered in you in relation to some people and situations—often when you least expect it. This is because bias is a frame through which we see the world, a frame that allows us to make fast decisions. As mentioned before, the problem is not the frame as such; we wouldn't be able to navigate the world—and its vast amount of information—without this framing. The problem is that the frame is defined through our culture and history—and that culture and history are built on gendered, racialised, heteronormative, neuro-normative, able-bodied, etc., norms and expectations. Thus, bias leads us to systematically prefer some people over others, see some skills and values in some people and not in others and feel more comfortable in some contexts rather than others.

The important learning is that we cannot get rid of our biases through bias training. But by converting biases from unconscious to implicit, by becoming aware of them, we will be better equipped to analyse when and in which situations bias risks influencing our decision-making negatively. Gaining such clarity makes it a lot easier to address bias-related issues and to block bias, as we detail in Chapter 5.

> *Making Connections: Poornima & Sara's Experiences*
> Sara worked with an executive of a large Danish organisation. She had for many years been very vocal about both gender and race discrimination and the overwhelming maleness and whiteness of the Danish business elite. As part of her job, she went as an expatriate to the US for two years. And here she discovered a bias she did not know she had. She was part of a recruitment process and sat at her desk, skimming through a pile of CVs to make a first assessment. Here, she discovered that she felt something was missing. The CVs didn't mention the candidates' age. In the Danish context, she was used to candidates stating their age or birth date on their CVs—even though Danish employment law has recently been changed to stop companies from registering age in the recruitment system. However, in the US context, it has for a longer time been illegal for an employer to know a candidate's age and therefore not customary to write one's age or birth date on the CV. The executive didn't know how it influenced her assessment, but she just felt that she really missed it and had difficulties relating to the candidates without this information. This is how she discovered she had an age bias—and, accordingly, that bias went from unconscious (and probably a bias that had influenced her decisions) to implicit. She still did not know exactly how it influenced her, but she could begin to take actions against it in recruitment situations—as, for instance, continuing the practice of not knowing candidates' age by actively removing this information from CVs in Denmark. (In Chapter 5, we'll go into details of masking CVs and many other ways to block bias.)

3.3 Expressions of Bias

Prejudice, Stereotypes and Discrimination

Our explicit and implicit biases express themselves as prejudice, stereotypes and discrimination. It can be helpful to think of these three terms as expressions of bias at different levels. Prejudice is bias expressed at an emotional level and is an opinion, prejudgement or attitude about a group or its individual members. Stereotypes are biases expressed at a cognitive level and are specific beliefs, images or distorted truths about a person or group. Stereotypes are a generalisation and simplification in an effort to reduce individuals or groups to certain dimensions that allow for little or no individual differences or social variation. These stereotypes reinforce harmful biases and perpetuate myths about certain groups and people and contribute to systemic bias and discrimination. Discrimination is bias expressed at the behavioural level and refers to behaviours that treat people unequally because of their group memberships. Discriminatory behaviours, ranging from insults to hate crimes, often begin with negative stereotypes and prejudices.

These terms are interlinked and reinforce each other (Image 3.3). One may have a deep-seated prejudice about a particular group based on prior experiences that would then lead to stereotyping all people who are identified as being part of that group, in turn leading to discriminatory behaviour against anyone from that group. It is important to note that this influence is not just a one-way process, as prejudice, stereotypes and discrimination can reinforce each other. So, discrimination acts to further reinforce the previously held prejudices and stereotypes. This cycle of influence continues subconsciously until and unless one becomes aware and consciously intervenes.

Overt and Subtle Biases: Microaggressions (Aka Termite Bias)

We see and experience overt biases around us, e.g. in the form of blatant racism, sexism, ageism and ableism and other types of discrimination. While biases can certainly manifest themselves as overt and obvious aggressions, unconscious bias is often expressed more subtly as microaggressions. Microaggression is a term coined by Dr. Chester Pierce in the 1970s in his work with African Americans. However, it was only in 2007 that the term resurfaced thanks to psychologist Derald Wing Sue. Here is the thing, we assume that overt bias causes significant harm to those being discriminated against. They do. However, research also shows us that subtle bias and discrimination have

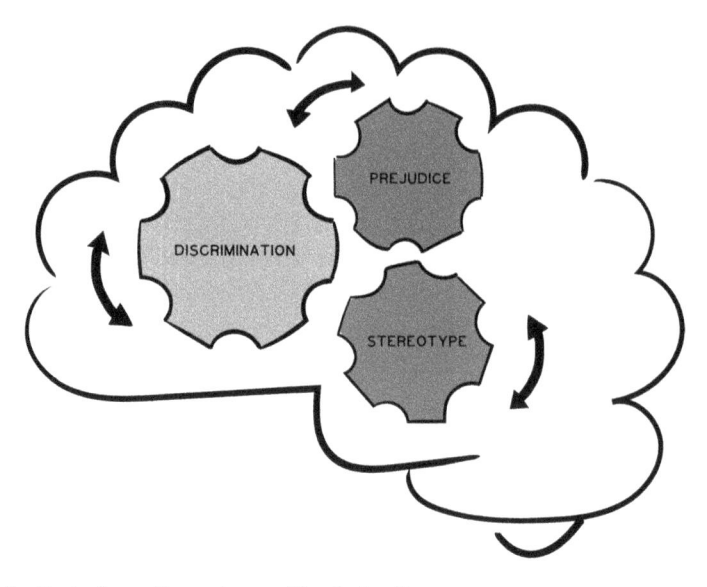

Image 3.3 Prejudice—Stereotype—Discrimination

an equally negative impact on our psychological and physical health, as well as work-related behaviours.[13] Microaggressions negatively impact psychological well-being, deplete our energy and lead to lower productivity and problem-solving capability.[14] This is why the term "microaggression" has in recent years received criticism for not fully capturing the extent of the negative impact, especially with the use of the word "micro" that suggests that it is somehow not as serious when, in fact, it absolutely is.[15]

These "micro" behaviours are much like a quiet disease, silently eating away at inclusion. While we both use the term microaggressions because it is a well-recognised term in the DEI field, we prefer to refer to these kinds of indirect, subtle and unintentional bias as *termite biases*, using the analogy of termites.[16] Termites do more damage to our economy than any other pest, but, crucially, you don't even know they are slowly eating away at your beautiful wooden cabinet until significant damage has been done—much like bias. While we are more aware and have greater understanding about the biases that manifest as overt and obvious aggressions, we are less aware and have limited understanding about the many times when our unconscious biases express themselves as *termite biases*.

Termite biases are often expressed unintentionally by people who may be well-intentioned. They can be mistaken for a casual comment, be brushed aside as humour, sound like a compliment or even be a well-intentioned remark. They may go unnoticed by others and even by the receiver. Termite biases are communicated through subtle language and may be indirectly communicated, making it difficult to know if you are committing one. If they sound relatively harmless, they aren't. Termite biases—when experienced repeatedly and frequently—make people feel undervalued, unappreciated and excluded. After all, it's often the little things that sting the most.[17]

Termite biases take many forms. Here are some examples of termite biases with explanations where necessary of why they are actual biases. As these biases may not be obvious, they can be challenging to spot:

- Saying to a woman who has been recently hired into a managerial/leadership role: "Congrats on your new role. You are so fortunate to be a woman, there are so many opportunities for you", assuming that the only reason she was hired was because of her gender identity, not because she was actually qualified for the role.
- Assuming that a woman is the secretary when actually she is the leader.
- Assuming that a new female colleague who "looks young" is an intern, based on the assumption that seniority of age is a prerequisite for seniority in hierarchy.
- Assuming that women would be willing to take minutes or notes of a meeting because that task is more suited for their gender.
- Calling a female colleague a "girl". Being "girled at work" refers to belittling, demeaning or excluding women through sexist language. More generally, it implies treating someone like a child or making them feel somehow less mature than others.[18]
- Pressing someone to answer, "Where are you actually from?" based on assumptions that someone who looks like them can't actually be from the place they say they are from.
- Asking someone wearing workwear from their culture (e.g. the Dashiki from West Africa or a Saree from India) or religious clothing such as a hijab, turban or bindi: "Is that really what you would wear to work in your home country?". This is based on a stereotypical definition of what professional work wear looks like, usually emanating from Western societies.
- Commenting to someone with natural or unstraightened curls: "Wow, your hair is so big today". This implies that some hairstyles are somehow more "professional" than others.
- Asking a parent who has returned to work after their parental leave if they have had a good vacation.
- Asking a mother why she wants a promotion, implying she should be focusing on her young children.

- Commenting to someone for whom English is their first language that "you speak English so well!" based on the assumption that someone who looks like them would not be a native English speaker.

When termite biases are pointed out, they are often dismissed by the person who is being held accountable for them. "I was actually complimenting you". "Oh come on, I was just joking". "You're being over-sensitive; it was just a casual comment". Very often, fearing these responses, those on the receiving end of termite biases may not bring them up. They may even rationalise the bias as being a one-off incident and tell themselves: "I'm sure they didn't mean it that way" or "I'm sure I'm overthinking this" or "I'm sure they were just joking".

We have all been at lunch or in a meeting where someone makes an inappropriate joke and others force a fake laugh. The room gets an uncomfortable vibe and people wriggle in their seats—you get the picture, right? The discomfort is usually only broken when someone changes the subject, because quite often we don't know how to react in such a situation, or we don't want to be labelled as the "woke police" with no sense of humour.

However, workplaces are not comedy studios—and we are not stand-up comedians. Yes, we need to have an environment of collegiality and be able to have fun at work, but humour at the expense of others should not be accepted in workplace cultures that promote inclusion—or anywhere for that matter. If humour at the expense of others has been normalised in organisational life, it is only because we have been socially conditioned to accept it and have not known how to address it. There must be more to joke about than other people, right? Even self-deprecating humour or self-irony can be tricky—when done about yourself and only yourself, that's your choice and absolutely acceptable. However, when it also stereotypes others of a group that you are a part of, it can reaffirm and propagate those very stereotypes and their associated bias. Jokes about invisible dimensions of diversity like sexual orientation, marital situations, neurodiversity and socio-economic backgrounds are particularly toxic because the target of the joke could be in the room without the person sharing the joke even knowing it—and that results in people hiding their identities, preventing people from bringing their whole unique selves to work.

What about compliments? How can something meant to be nice be harmful? When compliments are based on assumptions and expectations about someone, then they have the potential to reflect the underlying bias. Let us share a few examples: "Wow, you're so articulate" or "You don't speak with an accent". Such comments are based on an expectation that the person is someone who would have poor language competencies or an accent from the region of the world they are presumed to be from based on their physical appearances. This happens to many people of colour from non-English-speaking countries. Another example is when Asian students from China, Korea, India and other parts of Asia get asked for help with a maths or science question, based on a stereotype about a particular ethnic group being good at something—commonly referred to as the model minority myth.

What about the things that seem to be coming from a place of good intention like: "Everyone can succeed if they work hard enough" or "When I see you, I don't see colour" or "There is only one race, the human race"? Statements like these do not recognise that the world is experienced very differently by different people. Our deep desire to assume that life is experienced the same way, and our deep discomfort with accepting that it isn't, is often at the root of statements or comments like: "I can't be homophobic, I have gay friends" or "I can't be racist, I have friends who are people of colour".

Termite biases are not always expressed through what is often passed off as humour or as a compliment. They can also be expressed in other ways. For example, a White person clutching their bag tighter as a Black person passes by, the owner of a store following a person of colour around to check that nothing is stolen or when a White person waits to take the next elevator when a Black or Brown person is on it. All of these are based on the assumption that the person of colour is more likely to be dangerous, a threat or even a criminal.

There are also termite biases embedded in the casual comments or phrases that are frequently used. These usually make reference to a particular ethnic group or to a form of disability in a casual way. For example, "I am a slave to my work" or "these are Chinese whispers". They can also take the form of nicknames reflecting bias about certain groups. Phrases like "this is lame/dumb" or "blind recruitment"/"that's my blind spot" or "this is our team's handicap" perpetuate the perception that having a disability is a negative thing.

In the workplace, termite biases can take the form of the following behaviours[19]:

- *Interrupting*: Occurs when a member of a dominant group unnecessarily cuts off someone from an underrepresented group during a meeting or group discussion session. This often takes the form of "manterrupting". Did you know that women are interrupted 33% more frequently than men during meetings and panel discussions?[20]

- *Appropriating*: Occurs when a member of a dominant group takes credit for an idea shared by someone from an underrepresented group. This practice has inspired the colloquial term "bropropriating", which occurs, for instance, when a man takes credit for a woman's idea.
- *Splaining*: Occurs when a member of a dominant group explains something to someone from an underrepresented group in a condescending or patronising tone, based on the assumption that the person from the underrepresented group does not have the capability and knowledge about the issue at hand or is emotional and lacking rational thinking abilities. The most common form is "mansplaining", which was made famous in 2008 by author Rebecca Solnit's famous essay, "Men Explain Things to Me".
- *Tone Policing*: According to Dictionary.com, tone-policing is "a conversational tactic that dismisses the ideas being communicated when they are perceived to be delivered in an angry, frustrated, sad, fearful or otherwise emotionally charged manner".[21] This can take the form of being told to "calm down" or "use a nicer tone". The problem is that when someone is facing prejudice and discrimination, there are raw and hurtful emotions at play which can result in focusing on that rather than on the very cause of those emotions—bias.

While we have made some progress in becoming more aware and intentional in the language we use and, in our behaviours, when it comes to more obvious bias, we are sometimes oblivious to the termite biases embedded in the words we use and actions we take ourselves and those of people around us. These termite biases are the silent enemy when it comes to nurturing inclusive workplaces for all. If we do not address these, we do not stand a chance of progressing towards more diverse and inclusive environments.

Systemic Bias

Our workplaces have been built and sustained by those in power, very often (but not always) White cisgendered, heterosexual and able-bodied men. Because of this group's historical position of power, their implicit and explicit biases are expressed in the structures, systems, processes and policies in our organisations, what is known as systemic biases. These *systemic biases* are a significant barrier to achieving the vision of diverse and inclusive workplaces for all. Implicit bias and explicit bias have affected the way our organisational systems and processes have been set up. These biases and the consequential inequity are especially evident in key areas of our workplaces: our hiring and promotion practices; the way we compensate talent and provide benefits; the way talent is managed and led; the opportunities for talent development; and the kind of workplace cultures we have. These biases also impact the way we communicate and the language that we use. Over time, many of these biases have become systemic in nature. How many times have you heard someone bat away a bias with the excuse "this is the way things have always been done", without genuine critical questioning of the biases that lie beneath? Many systemic biases have even gone completely unnoticed and accepted as a norm. We need to address them urgently.

Now that we have a good understanding of what bias is, the layers of bias and how bias expresses itself, we are ready to explore the various biases themselves. Biases can take many forms, and while all biases are cognitive, they generally fall into two main categories: identity-related cognitive biases and situation-related cognitive biases. Identity-related cognitive biases arise as a reaction to a person's identity: one's diversity thumbprint, and these are further divided into two broad categories: (1) surface level identity biases (that arise from visible dimensions of diversity) and (2) deep level identity biases (that arise from invisible dimensions of diversity). Situation-related cognitive biases are biases that arise in situations when we process information in a systematic pattern of deviation from rationality in judgement. Because identity-related cognitive biases constitute the foundation for the way deviation from rationality occurs and thus the way cognitive biases are formed, we focus on identity-related cognitive biases in this chapter and discuss situation-related cognitive biases in the next chapter.

3.4 Identity-Related Cognitive Biases

In this section, we explore some of the many identity-related cognitive biases. We don't expect you to know all the biases out there (there are so many after all), but through the ones we have chosen to discuss here, we hope that you will understand how varied biases are and be better equipped to spot them. So, our goal is not to aim for clarity in the sense of knowing all of one's biases, but clarity in thinking, spotting and relating to bias.

It is crucial to keep in mind that each of these biases do not exist in isolation. Biases intersect with each other, depending on a person's identity and the dimensions of diversity in which they experience bias, forming overlapping layers of discrimination and marginalisation. With the intersection of our various identities, our experiences of bias and resulting discrimination also intersect and get compounded, forming intersectional bias. Different people are met with and understood through the lens of a range of these intersecting biases. For example, a White lesbian woman faces different biases than a Brown lesbian woman, and a Brown, Muslim woman is confronted with different biases than a White, Muslim woman, while a Black man faces different biases than those experienced by a White male wheelchair user.

Image 3.4 (and accompanying explanation of the terms), which is a further development of the diversity dimensions model we presented in Chapter 2, may be useful to understand the range of identity-related cognitive biases that exist in our workplaces and how they relate to our diversity thumbprint. The model is certainly not exhaustive, but these 15 biases are the ones we most commonly come across in workplaces, as they creep into our interactions with others and the decisions we make. Some of these biases are related to surface level (or visible) dimensions of our identity while others are deep level (or invisible) dimensions of our identity. As we have written in Chapter 2, and it is worth reemphasising here again, it is not always easy to identify which dimensions are visible and which are invisible, and some dimensions can be both or can be considered visible in some contexts but not others. Despite this, in this section, we divide them up broadly between surface level biases and deep level biases for ease of understanding though you, as a leader, should be aware of the nuance associated with this categorisation.

Before we take a deeper look at these biases, we'd like you to consider how many you can recognise in yourself, others and within the structures, systems and processes in your organisation.

Identity-Related Cognitive Bias
- Sexism and Transphobia: Bias and discrimination on the basis of sex and gender.
- Heterosexism/Bi- or Homophobia: Bias and discrimination on the basis of a person's sexual orientation.
- Ageism: Bias and discrimination against a person, based on their age.
- Ableism: Bias and discrimination against people with disabilities based on the belief that typical abilities are superior.
- Appearanceism/Lookism/Heightism/Weightism/Hairism: Bias and discrimination on the basis on how a person looks/their height/their weight/their natural hair.
- Education Bias: Bias and discrimination on the basis of a person's educational qualifications and where they attained that qualification from.
- Experience Bias: Bias and discrimination based on the work and life experiences that someone has. For example, having a criminal record or having a military background.

Image 3.4 Dimensions of diversity with corresponding biases

- Personality Bias: Bias and discrimination favouring certain personality types for certain roles.
- Neurodiversity Bias: Bias and discrimination on the basis of different ways of thinking and learning towards people who have dyslexia, dyspraxia, autism, Asperger's and attention deficit hyperactivity disorder (ADHD).
- Mental Health Bias: Bias and discrimination on the basis of a person's mental health conditions.
- Racism/Xenophobia/Colourism/Accentism: Bias and discrimination against people on the basis of their membership in a particular racial or ethnic group, typically one that is underrepresented or marginalised. Accentism is bias and discrimination on the basis of the way a language is spoken or written, usually by non-native speakers.

- Religious Bias: Bias and discrimination on the basis of people's religious beliefs and practices, including clothing, symbols and food.
- Marital/Parenthood Bias: Bias and discrimination on the basis of people's marital and parenthood choices.
- Location Bias: Bias and discrimination based on where someone lives, has lived or prefers living.
- Classism: Bias and discrimination on the basis of a person's socio-economic background.

Surface Level Identity Bias

Surface level bias is activated by a quick superficial evaluation of another person based on what that person looks like. We all do this, every time we meet a person. Superficial evaluation bias is in this sense a type of "über-bias". It is highly problematic in an organisational context, as it influences the way that we perceive another person's merits and values. As we will show through the rest of this chapter, the way we perceive merits and the personal values of a person is highly influenced by superficial bodily markers such as gender, race, age, looks, clothes, height, body weight and tattoos. Before you think rationally about a person, this person's appearance has already influenced your perception of them as people, their competencies, personalities, etc.

When it comes to surface level identity bias, gender and race biases are by far the most studied. It is by now very well documented, across a variety of contexts that we all—including women and people of colour—hold gender and race biases. As soon as we see a person, we register their gender and colour, and our preconceptions kick in. So let us begin with looking at those two dimensions—and their intersection—before moving to the other surface level identity biases. Where data and research are available, we will do our best to provide a view of the biases that result from an intersection of a person's identity dimensions. In understanding these surface level identity biases, keep in mind that even if research and data are not yet available, it does not mean that biases don't exist when those identity dimensions intersect.

Sexism or Gender Bias

Gender bias—or sexism—is a bias that is prevalent in countries across the world. Each year, the World Economic Forum releases their Global Gender Gap Report (GGGR)[22] which benchmarks 153 countries on their progress towards gender parity across four areas: economic participation and opportunity; educational attainment; health and survival; and political empowerment. The 2022 report reveals that at the current pace it will take us 132 years to achieve full gender parity, an increase from 99.5 years in 2020.

In workplaces, gender bias takes many different forms. We often hear from hiring managers that "there simply aren't enough women who are qualified enough". According to the World Economic Forum, in more than 100 countries in the world, women outnumber men in advanced education, suggesting that there should be no shortage of women in the talent pipeline. We also hear that "women are just not ambitious enough", but a 2021 survey of 1068 participants in the US by CNBC and Survey Monkey showed that 54% of working women reported that they were "very ambitious" with another 35% reporting that they were "somewhat ambitious".[23] What about: "women are not as competent as men"? An analysis of thousands of 360-degree reviews in 2019 showed that women outscored men on 17 of the 19 capabilities that differentiate excellent leaders from average or poor ones.[24] Finally, what about this comment: "women are too emotional". A 2021 study by Catalyst showed that employees reporting to leaders with high empathy experienced higher levels of creativity (61%) and engagement (76%) than those who reported to less empathic leaders (13% and 32%, respectively).[25] So, even if women are more emotional (which is not a given) that should not be a problem. Despite this, we see that women across the world—from the US, UK, to Brazil, Nigeria, India and Norway—are not adequately represented in leadership. In 2023, just 7% of CEOs leading the largest publicly listed companies were women, with just 10% of CEOs on the Fortune 500 list of companies being women and only 20% of companies in Norway, a leader in gender equality, having women CEOs.[26] So, what is going on? Why is this the case?

Let us begin with comparing how men and women are evaluated when they first engage with an organisation through a job application. Through a vast body of research, we know that women are consistently evaluated lower than men, the most famous of which are curriculum vitae (CV) studies. In these studies, CVs are sent out to a group of participants. All participants receive the exact same CV, except for the fact that half of them bear a female sounding name and the other half has a male sounding name. This setup has been adapted to different contexts to make the names as generic as possible and ensure that within those contexts, they don't signal class or race differences. Examples are John/Jenifer, Hans/Hannah, Martin/Maria and Greg/Emily. The results are very consistent across all contexts. If we think there is a man behind the CV, we have a tendency to evaluate his competencies to be higher and offer him a higher starting salary, and we are also more likely to offer to become his mentor, as we evaluate him to have more potential.

The latter is particularly interesting in the current gender equality debate, as this shows that it doesn't help to shift the rhetoric from competencies to potential, as many do in the attempt to hire more women. Potential is an empty concept that we can put anything into, and our superficial evaluation bias makes us see potential much more clearly in men than in other gender identities. Note, by the way, that we write "we" here. This is not something men "do" to women. This is something we all have a tendency to do, regardless of our own gender identity. This might explain why it is not guaranteed that women in leadership positions will hire qualified women. Women also exhibit gender bias that is skewed in favour of men. In fact, the studies do not find any significant gender difference when it comes to the evaluator of the CVs; the only consistency is that men are given better evaluations than women, for the exact same CV.[27]

Another set of very famous studies that demonstrate gender bias rests on a study of the American Symphony Orchestra's masked[28] audition.[29] For a long time, it was assumed that the fact that the orchestra mostly consisted of men was a sign of men's superiority in musical competencies. However, an experiment with masked auditions showed that if the musicians auditioned behind a curtain, the number of women who passed audition rose with 25%. An often forgotten but highly interesting detail of this study was that this increase didn't happen before the musicians took off their shoes when they walked onto the stage. Imagine a man walking up on the stage and after that a woman. Do they sound different from each other? Yes, because the norm for a woman attending an audition is to wear shoes with heels, which sound quite different from the flatter and softer sole of the typical male shoe. This additional twist of the study is interesting in a corporate context if you think about how women's heels and the sound they make are talked about in corporate settings.

What about feedback? Do men and women receive feedback differently? In a study published in 2022, the researchers asked 1,500 MBA students, full-time employees and managers based in the US and UK to imagine giving developmental feedback to an employee who needed to improve their performance.[30] The employee was described in exactly the same way to all participants, except that half of the participants were told the employee's name was Sarah, while the other half were told the employee's name was Andrew. While all the participants wanted to give candid feedback, the research found that participants consistently reported being more motivated to be kind when giving feedback to a woman than when giving it to a man. What is interesting is that this finding held strong regardless of the gender or political leanings of the person giving the feedback. You might be wondering why this is? Well, it is because women are stereotyped to be warmer than men, and people are naturally inclined to be kinder and more sympathetic towards others who are perceived to be warm. What is interesting to note about this study is that there was no evidence to suggest that managers are trying to hold women back, and this behaviour of being kind when giving feedback was not driven by a belief that women were less competent than men, a concern about seeming biased towards women, or a fear that women would not be able to handle negative feedback. The participants simply thought that it was more helpful to prioritise kindness when talking to women.[31] A study from MIT Sloan finds women receive higher performance assessment than men but 8.3% lower evaluation for potential, resulting in a 14% less likelihood of promotion for women.[32]

Gender bias, however, influences more than our view of people's competence. It also influences our perception of their likability. Studies show that female leaders are judged to be less likeable and not as nice compared to male leaders. One of the first studies to document this fact was conducted by Susan T. Fiske and colleagues in 2007.[33] They studied the perception of warmth and competence in a number of individuals. Here, they found that it is easier for people to see a man as both warm and competent, whereas this is not so with women. When women's perceived level of competence increases, we have a tendency to see them as not as nice, not as warm, not as likeable. This is a problem for female leaders, as likeability also has a positive influence on how we view a person's competences. So, the stereotype about the warm, nurturing, caring woman clashes with our stereotypical image of a leader, whereas our stereotype of the assertive and strong man certainly does match our stereotype of a leader. In a nutshell, this is the "think leader, think male" problematic coined by Virginia Schein and colleagues.[34]

A similar study was conducted at Columbia Business School by Professor Frank Flynn.[35] In an extended version of the CV studies, they analysed the competence and likeability levels of Heidi and Howard. Heidi Roizen is a successful Silicon Valley venture capitalist who became the subject of this study. Professor Frank Flynn presented half of his class with an original case study about Heidi Roizen. The second half of his class received an altered case study in which Heidi's name was changed to "Howard". The students rated Howard and Heidi as equally competent, but they found Howard to be more likeable than Heidi. Specifically, the students who received Howard's case study found him to be a smart and likeable leader, while the ones who received Heidi's case study considered her to be too aggressive. They thought Howard seemed like a nicer person and like someone they would like to hang out with and grab a Friday beer with. This might not directly influence the hire-ability of Heidi and Howard, but it does indirectly. What would you do, if you had two final candidates, equally qualified, where you just thought one was nicer and more likable than the other? Yes, you would probably hire the one you liked. As this study—and so many others—shows, even if we are able to rate competencies equally in men and women, we very often rate the likeability of male and female leaders differently.

Women, therefore, face a double bind as they aspire to occupy leadership positions: On the one hand, they are less often described using agentic traits (capable, competent, confident, common sense, intelligent, ambitious, assertive, competitive, decisive and self-reliant). On the other hand, if women do display agentic traits, they are seen as less likeable because they violate traditional gender stereotypes of women's communal traits (being good-natured, warm, empathetic, sincere, tolerant, happy, trustworthy, cooperative, patient, polite, sensitive and cheerful).[36] Research shows us that while confidence is a gender-neutral concept, it is weaponised against women. When women fail to achieve career goals, leaders are prone to attribute it to a lack of self-confidence. However, when women demonstrate high levels of confidence through behaviours like being extroverted or assertive, they risk being perceived as overdoing it and ironically as lacking confidence.[37] When we look at the intersection of gender and race, things get more complex. Research shows that Black women (and White men) are perceived more positively when they express agentic traits and dominance than White women (and Black men).[38]

This paradox is also referred to as the tightrope bias.[39] What the metaphor implies is that women leaders experience a very narrow socially accepted span of behaviour. If they become too assertive or strong in their leadership style, they quickly become labelled as "a bitch", "bossy", "too much", "mini-man", "more man than the men", etc. If they are nice and caring, they are not seen as leadership material. As such, they walk a thin line and have to balance their act very carefully. A male leader can be much more assertive and stronger in his leadership style before he is seen as "unnaturally bossy". Also, when male leaders display stereotypical feminine behaviour, such as caring for employees, organising the company off-site days or prioritising time with children, it is seen as impressive and further qualifies them as leaders. This, of course, only counts to a certain degree and applies more readily to men in the very top positions of an organisation. Men, too, experience bullying and harassment if they choose an active caretaker role or a caretaker profession (like being a nurse or stay-at-home dad). Men, therefore, also have to balance their behaviour according to what is perceived as socially accepted behaviours. They just have a slightly wider span of social acceptance; we could say that they walk a plank and not a tightrope. In working with bias, norms and inclusion, we argue, it is possible to widen the socially accepted span of behaviour for everyone. What if we all had a full road of opportunities? Wouldn't that be more equitable?

We also know from research that women receive shorter and less glowing (letters of) recommendations. This has been documented in qualitative studies of actual recommendations and in experimental studies where people are asked to write statements about fictive people.[40] From both these lines of study, we know that people have a tendency to talk more positively about men than women, and that they have a tendency to focus on the competencies if they (think they) are evaluating a man and on personality if they (think they) are evaluating a woman. In extended studies, which involve observing interview situations, we can see that people bring the same bias to interviews and have a tendency to ask men open-ended questions about their competencies, whereas women are asked more closed-ended questions about their personality and private life, questions in which the interviewee has a limited set of options from which to choose a response.[41] Hence, women do not have the same opportunity to demonstrate their competencies as men.

Women are also subject to what is known as the tall poppy syndrome in which people are attacked, resented, disliked, criticised or cut down because of their achievements and/or success. The Tallest Poppy 2023[42] is an international study across 103 countries that looks at thousands of working women from all demographics and professions to determine how their mental health, well-being, engagement and performance are affected by interactions with their clients, colleagues and leaders. The study, led by Dr. Rumeet Billan, reveals the consequences of this silent systemic syndrome and the impact it has on women in the workplace worldwide. According to the study's findings, 86.8% of respondents experienced this phenomenon at work. The Tallest Poppy reveals that women, who are successful, are being bullied and belittled, challenged on their successes and made to feel as though it's not their place to take up so much space. Disconcertingly, the study finds that men in higher leadership positions are more likely to penalise or undermine women below them in the hierarchy due to their success. Women, on the other hand, were more likely to cut down peers. This syndrome leads to stress, burnout, negative impact on mental health and lower self-confidence. In fact, a McKinsey report highlighted that female leaders experience much higher rates of burnout than men, 40% compared to 33%.[43]

Finally, research has shown how bias leads to associating successful entrepreneurship with men and not women.[44] This greatly influences who is successful in obtaining venture capital or other funding for their ideas and thus their probability of starting their own business. In Europe, according to the European Investment Bank (EIB), while women represent more than half the population, they account for less than a third of entrepreneurs.[45] Research shows us that investors ask very different questions to men and women. Investors tend to ask male entrepreneurs promotion-focused questions and female entrepreneurs prevention-focused questions. Naturally, these different approaches elicit different types of answers that may undermine the success of female entrepreneurs in raising higher amounts of funding, or any funding at all.[46] What is interesting is that despite receiving less than half of the investment capital of their male peers, female-founded companies deliver twice as much revenue per dollar invested. Within the venture capital space, the picture is particularly bleak. Female entrepreneurs in Europe received just 1% of venture capital investment in 2021.[47] The picture isn't much better across the Atlantic. Female entrepreneurs in the US received just 2% of overall venture capital funds in 2021—the smallest slice since 2016.[48] It doesn't stop there. Even when women succeed in setting up a venture, research from Copenhagen Business School shows that female founders do not only risk discrimination from external stakeholders like banks and investors, but they may also have to face discrimination from people on their own payroll, with employees making less effort for female than male employers.[49]

While most studies focus on the ways in which women are disadvantaged by gender bias, it is very important to understand that gender bias is not only a "women's thing". To the contrary, it influences everyone, just to varying frequencies, degrees and prevalence.

In studies of men and masculinity, it is found that men are bullied, teased or directly harassed if they choose to take a more active caretaker role by taking a long parental leave, working fewer hours or being a stay-at-home dad. They face stigmas, which stem from a lack of familiarity with the role, religious beliefs, opposing attitudes about gender roles and ignorance.[50] And more generally, not necessarily linked to children or caretaker roles, men who ask for a flexible schedule are seen as less masculine.[51] We are sure that you have observed that kindergarten and primary school educators tend to be women. Of the 506,400 full-time teachers in the UK, 30.5% of teachers are male and 69.5% are female.[52] Interestingly, at the primary school level, the teachers are 82.4% female. In the US, in 2018, about 76% of public school teachers were female and 24% were male, with a lower percentage of male teachers at the elementary school level (11%) than at the secondary school level (36%).[53] Similar data can be found across other OECD[54] countries. Why is this? Several studies state that men are underrepresented in early childhood education because of low salary, perceived lack of status, fear of child abuse allegations and scarcity of male camaraderie in the field.[55] In addition, early childhood education has been traditionally considered to be a female-oriented profession.[56] So, while women experience sexism and gender bias much more frequently, severely and pervasively, that does not mean men don't experience gender bias as well.

The majority of research on gender bias and sexism has largely focused on the binary, cisgender identities of men and women. What about employees with non-binary gender and transgender identities? What biases do they face? While there is limited research, existing studies find pervasive biases. In a study conducted by Business.com in 2023 who interviewed more than 400 non-binary Americans, it was found that over 80% of the interviewees "believed that identifying as nonbinary would hurt their job search".[57] Business.com also sent two "phantom" CVs to 180 job postings, both with a gender-neutral name, but one including "they/them" pronouns. Those with the non-binary pronouns received 8% less employer interest than those without. Then, Business.com followed up with hiring managers and found that they were less likely to wish to contact those who included "they/them" pronouns. Some claimed non-binary people would bring "drama" to the workplace. A 2021 McKinsey report shows that transgender adults in America are twice as likely as cisgender adults to be unemployed, and that people who identify as transgender feel far less supported in the workplace than their cisgender colleagues do. They report that it's more difficult to understand workplace culture and the compensation and benefit models, as well as harder to get promoted. They also feel less supported by their managers.

According to a study conducted by the National Human Rights Commission in India in 2018, 96% of transgender individuals are denied jobs and forced to take low paying or undignified work, like sex work and begging, for livelihood. The study also revealed that 92% of transgender individuals are deprived of the right to participate in any form of economic activity in India, with around 89% of transgender individuals saying they cannot get jobs that they are qualified for.

Racism or Ethnic Bias

Racism and ethnic bias are almost as well studied as sexism and gender bias. However, its acceptance as a leadership bias differs from context to context. Race is for many people still an extremely difficult subject to talk about, and many still deny the fact that most societies are built on a racial hierarchy, rooted in colonialism. While colonial history is exactly that, history, its influence on society and workplaces is still very much felt today. When countries were colonised by the Europeans hundreds of years ago, be it in Africa, US or Asia, the colonial powers introduced a stratification of society creating differences between those who had power (including wealth) and those who did not. Indigenous communities were forced into slavery and manual labour to fulfil the greed for power of the colonial "masters".

The concept of race was created by anthropologists and philosophers in the eighteenth century as a basis for geographically grouping people, based on their skin colour and physical traits. These groupings laid the foundation for the notion that some races are superior to others, which benefited White Europeans in slave trade, colonisation and accumulation of wealth while also promoting capitalism. Race has also been used as a basis for oppression during the Holocaust, the interethnic conflict in Rwanda and, most recently, the Rohingya genocide. According to the Merriam-Webster dictionary, racism is "a belief that race is the primary determinant of human traits and capacities and that racial differences produce an inherent superiority of a particular race". Closely related to racism is xenophobia, which is the dislike of or prejudice against people from other countries. While colonialism may well be a part of our history, its influence is very much present and felt in today's workplaces and societies.

Race, it should be emphasised, is not a biological construct. There is only one race—the human race—which is well researched to have begun in Africa. The differences in skin colour are a result of human adaptation that relate to where people moved to geographically about 50,000–80,000 years ago. Melanin is the skin's natural source of skin protection from the sun's UV rays of those closer to the tropics, while those further away from the equator in zones with less sunlight developed lighter skin. Race is a social construct, where certain skin colours and physical features have been assigned certain meanings.

In discussing racism and the impact of colonialism on racism, it is important for us to also address some of the ways in which racism shows up—through colourism, which according to the Oxford Language Dictionary is "prejudice or discrimination against individuals with a dark skin tone, typically among people of the same ethnic or racial group", and accentismand discrimination on the basis of the way a language is spoken or written, usually by non-native speakers. Research indicates that British colonialists who occupied the South Asian countries of India, Pakistan and Bangladesh showed preferential treatment for lighter-skinned individuals, exacerbating the view that lower classes were also of darker skin colour, a narrative that fit well with the racial narratives of the colonial masters.[58] Colourism is rampant across South Asia with fairness and bleaching skin products being extremely popular across the region. Very early on, young girls are conditioned to believe that being fair is a mark of beauty, intelligence and being able to fare better in life. This translates into a socio-economic stratification among the Global South Asian diaspora as those with lighter skin hold more power and privilege and are better treated socially and economically.[59] Just as gender bias tends to work against women, we know that there is a general tendency of associating light skin with competence and professionalism and dark skin with low competence, aggression and even criminality. Ekeoma Uzogara finds that "medium-skinned" Latinas perceive elevated levels of discrimination as compared to lighter-skinned Latinas.[60] Similarly, Laurie Rudman and Meghan McLean show the biased preference of Americans for lighter skin tones.[61]

Now let us look at accentism. Research has shown that most of us have a hierarchical sorting of accents based on what we perceive to be more socially and culturally acceptable.[62] This linguistic discrimination means that those with accents different from the majority feel ashamed of their accents and feel pressure at work to change the way they speak to "fit in". This can be mentally and emotionally exhausting, creating identity issues in people, along with anger and bitterness, as changing how you speak also changes who you are.[63]

In a survey in 2022, conducted by the BBC, which looked at university applicants, university students, early-career professionals and later career professionals, almost half of UK workers have had their accents mocked, criticised or singled out in a social setting. 31% of university attenders indicated that they were worried that their accents could have a negative impact on their future careers. 46% of workers have faced insults about their accents, with 25% reporting jokes at work. The survey also found that senior managers from working-class backgrounds were far more likely to worry that their accents could be barriers to their progression, with 29% highlighting such concerns compared to 22% from a "better off background".[64]

Race bias exists in all contexts, but it is most studied in so-called Western contexts. And before we continue to discuss those studies, let's dwell for a moment on the terms Western and non-Western. Try to pause for a second and imagine where on the globe the Western countries are located. North America, Europe, Australia and New Zealand… There isn't anything particularly Western about the location of these countries is there? And when we look at most maps, Europe is in the middle. Still, "Western" is a term many national registers use as a basis for data analysis.

More recently, research has been moving away from the terminology of "Western" and "non-Western" towards using the terms "global majority" and "global minority". If we could shrink the earth's population to a village of precisely 100 people, with all the existing human ratio remaining the same, data from 100people.org shows us that it would look like this (Image 3.5):

In the light of this, "global majority" is a more accurate collective term for ethnic groups which constitute approximately 85% of the global population, with the term "global minority" covering the remaining 15%. This means that people who have been considered to be ethnic minorities from a Western lens (Black, Asian, Brown, dual-heritage, indigenous to the Global South) are far from actually being minorities from a global standpoint. It is time to reframe this and move away from a colonial mindset of who is the majority and minority.

Having said that and because most register data analyses are based on the constructed distinction between Western and non-Western, let's get started with the research that we have on race bias in these locations. Unfortunately, studies show that such bias is ingrained from an early age. Research shows us that 3-month-old babies prefer faces from their own race,[65] and 9-month-olds only recognise other own-race faces, not other-race faces as familiar.[66] In the 1940s, psychologists Kenneth and Mamie Clark designed and conducted a series of experiments known colloquially as "the doll tests" to study the psychological effects of segregation on African American children. The results

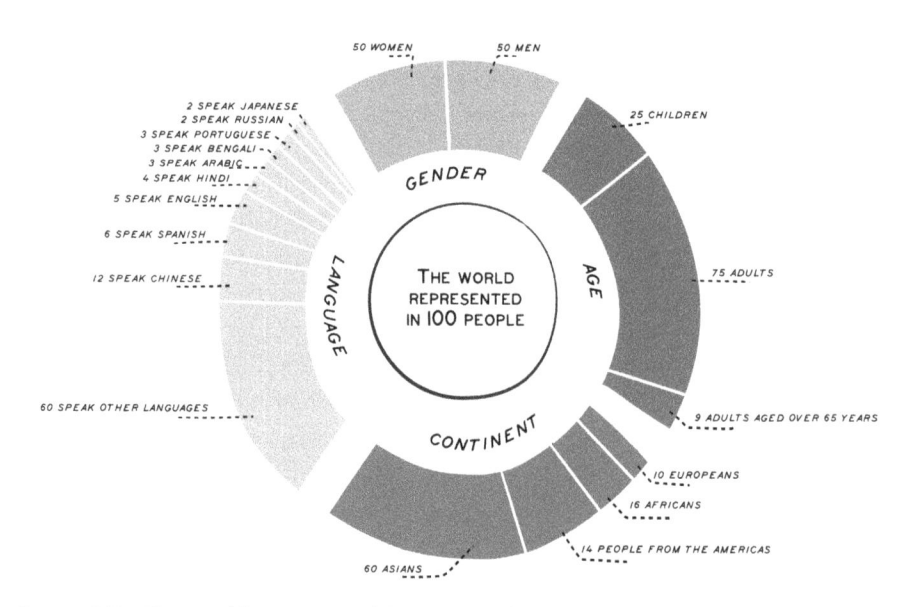

Image 3.5 The world represented in 100 people

showed the majority of Black children preferred White dolls to Black dolls. The dolls test has been repeated over the years, always yielding similar results. A 2021 study published in the Journal of Experimental Child Psychology[67] found that children were more likely to share their resources with White children than Black children. The effect did not appear to be motivated by in-group bias nor by feelings of warmth towards White children, but by a stereotype that White people are wealthier than Black people. From studies of kindergartens and primary schools, we know that teachers at this level already expect less of pupils with dark skin and dark hair.[68] A Danish study from 2022 asked 1.264 primary school teachers if they believed they could make room for one more pupil in their class. They were significantly more likely to answer yes, if the pupil's name was Mathias compared to if the pupil's name was Yousef.[69] This cannot but influence the possibilities and educational choices of pupils with names that are associated with a certain skin colour, religion and socio-economic background.

Once people reach the job market, race bias influences the recruitment process, as people with a "non-Western" sounding name in "Western" countries must send approximately 50% more applications to get to a job interview compared to people with "Western" sounding names with the exact same skills. A 2017 study published by S. Michael Gaddis, a sociology professor at UCLA, titled "How Black Are Lakisha and Jamal? Racial Perceptions from Names Used in Correspondence Audit Studies",[70] showed that when names like Lakisha and Jamal are used, they send signs about a person's social class and race. This study supports the findings of a 2004 study titled "Are Emily and Greg More Employable than Lakisha and Jamal?",[71] in which fictitious resumes were sent out in response to help-wanted ads in Chicago and Boston newspapers. The resumes were identical except for their names. The answer to the question in the title of the study is, unfortunately, a resounding "yes", with those resumes with African American sounding names needing to be sent out 50% more than those with European American sounding names before getting a call back. A similar study conducted at the University of Copenhagen in 2015 showed that applicants with Middle Eastern sounding names like Mohammed had to apply for 52% more positions to be called for an interview than someone with a Danish sounding name like Mads.[72] A Swedish study from 2007 found similar tendencies that the applicant with a Swedish sounding name had 50% more chance of being called for an interview compared to the applicant with a Middle Eastern sounding name.[73]

In a study researching job applications in the UK called the GEMM (Growth, Equal Opportunities, Migration and Markets) survey, researchers applied for over 3000 jobs, using different names from various ethnic backgrounds. All of the CVs and cover letters were otherwise identical. The study showed that only 15% of those from an underrepresented ethnic background received a call back compared to 24% of White applicants. The study also showed that applicants from an ethnic background had to send 60% more applications to get as many call backs as the White majority, and that British employers were the most discriminatory. What is also important to note is that the level of name discrimination faced by South Asians was as strong as it was at the end of the 1960s, despite these applicants being British-born or being British-educated from a young age, negating reasons of poor English language competence.

Studies have also linked race with how we perceive more personal competencies, such as service-mindedness. For example, a US study[74] has shown that Black service providers are required to exert higher levels of emotional labour to receive the same customer evaluations compared to their White peers. This means they must amplify positive expressions, smile more, be more friendly, etc., in order to satisfy customers. This has a direct link back to the race bias that assumes Black people are more aggressive than White people. Findings from a US study show that race bias also influences how people are punished for being late. Black employees experience fewer advancement opportunities the more often they are late—an effect that did not hold true for Hispanic and White peers.[75]

One of the most famous studies that looks at the prevalence of cultural stereotypes is the Princeton Trilogy task, referred to as a trilogy as the study was replicated across three generations of Princeton students. In the task, respondents were provided with a list of 84 trait adjectives and instructed "to read through the list of words and select those which seem to you typical of (target group)". The initial study found that there was a high level of consistency in the adjectives respondents associated with the Black stereotype. For instance, 85% of the students said that Blacks were superstitious. Other groups were similarly stereotyped; for example, 79% said that Jews were shrewd. At the same time, respondents were very positive towards their own group, reflecting in-group bias. Since most of the students did not have any personal contact with members of the ethnic groups they had to rate, it was suggested that stereotypes are learned through media and social conditioning.[76] Since that study in 1933, several studies have replicated this procedure in an effort to examine the amount of stability or change in stereotypes. What these studies found was that people were more uncomfortable with making generalisations about groups,[77] and that ethnic and national stereotypes increased rather than decreased, suggesting that current members of stereotyped groups may confront stereotypes more frequently than did previous members of stereotyped groups. While the studies showed that stereotypes may be confronted more frequently, they also found that over time stereotypes have become more favourable.[78]

A very recent study published in 2023 tested the well-supported hypothesis that in the US, the leaders of the highest valued companies, best-ranked universities and most-consumed media outlets are more likely to be White (that is, overrepresented as compared to White people's general share in the US population).[79] This gap has been explained by evidence that shows that US respondents' prototype of a leader is White by default—which in turn causes White (and not non-White) people to be promoted up the organisational ladder more quickly. Due to counter claims that US respondents no longer associate leaders—more than non-leaders—with being White, previous findings were tested through three experiments on the topic of whether leaders, more than non-leaders, continue to be associated with Whiteness (i.e. being categorised as White or being represented with stereotypically White qualities). The study found that associations between leaders and Whiteness hold up to scrutiny, but that detecting them may depend on what methods researchers employ. When researchers use direct methods of detecting racial assumptions (e.g. self-report measures), there appears to be no evidence of an association between leaders and Whiteness. However, when researchers use more indirect methods of detecting racial assumptions (e.g. a Princeton trilogy task), an association between leaders and Whiteness was clear. So, while respondents refrained from freely expressing associations they may harbour between leaders and Whiteness, these associations do not appear to have dissipated with time.

A Danish study recently demonstrated that male migrant workers from other "Western" countries earned on average 4% less than their Danish male co-workers and "Western" female workers on average earn 1.1% less than their Danish female co-workers. "Non-Western" male workers on average earn 8.4% less than their Danish male co-workers and "non-Western" female workers earn 3.1% less than their Danish female co-workers. Male migrant workers thus experience a significantly higher pay gap relative to their male native co-workers than female migrant workers do, especially migrant male workers from "non-Western" countries.[80] A study on stereotypes of East Asians in America showed that people disliked a dominant East Asian worker compared to a nondominant East Asian co-worker and compared to a White co-worker regardless of whether they were dominant or not. The study also showed that dominant East Asians were racially harassed at work more than nondominant East Asians and more than dominant and nondominant employees of other racial identities.[81]

What happens when we look at the intersection between race and gender identities? The bias that women face at work varies with race. Look around you in your organisation—who are the women who are getting opportunities to be hired, promoted or to join talent programs and other forms of employee development? Who are the women leaders in your organisation? Are they representative of the general population? Depending on where you are in the world, those women are likely to be from one of the well-represented race-related groups: White women, Indian women, Chinese women, African women or Latina women, and so on. They are also more likely to be cisgender heterosexual, able-bodied, from certain educational institutions and socio-economic backgrounds. Are we right?

Women are not a monolith and making efforts to support only some groups of women is in itself biased. The data paints a bleak picture for women of colour, particularly Black women. In corporate America, in 2023, just four women who identify as Black are in CEO positions of a Fortune 500 company.[82] According to the 2019 LeanIn.org and McKinsey & Company report, Black women in corporate America are more likely than other women to hear people express surprise when they demonstrate strong language skills or other abilities (26% vs. 11% of White women and 8% of men).[83] While Black women make up 7% of the total workforce, they account for 12% of minimum-wage earners[84] and while 21% of C-suite leaders are women, only 4% are women of colour, and only 1% are Black women.[85] For every 100 men promoted to manager, only 58 Black women are promoted.[86] 47% of Black transgender women report being fired, denied a promotion or not hired because of their gender identity.[87] Only 26% of Black women say they have equal access to sponsorship, compared with 32% of White women.[88] In meetings and other common workplace scenarios, 54% of Black women are often the only or one of the only people of their race/ethnicity in the room[89] with Black women being required to represent their entire race, constantly proving that they are competent and capable.

A report published in 2023 by Catalyst studied 2,734 women from marginalised racial and ethnic groups in the US, the UK, Canada, Australia and South Africa. The study found that women with darker skin tones were more likely to experience discrimination compared to those with lighter skin tones. Queer (63%) and transgender (67%) women are particularly likely to experience racism at work, compared with cisgender heterosexual women (49%). What was also particularly noteworthy is that 25% of the participants of the study believed that senior leaders in their organisation would discriminate against an employee based on their ethnicity, race or culture and that this discrimination could take the form of overt and covert racism that included negative assumptions, belittling insults, disparaging remarks, discriminatory actions and outright racial slurs.[90]

So, what do people do to cope with racism, particularly accentism and name discrimination? They code-switch. Code-switching "involves adjusting one's style of speech, appearance, behaviour, and expression in ways that will optimize the comfort of others in exchange for fair treatment, quality service, and employment opportunities".[91] The term code-switching was originally created to refer specifically to linguistics when the speaker alternates between two or more languages, language varieties, accents or informal mixtures of language within a single conversation. This happens often in multicultural workplace environments. However, code-switching involves much more than just speech, including any behaviour in an effort to "fit in". Altering one's name is one aspect of code-switching.

Ageism

Ageism is the form of discrimination that is most likely to affect all of us in some form at some point in our lives.[92] Nonetheless, there has been surprisingly little research on age-based discrimination in comparison with the rich insights on gender and race bias. This is particularly problematic as we face an ageing population, and thus a decline in young skilled individuals. This leads to skills shortages in a range of occupations and has intensified the fight for talent, resulting in highly competitive and dynamic job markets.[93]

However, according to a WHO analysis, every other person in the world is assumed to hold age bias against older people. Several research studies have demonstrated age discrimination against older people, where age has been associated with lack of energy, competence and willingness to "put in the work".[94] Older workers with the same qualifications as younger peers often receive lower subjective evaluations on performance in job interviews or in job performance reviews.[95]

Most studies of ageism have, therefore, concentrated on the discrimination of older people or the positive effect that looking young might have. Here, studies have shown a positive relation between perceived competencies and potential and what researchers have called "having a baby face". This means that people who look younger than their age are judged more favourably compared to people, who look their age or older. Other studies have shown that older people who look younger than they are will not only be seen as more competent but also as less hostile and more trustworthy.[96]

All of these results could make us believe that it's an advantage to be young, but that is not always the case. It depends on how young you look—as well as your gender. Ageism goes both ways, so to speak. A 2019 Diversity and Inclusion Study by Glassdoor in the US, UK, France and Germany showed that younger employees (52% of ages 18–34) are more likely than older employees (39% of ages 55+) to have witnessed or experienced ageism.[97] In this regard, you might recall the May 2013 *TIME* Magazine cover "The Me Me Me Generation", which declared that "Millennials are lazy, entitled narcissists".

Ageism against younger individuals occurs mostly in institutions such as the workplace as well as in legal and political systems. In Europe, it even seems to be more prevalent than ageism against older people. Furthermore, ageism towards younger women is stronger than age-based discrimination of young men, implying intersectional effects.[98] Similarly, it has been shown that 65+-year-old women are more often than 65+-year-old men seen as "too old" to be leader material. We don't have to look far in either political or commercial leadership roles to see this tendency. In a study of voting behaviours in Ireland, researchers found that being young can provide a net electoral advantage to male candidates. In contrast, young female candidates appear to be advantaged by their age but penalised by their gender.[99] So, in this study although young age was a benefit for men and women, it benefitted male individuals more than females.

Because of the complex perception of age and how perception of age is influenced by one's profession, looks, gender and race, age as a numerical concept can be difficult to operationalise. Instead, studies have shown that it is better to work with life events categories, which are not stable but performed in social interactions and dependent on individual life experiences.[100] If a life event approach is used, you would as a leader not assume that a woman in her late 20s and early 30s would want to be a parent, but that individuals of all genders and all ages could choose to be a parent at a point in their lives. Similarly, you would not assume that a 65+-year-old person was ready to take it easier or retire, but discuss with each individual, regardless of their age, when they need to slow down or speed up their career.

Appearancism/Lookism

How we look is also a source of bias. Several studies document that we judge attractive people as more competent and healthier as well as less hostile and more trustworthy.[101] At work, many of us draw on physical appearance stereotypes when we interact with others and assume that physically attractive people also possess other socially desirable traits.[102] It gets more complicated when we also take the cultural element into consideration. In individualistic "Western" cultures, studies have shown that people believe and listen to those who are more physically attractive[103], and in more collectivist societies, e.g. Taiwan, physical attractiveness is associated with intellectual competence and trust that collectively play a role in determining satisfaction and loyalty.[104]

In Korea, university students associated being beautiful with being trustworthy and showing a greater degree of concern for others but did not share the North American association that physically attractive people are more dominant and assertive than those who are not.[105] This stereotype acts as a self-fulfilling prophecy. Being more attractive is perceived to be of more value to society, leading attractive individuals to receive greater benefits and preferential treatment,[106] and research shows a correlation between physical attractiveness and higher income, social skills and self-confidence.[107] This contributes towards attractive jobseekers standing out to employers.[108]

In recent research, it was found that it is not just those who are very attractive who seem to be reaping the fruits, "very ugly" people also do well and may even have an advantage. While "ugliness" (as well "attractiveness") is absolutely subjective, it was found that the least attractive 3% of the population earned more than the 50% of the population who were considered to be average looking or "sort of ugly".[109] Peggy Drexler, in an opinion piece written for CNN,[110] attributes this to sinister motives of intra-gender sexism and female misogyny. She suggests that women hold other women back in an effort of self-preservation, fighting for the few spots at the top of the corporate ladder. Supporting and rewarding the "very ugly" is an unthreatening way to keep the threatening women, who are more attractive, smarter or wealthier, down.

A 2018 study published in the *Journal of Personality and Social Psychology* showed that perceptions that attractive individuals have a greater sense of entitlement can result in negative treatment of attractive people.[111] Margaret Lee, co-author of the study, says we "perceive attractive individuals to feel more entitled to good outcomes than unattractive individuals".[112] A study looking at situations where attractiveness can be detrimental for women found that attractive women, when applying for masculine jobs where physical appearance is not important (e.g. security guard), are discriminated against.[113]

What about tattoos and other aspects of how we look? In a study where half of the participants were shown pictures of tattooed individuals and the other half pictures with the tattoos edited out, the researchers found something interesting. Whereas the participants judged the individuals with tattoos (both men and women) to be less intelligent, more heavy drinkers as well as more likely to be a criminal, they also found them, especially women, to be stronger and more independent than their counterparts without tattoos.[114] However, other studies also find this stigma to vary across industries. In the creative industries, it has been shown that tattooed individuals hold an advantage.[115] On the other hand, the HR Director publication[116] refers to a study that showed that recruiters said they would feel uncomfortable hiring someone wearing clothing that is too casual (34%), having visible piercings (26%) and having brightly dyed hair (21%).

In the first of its kind, large-scale comparative field experiment on appearance-based racial discrimination in Europe, which was published in 2023, researchers sent about 13,000 fictitious CVs to real job openings in Germany, the Netherlands and Spain. The applicants were young adults born to parents from over 40 different countries of ancestry.[117] They randomly varied the applicants' ethnic ancestry signalled by name and their racial appearance signalled by photographs. This is what they found: Applicants' racial appearance triggers discriminatory behaviour in all the three countries studied with Black applicants tending to receive the lowest call back rates on average while White applicants receive the highest. It should be noted that the call back rates for Black applicants were only marginally different from those found for other non-White groups (Asian/Indigenous, Dark-Skinned Caucasian). The authors highlight that with a large pool of second-generation applicants entering employment in Europe, the number of new Europeans at risk of suffering appearance-based racial discrimination is on the rise.

Heightism

A large experimental study confirmed what other studies had also found, namely that physical height is significantly related to measures of social esteem, leader skills and performance. Furthermore, the same study also showed that being taller is positively related to income, even after controlling for sex, age and weight.[118] It is perhaps not surprising that the positive effect is stronger for men than women. This probably relates to the tightrope bias, discussed earlier. Very tall women (or women taller than men) might be punished for exhibiting attributes not stereotypically associated with femininity.

Malcolm Gladwell, in his bestselling book *Blink*, presents an analysis among the Fortune 500 firms in which he found that the average CEO was 6′ tall, whereas the average American is 5′9″. This means that the Fortune

500 CEOs on average are 3 inches taller than the average American. In the US population, about 14.5% of all men are more than 6′ tall. However, 58% of male Fortune 500 CEOs are more than 6′ tall. Also, while 3.9% of adult American men are 6′2″ or taller, 30% of Fortune 500 CEOs are 6′2″ or taller.

What is also worth noting is that a study published in 2004 in the *Journal of Applied Psychology* showed that every inch above average in height may be worth $789 per year in earnings.[119] The study also found that someone who is 6′ tall earns, on average, nearly $166,000 more during a 30-year career than someone who is 5′5″—even when controlling for gender, age and weight.

Hairism

Did you know that our natural hair can be a source of bias? A publication from August 2020 in *Social Psychology and Personality Science* showed that the hair-related bias in recruitment against Black women with natural hairstyles is very real.[120] In the study, participants from various diasporas evaluated the profiles of Black and White female job applicants across a variety of hairstyles. The study found that Black women with natural hairstyles were perceived to be less professional, less competent and less likely to be recommended for a job interview than Black women with straightened hairstyles and White women with either curly or straight hairstyles. In industries with conservative dressing norms, Black women with natural hairstyles received more negative evaluations when applying for jobs. In one of the experiments of the study, participants reviewed Black women with natural hairstyles and Black women with straightened hair for the same employment opportunity. The Black women with straightened hair were consistently reported to be more professional, with professionalism being defined as "refined, polished, and respectable", leading to more positive recommendations for an interview for those women. In a US 2023 survey of 1000 Black women between the ages of 25 to 64, commissioned by Dove and LinkedIn to support the CROWN (Creating a Respectful and Open World for Natural Hair) Act to end hair biases and discrimination, Black women's hair is 2.5 times more likely to be perceived as unprofessional. 66% of the respondents said that they had changed their hair for a job interview to reduce the chances of being discriminated on the basis of their hair, with 41% saying they changed their hair from curly to straight and over 20% reporting they were sent home from work because of their hair. 44% of Black women under age 34 feel pressured to have a headshot with straight hair.[121]

The consequence of this is that Black women spend a greater amount of time and money on hair products to help them manage their hair in a way that conforms to other peoples' standards of appropriateness. This was documented in a "good hair" survey conducted by Perception Institute in 2016,[122] which found that White women show explicit bias against Black women's textured hair. This bias resulted in one in five Black women feeling a social pressure to straighten their hair for work—twice as many as White women. This pressure also has some serious health consequences, with the use of chemical relaxers to straighten the hair increasing the risk of developing uterine cancer.[123]

Weightism or Fatphobia

In the US, 70% of adults are overweight, and 40% of those are obese[124] while the number is one in four for UK adults.[125] In urban areas of China, obesity rates are over 20%.[126] India has seen a surge in obesity in recent years, with 135 million individuals affected by obesity.[127] With a growing percentage of the global population being overweight, this bias is an extremely relevant one to consider. A review of research in this area shows that overweight individuals face negative perceptions and stigmatisation in the workplace at every stage of the employment cycle, from selection, placement, compensation, assignments, promotions, assessments, discipline and termination.[128] Obesity is a key factor in unequal treatment at work and can be seen in inequity in pay, unequal treatment by superiors and lower social acceptance in the workplace. It is found to be a barrier to professional success and results in fewer prospects for promotions.[129]

In a study conducted in 2015, research assistants wore "fat suits" when applying for jobs at retail stores.[130] These job applicants observed more discrimination in the form of subtle interpersonal behaviours such as less nodding and smiling, more interpersonal distance and shorter interactions when they were wearing the suits than when they were not. This discrimination is also experienced once the person is hired as an employee. Studies show that people have lower expectations from trainees who are obese.[131] There seems to be an added gender bias: Weight gain for women is significantly related to lower salaries, but only affects the salaries for men when they are very obese.[132] Research also shows that senior leaders, CEOs, senior Vice-Presidents and board members are not spared from weight bias. Supervisors, subordinates and peers of senior executives rated obese leaders more negatively, in terms of both task and interpersonal performance, than thin leaders.[133]

Ableism

Disabled World defines ableism as "discrimination action against people based on the physical ability of their body, especially against people with disabilities in favour of people who are not disabled". [134] We live in an ableist society where those of us who do not have disabilities—both those that are visible (physical, mental or neurological condition that is visible from the outside and limits or challenges a person's movements, senses or activities) and invisible (physical, mental or neurological conditions that are not visible from the outside, yet can limit or challenge a person's movements, senses or activities)—determine what are considered "normal ways of living".

While the law seems to be on the side of people who are physically disabled, they remain an underrepresented group in our workplaces. In 2018, only 29% of working-age Americans with disabilities (between ages 16 and 64) participated in the workforce, compared with 75% of Americans without a disability. In 2018, there were 15.1 million people of working-age living with disabilities in the US and a report by Accenture suggested that if companies embrace disability inclusion, they would have access to a new talent pool of more than 10.7 million people.[135]

We have seen some progress in the UK. In 2019, over 4.2 million disabled people were employed, an increase from 2013 when the number employed was just 2.9 million.[136] Also, the employment rate gap between disabled men and disabled women has reduced, with more disabled women being employed, and the overall unemployment rate for disabled people has roughly halved between 2013 and 2019.

So, what is standing in the way from employing someone with a physical disability? The reasons cited by managers and leaders are many. Fears about the added risk, additional healthcare costs, accommodation costs of accessibility features and training, as well as legal issues are listed as some of the reasons. While numerous studies show that these fears are not substantiated,[137] one of the biggest barriers to hiring and retaining people with physical disabilities is people's biased attitude.[138] These biases towards those with physical disabilities affect the entry and progression of people with disabilities.[139] At the same time, there is a clear lack of support and prioritisation from organisational leadership. According to the 2018 annual global CEO survey, disability was addressed by only 7.2% of the CEOs surveyed in their D&I strategies.[140]

In fact, very few people openly acknowledge that they have bias against people with disabilities because of the guilt experienced for even having this bias, making it easier to not talk or think about it. While we may not openly acknowledge it, many of us have bias against those who are physically disabled. A 2019 study conducted using data from 300,000 participants, gathered over 13 years, showed that even though people were positive towards others with disabilities, their unconscious or implicit bias grew over time and with age.[141] People with physical disabilities face bias and discrimination every day. Over one in three people show an unconscious bias against those with a disability, making this higher than levels of bias on the basis of gender or race.[142]

Religious Bias

Religious bias can take the form of bias against someone's faith-based more visible religious symbols or less visible food habits. A Carnegie Mellon study found that Muslim job candidates experienced more discrimination than Christian job candidates during the hiring process. For Muslim job candidates, there was a 13% lower call back rate compared to Christian job candidates.[143] Research shows that there is evidence of formal discrimination in job call backs and permission to complete applications, interpersonal discrimination through perceived negativity and low expectations to receive job offers in the workplace for those wearing a hijab. This is sometimes referred to as hijabophobia, discrimination against women wearing Islamic veils—the hijab, chador, niqab and burqa. Furthermore, the research also found that those wearing a hijab were less likely to receive call backs when there was low employee diversity as compared to when there was higher employee diversity.[144] Similar incidents have also been experienced by those wearing a Sikh turban. Turban Myths, a 2013 study by Stanford University Peace Innovation Lab and the Sikh American Legal Defense and Education Fund, showed that "the turban – an article of faith for the Sikhs – is associated with personalities that provoke great animosity among Americans in the post-9/11 era".

Religious practices also influence people's food choices. For example, practising Hindus do not eat beef, practising Muslims do not eat pork, eat halal meat and observe the fasting month of Ramadan and practising Jews who eat food that is Kosher observe a series of rules in terms of what to eat and how to prepare it. Religious bias often shows up as the lack of food choices available to these groups at the office canteen or during work events.

In a cross-national field experiment on ethnic discrimination, conducted by the Growth, Equal Opportunities, Migration and Markets (GEMM) project in Germany, the Netherlands, Norway, Spain and the UK, job applications were sent from fictitious job candidates to real job openings. The fictitious job candidates were either natives or had an immigrant background in one out of 52 different countries of origin. In all 5 countries, the study found clear differences in the call back rates of the majority population and minority applicants, confirming that minority applicants are discriminated against in the hiring process, similar to studies we have looked at earlier in this chapter. The study also found that the call back rates were higher for applicants from countries with a low share of Muslim population.[145]

> **Making Connections: Poornima & Sara's Experiences**
> During one of our classes, Poornima was struck by the experience that a student in Denmark shared. She is a Muslim woman who wears a hijab. She applied for student internship positions—as is common practice in Denmark—in some of the largest Danish companies. She noticed that her peers were getting invitations for interviews and she was not. Her grades and CV looked very similar to theirs with one difference—her photo (yes, we still have photos on CVs in Denmark) was of her in a hijab. Out of sheer frustration, she took off her hijab, took a new photo, added it to her CV and sent out the applications once again as the calls for applicants were still open. Guess what? Once the hijab was removed, she got multiple calls for interviews. In a separate interaction with a senior leader of Indian origin in Denmark, he expressed to Poornima that he is often asked if he is Muslim simply because of his skin colour and the way he looks. Over time, he shared that he has become better able to respond to such questions with "how does it matter?".

Deep Level Identity Bias

Deep level identity bias refers to the biases that are invisible, assumed to be invisible or at least not automatically activated by bodily or material differences. Deep level identity biases are connected to the way we live, the choices we make, the preferences we have and our various abilities.

Heterosexism and Sexual Orientation Bias

Sexual orientation bias encompasses all negative attitudes based on sexual orientation, whether the target is homosexual, bisexual or heterosexual,[146] but given the deeply embedded "acceptable" norms of behaviour, sexual prejudice is almost always directed at non-heterosexual people.[147] Heterosexism or heteronormativity is a "belief system that values heterosexuality as superior to and/or more 'natural' than homosexuality".[148] It is a term similar to sexism and racism, describing an ideological system that denies, denigrates and stigmatises any non-heterosexual form of behaviour, identity, relationship or community.[149] It includes the assumption that all people are heterosexual and denies or rejects the possibility of being other than straight. It is the idea that everyone is, or should be, heterosexual or straight and can be thought of as a more subtle and pervasive form of homophobia.

Sexual orientation bias can for example take the form of homophobia and biphobia. The Merriam-Webster dictionary defines homophobia as "irrational fear of, aversion to, or discrimination against homosexuality or homosexuals". Biphobia, which is an aversion towards bisexuality and towards bisexual people as a social group or as individuals, is a subset of homophobia.

The 2019 Glassdoor Diversity and Inclusion Study was conducted in the US, UK, France and Germany.[150] When compared to the other countries in the study, the percentage of employees reporting having experienced or witnessed workplace discrimination related to their LGBTQ identity was highest in the US at 33% compared to the UK (25%), France (22%) and Germany (15%). Among US employees, one in three (33%) has experienced or witnessed LGBTQ discrimination at work. The study also showed that in the US, younger employees (43% of ages 18–34) are more likely than older employees (18% of ages 55+) to have experienced or witnessed LGBTQ discrimination. In addition, employed LGBTQ identified men (38%) are more likely than employed LGBTQ identified women (28%) to have experienced or witnessed discrimination at work. When it comes to LGBTQ discrimination among younger workers, specifically, younger employed LGBTQ identified men (51% of ages 18–34) are significantly more likely than younger employed LGBTQ identified women (34% of ages 18–34) to have experienced or witnessed it.

Globally, about 40% of LGBTQ employees are closeted at work and 75% have reported experiencing negative day-to-day workplace interactions related to their LGBTQ identity in the past year.[151] 36% of employees who have come out of the closet have lied or "covered" parts of their identities at work in the past year, while 54% of employees who are out at work remain closeted to their clients and customers.[152] When employees cannot bring all aspects of who they are to work, it has a huge psychological impact on them, affecting their emotional and mental well-being in the workplace as well as how "authentic" they are perceived as being. When people are not perceived as behaving authentically or as if they are "hiding something", they are also seen as less of a "fit" with the organisation's culture. In a 2011 study, LGBTQ participants described that when they experienced microaggressions, they felt depressed, anxious and even traumatised.[153]

> **Making Connections: Poornima & Sara's Experiences**
> Sara facilitated a DEI workshop for a group of directors from a large Danish public organisation. When she presented the data above, one of the participants said that she didn't understand why homosexual people always had to make a fuss about their sexual orientation. Recently, the director had reviewed applications for a job opening and one of the applicants had written in her CV that she was a lesbian. The director had felt a little annoyed by this information. Not that she felt that there was something wrong with the applicant being a lesbian, but that she had to be so direct about it in the CV felt a little silly to her. However, one of her male colleagues responded promptly that he completely understood why the woman had written this in her CV, and then he told a story. He had recently been part of an interview panel. His colleague had asked a question to a candidate in which he had gendered her partner (e.g. what does your husband think about this?). The applicant had responded politely, but firmly, that she did not have a husband, she had a wife. The colleague in the interview panel got all flustered and didn't ask any more questions. After the interview, he had told the director that after that information "he couldn't concentrate". So, as the director said to the group, he completely understood why people would write this in a CV. It will save them and the interviewer the embarrassment of a mistake and the following awkwardness.

Education Bias

Many companies have a *"university bias"* in recruitment, preferring people who hold university degrees and whose degrees are from esteemed institutions, based on the assumption that students from these educational institutions are smarter, have undergone better training, are more hard-working or even innovative.[154] The problem is that the higher education system in the US, which many other universities around the world are modelled on, is highly stratified; so much so that it has been referred to as the caste system of the US.[155] In the US, tertiary education can range between $5000 and $50,000, while in the UK it is about $11,000. An Ivy League education will set a student and their parents back a substantial amount, making it available to just a select few: those who have such resources available, those fortunate or talented enough to obtain a scholarship or those who are eligible for bursary funding. However, even in countries where education is free, it is not equally available. This is often due to the extra layer of classism or socio-economic bias, which we explain further below.

Experience Bias

We also have bias against people's life experiences, for example against those who have a criminal record. In the UK, only 17% of ex-offenders manage to get a job within a year after release from prison.[156] The main barrier is discrimination and the resulting lack of opportunities.[157]

Another group of people in our society who are often discriminated against are veterans. Veterans, also known as ex-servicemen and women, are those who have served as part of the Armed Forces of a country, usually for an extended period, and who have been discharged from their duties under conditions that were not dishonourable. Veterans often face discrimination in hiring processes by employers who may be concerned about their physical or even mental abilities. This could be because a significant number of veterans experience Post-Traumatic Stress Syndrome (PTSD) due to the traumatic nature of their service in hostile conditions. While there are laws that protect veterans, making discrimination against them illegal, discrimination still exists.

> **Making Connections: Poornima & Sara's Experiences**
> Poornima was having a conversation with a White man in his early 50s. On the surface of it, this person should have had a fairly privileged existence. Yet, given that he had served in the army of his country during the Gulf War in the early 1990s, he struggled to find a job when he returned home due to companies not willing to pay for the potential insurance claims that could possibly occur due to PTSD (Post-Traumatic sStress Disorder).

Personality Bias

A study done in 2015 looked at how our personality influences our careers—whether certain kinds of people make more money, why certain kinds of personalities tend to end up in that nice corner office and so on.[158] The study looked at the 16 Myers-Briggs personality types and found the following results: Extrovert, Sensor, Thinker and Judger (ESTJ) made more money than other personality types; Extrovert, Sensor, Feeler and Judger (ESFJ) were more satisfied at work; Extroverts tend to manage larger teams as do Thinkers and Judgers. The study supported previous work that showed that personality types that are especially ambitious and inclined to leadership are the ENTJ (Extroverts, Intuitive, Thinker and Judger). Those who are ESTJ and ENTPs (Extroverts, Intuitive, Thinker and Perceiving) tend to be more entrepreneurial, while ESFJs are nurturing and tend to be focused on the task of parenting. As we can see, our organisations seem to favour extroverts rather than introverts.

Neurodiversity Bias

Neurodiversity refers to the infinite variety of cognitive styles of thinking and learning. Our workplaces have been created by and for people who fit into the neurotypical ways of thinking and learning. Neurodivergent talent struggles to fit the profiles sought by employers and profiles that include being a good communicator, being a team player, having high emotional intelligence, being persuasive, being extroverted, and having the ability to build relationships and networks. This automatically screens out neurodivergent talent who do not fit the prototype.

Many people with dyspraxia, dyslexia, ADHD, Asperger's, social anxiety disorders and autism have higher-than-average abilities and often have extraordinary skills, including superior problem-solving skills,[159] pattern recognition, memory and mathematics as well as bringing different perspectives to the workplace.[160] Research suggests that autistic employees are as much as 140% more productive than their neurotypical colleagues because of their increased ability to focus on certain tasks and ability to concentrate for an extended period of time.[161] With about 10–17% of the global population being neurodivergent, it is high time we embraced this talent pool in our organisations.

Mental Health and Invisible Disabilities Bias

Invisible disabilities can include anxiety, eating disorders, vision or hearing impairment or diabetes, among many others. They are invisible because they are not obvious to the naked eye. According to the World Health Organisation (WHO), one in every eight people, or 970 million people around the world, was living in 2019 with a mental health disorder, with anxiety and depressive disorders being the most common.[162] In 2020, the number of people living with anxiety and depressive disorders rose significantly because of the COVID-19 pandemic. In the US, according to a 2021 study of the National Institute of Health (NIH), nearly half of Americans surveyed reported recent symptoms of an anxiety or depressive disorder.[163] In India, the WHO says that about 20% of Indians suffered from mental diseases at the end of 2022, forecasting that India will lose $1.03 trillion in economic value owing to mental health issues between 2012 and 2030.[164]

Despite discrimination against employees because of their health—including mental health—being illegal in many countries, McKinsey & Company[165] shows that bias or stigma exists at three levels. The first is "self-stigma", which occurs when individuals internalise and accept negative stereotypes. The second is "public or social stigma", which refers to the negative attitude of society towards a particular group of people. In the case of behavioural-health conditions, it creates an environment in which those with such conditions are discredited, feared and isolated. Finally, "structural stigma" refers to system-level discrimination—such as cultural norms, institutional practices and healthcare policies—that constrains resources and opportunities and therefore impairs well-being.

Marital and Parenthood Choice Bias

Sociologists have shown that women have had to contend with the patriarchal nature of workplace environments, which reinforces the perception that being an "ideal worker" is incompatible with being a "good mother".[166] Women are confronted with the motherhood penalty—arising from "maternal wall bias".[167] Maternal wall bias occurs when decision-makers and colleagues view mothers or pregnant women as being less competent and less committed to their jobs. Discrimination against employees who are caregivers is on the rise for both men and women and is particularly damaging for women.[168] Even women of childbearing age who do not have children—some of whom may never want or be able to—face this bias. We have heard from so many women around the world who are 30 years old and above that they face daily invasive questions about their marital and parenthood status at work.

Organisations have a parenthood bias in which employees are expected to be either committed to their work or to their families. We have an implicit assumption that employees cannot do both. Mothers are less likely to be offered a job and promoted and are offered a lower salary compared to women without children, whereas fathers are more likely to be hired and promoted and receive a higher starting salary compared to men without children.[169] Interestingly, when mothers present themselves as the primary breadwinner, the motherhood penalty can become a breadwinner bonus.[170]

A further extension of the CV studies, which we looked at earlier in this chapter, shows us that people have a tendency to think that leaders who are mothers are constantly met with doubt about whether they can balance work and private life, and whether they are sure they want to compromise time with their family in order to succeed at work. It does not stop there. From friends and family, teachers and caretakers, their choice is met with suspicion about how they can spend so much time away from their children. Male leaders do not receive this kind of reaction to their choices. Whereas such reactions sometimes can be masked as "care" for women, this "care" risks constraining women, constructing them as fragile and thus needing to forgo work opportunities.[171]

In a field experiment conducted in the two large Spanish cities of Barcelona and Madrid, two pairs of fictitious CV (a man's and a woman's) were sent to 1,372 job offers from a broad selection of occupations.[172] In one pair, candidates had equivalent CVs except for their sex and their qualifications (either meeting standards or higher). In the second pair, candidates differed by sex and parenthood status (either with or without children). The researchers concluded that the observed differences in favour of men signalled gender bias in recruitment. This bias is reduced when women have higher qualifications and increased when they have children.

Fathers and/or parents from the LGBTQ+ community also face parental bias. Even though male employees who are fathers may be more likely to be hired, promoted and even get a higher starting salary, this is only when they conform to the prototype of who is an ideal worker. A male employee who leaves work earlier than others to attend their child's sport or dance lesson is seen to be less "professional" than others. A 2023 State of the Future of Work report in Australia by Melbourne University showed that 55% of male caregivers believe that they are treated unfairly at work and 31% believe that they lost their jobs because of caregiving, compared with 22% of working mothers. In another study by Australia's national caregiver consultancy Circle In, 73% of fathers want to take parental leave but 40% of employers offer none and 72% of fathers said their workplace or manager had discouraged them from doing so.

In another study, when candidates explicitly shared information about them being the breadwinner, it eliminated discrimination on pay for the female candidate, and when candidates explicitly shared information about their caregiver status, it eliminated discrimination on needing a flexible schedule for the male candidate. However, a male candidate's caregiver status decreased his likelihood of being offered a leadership training program (with no effect for the female candidate), and a female candidate's breadwinner status increased the perception that the female candidate's spouse or partner was incompetent (with no effect for the male candidate).[173] These parenthood biases and penalties exist because of the requirement of people to conform to a prototype of what is expected of them at work and in society.

Location Bias

Location bias relates to where someone belongs or comes from and has an impact on job prospects. This aspect of bias has not yet been well researched, but there is a growing interest in bias based on where one lives or chooses to live. A research study, conducted by University of Notre Dame economics professor David Phillips,[174] tested the effect that commuting distance has on an applicant's chance of being hired. It found that hiring managers are biased against those who live farther away. This involved sending more than 2,000 fictional resumes to low-wage employers in Washington, DC. Phillips carefully chose resumes addresses for each job opening and balanced the mix of applicant-workplace proximity and the affluence of the job seeker's neighbourhood to see how the location of the applicant's home influenced invitations to interview. The study found that hiring managers were biased against those who live farther away, and applicants living five or six miles farther from the job received one-third fewer call backs than those who lived closer.

Classism or Socio-Economic Bias

Classism or class discrimination refers to the prejudices we hold and the discriminatory behaviour we display based on social class—a hierarchy based on wealth, income, education, occupation and social networks. A report from the Social Mobility Commission in the UK[175] found that those from more affluent backgrounds are 80% more likely to be in a professional job than their working-class peers. In the UK, poor social mobility and workplace discrimination are estimated to cost the economy £270 billion each year.[176]

In a study done in the UK, students from poorer families are less likely to take science subjects in grades 11 and 12, and those who do are less likely to obtain grades high enough to encourage further study of the subject.[177] The reasons for this are not clear, with possible explanations including fewer opportunities and lack of role models at home and in workplaces. What is clear, however, is that as we think about how to ensure a diverse future talent pipeline for companies in the STEM industries, this is a concern we must address.

In this chapter, we have looked at the fundamentals of bias that you need to know to understand what bias is. Further, we have presented the many identity biases that exist. What has been covered here is, however, by no means exhaustive; there are many other biases, but hopefully you are now able to recognise and identify a range of different identity biases, even when you experience biases that are not mentioned in this chapter. What is crucial to remember is that these biases don't exist in isolation; they intersect with each other, depending on our diversity thumbprint. Also, your journey in exploring bias does not end here. In the next chapter, we continue building the ability to lead with clarity, turning our attention to situation-related cognitive bias.

Self-Reflection Exercise: My Bias

Refer back to the "My intersectional identity" exercise in Chapter 2. Reflect on the biases you experience based on your identity. Which dimensions of diversity do you experience bias in because of your identity?

_____

_____

_____

_____

_____

_____

_____

_____

_____

_____

Reflect on how these biases intersect with each other. What is the impact of this intersection of biases on you?

After learning more about bias, have you discovered any biases (including stereotypes) that you may hold against particular identities/social groups? List them below and consider when they occur.

What have you done so far to address bias that you witness or experience?

Notes

1. https://www.forbes.com/sites/daviddisalvo/2013/06/22/your-brain-sees-even-when-you-dont/#3eb381a8116a.
2. Thaler, R. H., & Sunstein, C. R. (2009). *Nudge: Improving Decisions about Health, Wealth and Happiness.* Penguin Books. Kahneman, D., Lovallo, D., & Sibony, O. (2011). Before You Make That Big Decision. *Harvard Business Review,* 89(6), 50-60. Tversky, A., & Kahneman, D. (1974, September 27). Judgment Under Uncertainty: Heuristics and Biases. *Science,* 185(4157), 1124–1131.
3. Slowman, S., & Fernbach, P. (2017). *The Knowledge Illusion: Why We Never Think Alone.* Riverhead Books.
4. Jost, J. T., Rudman, L. A., Blair, I. V., Carney, D. R., Dasgupta, N., Glaser, J., & Hardin, C. D. (2009). The Existence of Implicit Bias Is Beyond Reasonable Doubt: A Refutation of Ideological and Methodological Objections and Executive Summary of Ten Studies That No Manager Should Ignore. *Research in Organizational Behavior,* 29, 39–69.
5. Tversky, A., & Kahneman, D. (1974, September 27). Judgment Under Uncertainty: Heuristics and Biases. *Science,* 185(4157), 1124–1131.
6. Kahneman, D. (2019). *Thinking, Fast and Slow.* Farrar, Straus and Giroux.
7. Butler, J. (1990). *Gender Trouble.* Routledge.
8. Slowman, S., & Fernbach, P. (2017). *The Knowledge Illusion: Why We Never Think Alone.* Riverhead Books.
9. Willard, G., Isaac, K. J., & Carney, D. R. (2015). Some Evidence for the Nonverbal Contagion of Racial Bias. *Organizational Behavior and Human Decision Processes,* 128, 96–107.
10. Madl, T., Baars, B. J., & Franklin, S. (2011, April 25). The Timing of the Cognitive Cycle. *PLoS One,* 6(4), e14803.
11. Wilson, T. D., Lindsey, S., & Schooler, T. Y. (2000). A Model of Dual Attitudes. *Psychological Review,* 107, 101–126.
12. Hagiwara, N., Dovidio, J. F., Eggly, S., & Penner, L. A. (2016). The Effects of Racial Attitudes on Affect and Engagement in Racially Discordant Medical Interactions between Non-Black Physicians and Black Patients. *Group Processes and Intergroup Relations,* 19(4), 509–527.
13. Jones, K. P., Peddie, C. I., Gilrane, V. L., King, E. B., & Gray, A. L. (2016). Not So Subtle: A Meta-Analytic Investigation of the Correlates of Subtle and Overt Discrimination. *Journal of Management,* 42(6), 1588–1613.
14. https://hbr.org/2022/03/we-need-to-retire-the-term-microaggressions.
15. https://hbr.org/2022/03/we-need-to-retire-the-term-microaggressions.
16. Luthra, P. (2022). *The Art of Active Allyship.* København: TalentED.
17. Luthra, P. (2022). *The Art of Active Allyship.* København: TalentED.
18. https://www.abc.net.au/news/2016-06-01/words-you-should-avoid-using-about-women-in-the-workplace/7467848.
19. Luthra, P. (2022). *The Art of Active Allyship.* København: TalentED.

20. Hancock, A. (2014). Influence of Communication Partner's Gender on Language. *Journal of Language and Social Psychology*, 34(1), 46–64.
21. https://www.dictionary.com/browse/tone-policing.
22. http://www3.weforum.org/docs/WEF_GGGR_2022.pdf.
23. https://www.cnbc.com/2020/03/05/why-women-are-locked-out-of-top-jobs-despite-having-high-ambition.html.
24. https://hbr.org/2019/06/research-women-score-higher-than-men-in-most-leadership-skills.
25. https://www.catalyst.org/media-release/empathic-leaders-drive-employee-engagement-and-innovation-media-release/.
26. https://fortune.com/2023/01/12/fortune-500-companies-ceos-women-10-percent/.
27. Moss-Racusin, C. A., Dovidio, J. F., Brescoll, V. L., Graham, M., & Handelsman, J. (2012). Science Faculty's Subtle Gender Biases Favor Male Students. *PNAS: Proceedings of the National Academy of Sciences for the United States of America*, 109(41), 16474–16479. Moss-Racusin, C. A., Molenda, A. K., & Cramer, C. R. (2015). Can Evidence Impact Attitudes? Public Reactions to Evidence of Gender Bias in STEM Fields. *Psychology of Women Quarterly*, 39(2), 194–209.
28. Poornima & Sara prefer to use the word "masked" instead of "blind" due to the underlying bias that is associated with people who are visually impaired.
29. Goldin, C., & Rouse, C. (2000). Orchestrating Impartiality: The Impact of "Blind" Auditions on Female Musicians. *The American Economic Review*, 90(4), 715–741.
30. Jampol, L., Rattan, A., & Wolf, E. B. (2022). A Bias Toward Kindness Goals in Performance Feedback to Women (vs. Men). *Personality and Social Psychology Bulletin*, 49(10), 1423–1438.
31. https://hbr.org/2023/01/women-get-nicer-feedback-and-it-holds-them-back.
32. https://mitsloan.mit.edu/ideas-made-to-matter/women-are-less-likely-men-to-be-promoted-heres-one-reason-why.
33. Fiske, S. T., Cuddy, A. J. C., & Glick, P. (2007). Universal Dimensions of Social Cognition: Warmth and Competence. *Trends in Cognitive Sciences*, 11(2), 77–83.
34. Schein, V. E., Mueller, R., Lituchy, T., & Liu, J. (1996). Think Manager – Think Male: A Global Phenomenon? *Journal of Organizational Behavior*, 17(1), 33–41.
35. https://www.gsb.stanford.edu/experience/news-history/gender-related-material-new-core-curriculum.
36. Tan, X., Zuo, B., Wen, F., Xie, Z., & Song, S. (2021). Fear of Backlash Moderates Female Senior Executives' Communion (but Not Agency) as Compared to Female Lecturers. *Frontiers in Psychology*, 12, article 520590.
37. https://hbr.org/2022/10/how-confidence-is-weaponized-against-women.

38. Livingston, R. W., Rosette, A. S., & Washington, E. F. (2012). Can an Agentic Black Woman Get Ahead? The Impact of Race and Interpersonal Dominance on Perceptions of Female Leaders. *Psychological Science*, 23(4), 354–358.
39. Muhr, S. L. (2019). Ledelse af Køn. København: DJØF Forlag. Williams, J. C. (2021, October). *Bias Interrupted: Creating Inclusion for Real and for Good*. Harvard Business Press. Williams, Joan C. (2014). Hacking Tech's Diversity Problem. *Harvard Business Review*, pp. 94–100.
40. Schmader, T., Whitehead, J., & Wysocki, V. H. (2007). A Linguistic Comparison of Letters of Recommendation for Male and Female Chemistry and Biochemistry Job Applicants. *Sex Roles*, 57(7–8), 509–514.
41. Dana, J., Dawes, R., & Peterson, N. (2013, September). Belief in the Unstructured Interview: The Persistence of an Illusion. *Judgment and Decision Making*, 8(5), 512–520.
42. https://www.womenofinfluence.ca/tps/.
43. https://www.mckinsey.com/featured-insights/diversity-and-inclusion/women-in-the-workplace.
44. Ahl, H., & Marlow, S. (2012). Exploring the Dynamics of Gender, Feminism and Entrepreneurship: Advancing Debate to Escape a Dead End? *Organization*, 19(5), 543–562.
45. https://www.eib.org/en/publications/why-are-women-entrepreneurs-missing-out-on-funding-report.
46. Kanze, D., Huang, L., Conley, M., & Higgins, E. (2018). We Ask Men to Win and Women Not to Lose: Closing the Gender Gap in Startup Funding. *The Academy of Management Journal*, 61(2), 586–614.
47. https://www.eib.org/en/stories/investment-in-women-entrepreneurs.
48. https://www.eib.org/en/stories/investment-in-women-entrepreneurs.
49. Kacperczyk, O., Younkin, P., & Rocha, V. (2022). Do Employees Work Less for Female Leaders? A Multi-Method Study of Entrepreneurial Firms. *Organisation Science*, 34(3), 987–1352.
50. Rochlen, A., McKelley, R., & Whittaker, T. (2010). Stay-at-Home Fathers' Reasons for Entering the Role and Stigma Experiences: A Preliminary Report. *Psychology of Men & Masculinity*, 11, 279–285.
51. Williams, J. C. Glass, J., Correll, S., Berdahl, J. L., Levy, S. R. (2013). *The Flexibility Stigma*. Wiley-Blackwell; Rudman, L. A., & Mescher, K. (2013). Penalizing Men Who Request a Family Leave: Is Flexibility Stigma a Femininity Stigma? *Journal of Social Issues*, 69(2), 322–340.
52. UK Department of Education: https://www.besa.org.uk/key-uk-education-statistics/.
53. U.S. Department of Education: https://nces.ed.gov/surveys/ntps/tables/ntps1516_19031801_t1n_rev.asp).
54. https://data.oecd.org/teachers/women-teachers.htm#indicator-chart.

55. Klecker, B. M., & Loadman, W. E. (1999). Male Elementary School Teachers' Ratings of Job Satisfaction by Years of Teaching Experience. *Education, 1*(19), 131 504-513.
56. Barnard, C., Hovingh, L., Nezwek, M., Pryor-Bayard, D., Schmoldt, J., Stevens, J., Sturrus, W., Wabeke, S., & Weaver, L. (2000). *Recommendations for Improving the Recruitment of Male Early Childhood Education Professionals: The Female Viewpoint.*
57. https://www.business.com/hiring/nonbinary-discrimination-job-market-report/.
58. Osuri, G. (2008, October). *Ash-Coloured Whiteness: The Transfiguration of Aishwarya Rai*, pp 109–123; Mishra, N. (2015). *India and Colorism: The Finer Nuances.*
59. https://www-psychologytoday-com.cdn.ampproject.org/c/s/www.psychologytoday.com/intl/blog/the-psychology-of-the-south-asian-diaspora/202303/south-asian-women-seeking-fair-and-lovely?amp.
60. Uzogara, E. E. (2019). Who Desires in-Group Neighbors? Associations of Skin Tone Biases and Discrimination with Latinas' Segregation Preferences. *Group Processes and Intergroup Relations*, 22(8), 1196–1214.
61. Rudman, L. A., & McLean, M. C. (2016). The Role of Appearance Stigma in Implicit Racial Ingroup Bias. *Group Processes and Intergroup Relations*, 19(3), 374–393.
62. https://www.forbes.com/sites/pragyaagarwaleurope/2018/12/30/bias-is-your-accent-holding-you-back/?sh=1534c95c1b5a.
63. http://www.bbc.co.uk/newsbeat/article/28225710/accentism-similar-to-racism-suggests-new-research.
64. https://www-bbc-com.cdn.ampproject.org/c/s/www.bbc.com/news/uk-63494849.amp.
65. Kelly, D. J., Quinn, P. C., Slater, A. M., Lee, K., Gibson, A., Smith, M., Ge, L., Pascalis, O. (2005, November). Three-Month-Olds, but not Newborns, Prefer Own-Race Faces. *Developmental Science*, 8(6), F31-6.
66. Lee, K, Quinn, P. C., Pascalis, O. (2017, June). Face Race Processing and Racial Bias in Early Development: A Perceptual-Social Linkage. *Current Directions in Psychological Science*, 26(3), 256–262.
67. Mandalaywala, T., Benitez, J., Sagar, K., & Rhodes, M. (2021). Why Do Children Show Racial Bias in Their Resource Allocation Decisions? *Journal of Experimental Child Psychology*, 211, 105, 224.
68. Lagerman, L.C. (2019). *Farvede Forventninger*. Århus Universitetsforlag.
69. https://videnskab.dk/kultur-samfund/folkeskolelaerere-diskriminerer-drenge-med-mellemoestlige-navne.
70. Gaddis, S. M. (2017). How Black Are Lakisha and Jamal? Racial Perceptions from Names Used in Correspondence Audit Studies. *Sociological Science*, 4, 469–489.

71. Bertrand, M., & Sendhil M. (2004, September). Are Emily and Greg More Employable Than Lakisha and Jamal? A Field Experiment On Labor Market Discrimination. *American Economic Review*, 94(4), 991–1013.
72. https://politiken.dk/debat/art5731006/Danske-arbejdsgivere-v%C3%A6lger-%E2%80%99Mads%E2%80%99-frem-for-%E2%80%99Muhammed%E2%80%99.
73. Carlsson, M., & Rooth, D.-O. (2007). Evidence of Ethnic Discrimination in the Swedish Labor Market Using Experimental Data. *Labor Economics*, 14, 716–729.
74. https://journals.sagepub.com/doi/abs/10.1177/0149206318757019?journalCode=joma.
75. Luksyte, A., Waite, E., Avery, D. R., & Roy, R. (2013). Held to a Different Standard: Racial Differences in the Impact of Lateness on Advancement Opportunity. *Journal of Occupational and Organisational Psychology*, 86, 142–165.
76. Katz, D., & Braly, K. W. (1933). Racial Stereotypes of One Hundred College Students. *The Journal of Abnormal and Social Psychology*, 28(3), 280–290.
77. Gilbert, G. M. (1951). Stereotype Persistence and Change Among College Students. *The Journal of Abnormal and Social Psychology*, 46(2), 245–254.
78. Madon, S., Guyll, M., Aboufadel, K., Montiel, E., Smith, A., Palumbo, P., & Jussim, L. (2001). Ethnic and National Stereotypes: The Princeton Trilogy Revisited and Revised. *Personality and Social Psychology Bulletin*, 27, 996–1010.
79. Petsko, C. D., & Rosette, A. S. (2023). Are Leaders Still Presumed White by Default? Racial Bias in Leader Categorization Revisited. *Journal of Applied Psychology*, 108(2), 330–340.
80. Henriksen, L, Holck, L. & Muhr, S. L. (2023). *Organizing Against Inequality: Wage Gaps and Workplace Unionization Amongst High-Skilled Male and Female Migrants*. Working Paper. Frederiksberg, DK: Copenhagen Business School.
81. Berdahl, J. L., & Min, J.-A. (2012). Prescriptive Stereotypes and Workplace Consequences for East Asians in North America. *Cultural Diversity and Ethnic Minority Psychology*, 18(2), 141–152.
82. https://www.forbes.com/sites/christinecarter/2022/11/14/these-two-black-female-ceos-are-also-working-moms-that-didnt-stop-them-from-rising-to-the-top/?sh=6070625120ef.
83. Women in the Workplace 2019. McKinsey & Company: https://www.mckinsey.com/~/media/McKinsey/Featured%20Insights/Gender%20Equality/Women%20in%20the%20Workplace%202019/Women-in-the-workplace-2019.ashx.
84. American Association of University Women, "Black Women and the Pay Gap," https://www.aauw.org/resources/article/black-women-and-the-pay-gap/.

85. Women in the Workplace 2019. McKinsey & Company: https://www.mckinsey.com/~/media/McKinsey/Featured%20Insights/Gender%20Equality/Women%20in%20the%20Workplace%202019/Women-in-the-workplace-2019.ashx.
86. Women in the Workplace 2019. McKinsey & Company: https://www.mckinsey.com/~/media/McKinsey/Featured%20Insights/Gender%20Equality/Women%20in%20the%20Workplace%202019/Women-in-the-workplace-2019.ashx.
87. James, S. E., Brown, C., & Wilson, I. (2015). *U.S. Transgender Survey: Report on the Experiences of Black Respondents.* https://www.transequality.org/sites/default/files/docs/usts/USTS-Black-Respondents-Report.pdf.
88. Women in the Workplace 2019. McKinsey & Company: https://www.mckinsey.com/~/media/McKinsey/Featured%20Insights/Gender%20Equality/Women%20in%20the%20Workplace%202019/Women-in-the-workplace-2019.ashx.
89. Women in the Workplace 2019. McKinsey & Company: https://www.mckinsey.com/~/media/McKinsey/Featured%20Insights/Gender%20Equality/Women%20in%20the%20Workplace%202019/Women-in-the-workplace-2019.ashx.
90. https://www.catalyst.org/reports/antiracism-workplace-leadership/.
91. https://hbr.org/2019/11/the-costs-of-codeswitching.
92. https://www.who.int/teams/social-determinants-of-health/demographic-change-and-healthy-ageing/combatting-ageism/global-report-on-ageism.
93. Bieling, G., Stock, R. M., & Dorozalla, F. (2015). Coping with Demographic Change in Job Markets: How Age Diversity Management Contributes to Organisational Performance. *German Journal of Human Resource Management*, 29(1), 5–30.
94. Buttigieg, D. (2011). The Business Case for an Age-diverse Workforce. In E. Parry & S. Tyson (Eds.), *Managing an Age-Diverse Workforce*. Palgrave Macmillan. Cutcher, L., Riach, K., & Tyler, M. (2022). Splintering Organizational Subjectivities: Older Workers and the Dynamics of Recognition, vulnerability and Resistance. *Organization Studies*, 43(6), 973–992. Li, Y., Gong, Y., Burmeister, A., Wang, M., Alterman, V., Alonso, A., & Robinson, S. (2021). Leveraging Age Diversity for Organizational Performance: An Intellectual Capital Perspective. *Journal of Applied Psychology*, 106(1), 71.
95. Posthuma, R. A., Fernanda Wagstaff, M., & Campion, M. A. (2012, September 18). Age Stereotypes and Workplace Age Discrimination: A Framework for Future Research. In W. C. Borman & J. W. Hedge (Eds.), *The Oxford Handbook of Work and Aging*. Oxford Library of Psychology (online edn, Oxford Academic). Riach, K. (2009). Managing 'difference': Understanding age diversity in Practice. *Human Resource Management Journal*, 19(3), 319–335.
96. Zebrowitz, L. A., & Franklin, R. G. (Jr.). (2014). The Attractiveness Halo Effect and the Babyface Stereotype in Older and Younger Adults:

Similarities, Own-age Accentuation, and Older Adult Positivity Effects. *Experimental Aging Research*, 40(3):375–393.
97. https://www.glassdoor.com.
98. https://www.who.int/teams/social-determinants-of-health/demographic-change-and-healthy-ageing/combatting-ageism/global-report-on-ageism.
99. Belschner, J. (2022). Youth Advantage Versus Gender Penalty: Selecting and Electing Young Candidates. *Political Research Quarterly*, 76(1), 90–106.
101. Cutcher, L., Riach, K., & Tyler, M. (2022). Splintering Organizational Subjectivities: Older Workers and the Dynamics of Recognition, Vulnerability and Resistance. *Organization Studies*, 43(6), 973-992. Previtale, F., & Spedale, F. (2021). Doing Age in the Workplace: Exploring Age Categorization in Performance Appraisal. *Journal of Aging Studies*, 59, article 100973. Riach, K., & Kelly, S. (2015). The Need for Fresh Blood: Understanding Organizational Age Inequality Through a Vampiric Lens. *Organization*, 22(3), 287–305.
101. Zebrowitz, L. A., Franklin, R. G. Jr. (2014). The Attractiveness Halo Effect and the Babyface Stereotype in Older and Younger Adults: Similarities, Own-Age Accentuation, and Older Adult Positivity Effects. *Experimental Aging Research*, 40(3), 375–393.
102. Cialdini, R. B. (1993). *Influence: Science and Practice*. HarperCollins College Publishers.
103. Dion, K., Berscheid, E., & Walster, E. (1972). What Is Beautiful Is Good. *Journal of Personality and Social Psychology*, 24(3), 285–290; Miller, A. G. (1970). Role of Physical Attractiveness in Impression Formation. *Psychonomic Science*, 19(4), 241–243.
104. Yeh, W.-C., Lee, C.-C., Yu, C., Wu, P.-S., Chang, J.-Y., & Huang, J.-H. (2020). The Impact of the Physical Attractiveness and Intellectual Competence on Loyalty. *Sustainability*, 12(10), 3970.
105. Wheeler, L., & Kim, Y. (1997). What is Beautiful is Culturally Good: The Physical Attractiveness Stereotype has Different Content in Collectivistic Cultures. *Personality and Social Psychology Bulletin*, 23(8), 795–800.
106. Hamermesh, D. S., & Biddle, J. E. (1994). Beauty and the Labor Market. *The American Economic Review*, 84(5), 1174–1194.
107. Berscheid, E., & Walster, E. (1969). *Interpersonal Attraction*. Addison-Wesley.
108. Judge, T. A., Hurst, C., & Simon, L. S. (2009, May 16). Does It Pay to Be Smart, Attractive, or Confident (or All Three)? Relationships Among General Mental Ability, Physical Attractiveness, Core Self-Evaluations, and Income. *Journal of Applied Psychology*, 94(3), 742–755.
109. Kanazawa, S., & Still, M. C. (2018). Is There Really a Beauty Premium or an Ugliness Penalty on Earnings? *Journal of Business and Psychology*, 33, 249–262.
110. https://edition.cnn.com/2017/07/28/opinions/ugliness-premium-opinion-drexler/index.html.

111. Lee, M., Pitesa, M., Pillutla, M. M., & Thau, S. (2018). Perceived Entitlement Causes Discrimination Against Attractive Job Candidates in the Domain of Relatively Less Desirable Jobs. *Journal of Personality and Social Psychology*, 114(3), 422–442.
112. https://qz.com/work/1115220/are-attractive-people-more-likely-to-get-hired-not-always-says-new-london-school-of-business-study/.
113. Johnson, S. K., Podratz, K. E., Dipboye, R. L., & Gibbons, E. (2010). Physical Attractiveness Bias in Ratings of Employment Suitability: Tracking Down the "Beauty is Beastly" Effect. *The Journal of Social Psychology*, 150(3), 301–318.
114. Broussard, K. A., & Harton, H. C. (2018). Tattoo or Taboo? Tattoo Stigma and Negative Attitudes Toward Tattooed Individuals. *The Journal of Social Psychology*, 158(5), 521–540.
115. Ruggs, E.N. & Hebl, M. (2022). Do Employees' Tattoos Leave a Mark on Customers' Reactions to Products and Organisations? *Journal of Organizational Behavior, 43*(6), 965–982.
116. https://www.thehrdirector.com/features/policies-and-procedures/employer-bias-tattoos/.
117. Polavieja, J. G., Lancee, B., Ramos, M., Veit, S., & Yemane, R. (2023). In Your Face: A Comparative Field Experiment on Racial Discrimination in Europe. *Socio-Economic Review*, 22(1), 1551–1578.
118. Judge, T. A., & Cable, D. M. (2004). The Effect of Physical Height on Workplace Success and Income: Preliminary Test of a Theoretical Model. *Journal of Applied Psychology, 89*(3), 428–441.
119. Judge, T. A., & Cable, D. M. (2004). The Effect of Physical Height on Workplace Success and Income: Preliminary Test of a Theoretical Model. *Journal of Applied Psychology, 89*(3), 428–441.
120. Koval, C. Z., & Rosette, A. S. (2020). The Natural Hair Bias in Job Recruitment. *Social Psychological and Personality Science*, 12(5), 741–750.
121. https://www.thecrownact.com/.
122. https://perception.org/goodhair/results/.
123. Chang, C. J., O'Brien, K. M., Keil, A. P., Gaston, S. A., Jackson, C. L., Sandler, D. P. & White, A. J. (2022). Use of Straighteners and Other Hair Products and Incident Uterine Cancer. *JNCI: Journal of the National Cancer Institute, 114*(12), 1636–1645.
124. Centers for Disease Control and Prevention: https://www.cdc.gov/nchs/fastats/obesity-overweight.htm.
125. National Health Service: https://www.nhs.uk/conditions/obesity/.
126. https://www.economist.com/graphic-detail/2019/10/28/china-worries-about-its-bulging-waistlines.
127. Ahirwar, R., & Mondal, P. (2018). Prevalence of Obesity in India: A Systematic Review. *Diabetes & Metabolic Syndrome: Clinical Research & Reviews, 13*(1), 318–321.

128. Nowrouzi-Kia, B., Mcdougall, A., Gohar, B., Nowrouz-Kia, B., & Casole, J. (2015). Weight Bias in the Workplace: A Literature Review". *Occupational Medical Health Affairs, 3*(3), 206.
129. Giel, K. E., Thiel, A., Teufel, M., Mayer, J., & Zipfel, S. (2010). Weight Bias in Work Settings—A Qualitative Review. *Obesity Facts, 3*(1), 33-40.
130. Ruggs, E. N., Hebl, M. R., & Williams, A. (2015). Weight Isn't Selling: The Insidious Effects of Weight Stigmatization in Retail Settings. *Journal of Applied Psychology,* 100(5), 1483–1496.
131. Shapiro, J. R., King, E. B., & Quinones, M. A. (2007). Expectations of Obese Trainees: How Stigmatized Trainee Characteristics Influence Training Effectiveness. *Journal of Applied Psychology,* 92(1), 239–249.
132. Judge, T. A., & Cable, D. M. (2011). When It Comes to Pay, Do the Thin Win? The Effect of Weight on Pay for Men and Women. *Journal of Applied Psychology,* 96(1), 95–112.
133. King, E. B., Rogelberg, S. G., Hebl, M. R., et al. (2016). Waistlines and Ratings of Executives: Does Executive Status Overcome Obesity Stigma? *Human Resource Management,* 55(2), 283–300.
134. https://www.disabled-world.com/.
135. https://www.accenture.com/content/dam/accenture/final/a-com-migration/pdf/pdf-142/accenture-enabling-change-getting-equal-2020-disability-inclusion-report.pdf; https://www.accenture.com/content/dam/accenture/final/a-com-migration/pdf/pdf-89/accenture-disability-inclusion-research-report.pdf.
136. Office of National Statistic: https://www.ons.gov.uk/.
137. https://risepeople.com/blog/why-dont-employers-hire-people-with-disabilities/.
138. Boni-Saenz, A., Heinemann, A., Crown, D., & Emanuel, L. (2006). The Business of Employing People with Disabilities: Four Case Studies. *Organizational Ethics: Healthcare, Business and Policy, 3*(1), 3–18.
139. Bonaccio, S., Connelly, C. E., Gellatly, I. R., et al. (2020). The Participation of People with Disabilities in the Workplace Across the Employment Cycle: Employer Concerns and Research Evidence. *Journal of Business and Psychology,* 35, 135–158.
140. https://www.pwc.com/gx/en/ceo-survey/2015/assets/pwc-18th-annual-global-ceo-survey-jan-2015.pdf.
141. Harder, J., Keller, V., & Chopik, W. (2019). Demographic, Experiential, and Temporal Variation in Ableism. *Journal of Social Issues, 75*(3), 683–706.
142. Disability: A Research Study on Unconscious Bias. ENEI 2014, www.enei.org.
143. Acquisti, A., & Fong, C. (2012). An Experiment in Hiring Discrimination Via Online Social Networks. *Management Science, 66*(3), 1005–1024.
144. Ghumman, S., & Ryan, A. (2013). Not Welcome Here: Discrimination Towards Women Who Wear the Muslim Headscarf. *Human Relations,* 66, 671–698.

145. https://home-affairs.ec.europa.eu/system/files/2020-09/201712_gemm_l egal_migration_consultation_en.pdf.
146. Rivera, D. P. (2011). Sexual Prejudice. In S. Goldstein & J. A. Naglieri (Eds.), *Encyclopedia of Child Behavior and Development*. Springer.
147. Herek, G. M. (2000). The Psychology of Sexual Prejudice. *Current Directions in Psychological Science*, 9, 19–22.
148. Morin, S. F. (1977). Heterosexual Bias in Psychological Research on Lesbianism and Male Homosexuality. *American Psychologist*, 32(8), 629–637.
149. Herek, G. M. (1990). The Context of Anti-Gay Violence: Notes on Cultural and Psychological Heterosexism. *Journal of Interpersonal Violence*, 5, 316–333.
150. https://www.prnewswire.com/news-releases/glassdoor-survey-finds-three-in-five-us-employees-have-experienced-or-witnessed-discrimination-based-on-age-race-gender-or-lgbtq-identity-at-work-300943513.html.
151. https://www.bcg.com/publications/2020/inclusive-cultures-must-follow-new-lgbtq-workforce.
152. https://www.bcg.com/publications/2020/inclusive-cultures-must-follow-new-lgbtq-workforce.
153. Nadal, K. L., Wong, Y., Issa, M., Meterko, V., Leon, J., & Wideman, M. (2011). Sexual Orientation Microaggressions: Processes and Coping Mechanisms for Lesbian, Gay, and Bisexual Individuals. *Journal of LGBT Issues in Counseling*, 5(1), 21–46.
154. https://hbr.org/2020/09/graduates-of-elite-universities-get-paid-more-do-they-perform-better.
155. Courtice, A. J. (2016). *Education: The American Caste System*. Strategic Book Publishing.
156. https://www.gov.uk/government/publications/unlock-opportunity-employer-information-pack-and-case-studies/employing-prisoners-and-ex-offenders.
157. https://www.cnbc.com/2018/09/18/why-companies-are-turning-to-ex-cons-to-fill-slots-for-workers.html.
158. https://www.truity.com/sites/default/files/PersonalityType-CareerAchievementStudy.pdf.
159. https://stackrecruitment.org/2020/05/12/7-benefits-of-employing-autistic-individuals/.
160. https://hbr.org/2017/05/neurodiversity-as-a-competitive-advantage.
161. https://stackrecruitment.org/2020/05/12/7-benefits-of-employing-autistic-individuals/.
162. https://www.who.int/news-room/fact-sheets/detail/mental-disorders.
163. https://covid19.nih.gov/covid-19-topics/mental-health.
164. https://timesofindia.indiatimes.com/blogs/voices/mental-health-care-analysis/.

165. https://www.mckinsey.com/industries/healthcare/our-insights/overcoming-stigma-three-strategies-toward-better-mental-health-in-the-workplace.
166. Fuegen K., Biernat M., Haines E., & Deaux K. (2004). Mothers and Fathers in the Workplace: How Gender and Parental Status Influence Judgments of Job-Related Competence. *Journal of Social Issues*, 60, 737–7; Byron R. A., & Roscigno V. J. (2014). Relational Power, Legitimation, and Pregnancy Discrimination. *Gender & Society*, 28, 435-462; Benard S., & Correll S. J. (2010). Normative Discrimination and the Motherhood Penalty. *Gender & Society*, 24, 616–646; Ridgeway, C. L., & Correll S. J. (2004). Motherhood as a Status Characteristic. *Journal of Social Issues*, 60, 683–700.
167. Bear, J. B., & Glick, P. (2017). Breadwinner Bonus and Caregiver Penalty in Workplace Rewards for Men and Women. *Social Psychological and Personality Science*, 8(7), 780–788; Williams, J. C. (2021). *Bias Interrupted: Creating Inclusion for Real and for Good*. Harvard Business Press.
168. Hirsh, C. E., Treleaven, C., & Fuller, S. (2020). Caregivers, Gender, and the Law: An Analysis of Family Responsibility Discrimination Case Outcomes. *Gender & Society*, 34(5), 760–789.
169. Correll, S. J., Benard, S., & Paik, I. (2007). Getting a Job: Is There a Motherhood Penalty? *Amarican Journal of Sociology, 112*(5), 1297–1338.
170. Bear, J. B. & Glick, P. (2017). Breadwinner Bonus and Caregiver Penalty in Workplace Rewards for Men and Women. *Social Psychological and Personality Science, 8*(7), 780–788.
171. Storm, K., & Muhr, S. L. (2022). Work-Life Balance as Gaslighting: Exploring Repressive Care in Female Accountants' Careers. *Critical Perspectives on Accounting*, 95, Article 102484.
172. González, M. J., Cortina, C., & Rodríguez, J. (2019). The Role of Gender Stereotypes in Hiring: A Field Experiment. *European Sociological Review*, 35(2), 187–204.
173. Bear, J., & Glick, P. (2016). Gendered Rewards: Breadwinner versus Caregiver Status Affects Workplace Rewards for Men and Women. *Academy of Management Proceedings*, 2016(1), 11559.
174. Phillips, D. C. (2020). Do Low-Wage Employers Discriminate Against Applicants with Long Commutes?: Evidence from a Correspondence Experiment. *Journal of Human Resources*, 55(3), 864–901.
175. https://www.hrmagazine.co.uk/content/news/state-of-the-nation-report-employers-must-do-more-on-social-mobility.
176. https://www.hrmagazine.co.uk/content/news/businesses-must-do-more-on-social-mobility.
177. Gorard, S., & See, B. (2009). The Impact of Socio-Economic Status on Participation and Attainment in Science. *Studies in Science Education*, 45(1), 93–129.

4

Leading With Clarity (Part 2: Situation-Related Cognitive Bias and the Impact of Bias)

In this chapter, we continue to establish the basis for leading with clarity. Having a solid understanding of biases and having looked at identity-related cognitive biases in the previous chapter, we are now ready to move on to exploring situation-related cognitive bias. Towards the end of this chapter, we will consider the impact of bias on organisations and employees.

4.1 Situation-Related Cognitive Bias

Situation-related cognitive biases arise because of the way our brain functions when processing information in situations, creating shortcuts to manage the enormous amount of information coming our way every moment. These cognitive biases can be thought of as systematic thought processes caused by the tendency of the human brain to simplify information processing through a filter of past experiences and preferences. The vast majority of the shortcuts are most frequently used in four situations: (1) when deciding what we should remember amongst the vast amount of information available, (2) when there is too much information, (3) when there is information lacking and (4) when we need to make decisions as fast as possible. Regardless of our identity and diversity thumbprint, we all hold situation-related cognitive biases. There are in fact over 50 situation-related cognitive biases, and we have chosen to present some of these cognitive biases that we believe are most relevant in today's workplaces and for leaders to know in order to be able to lead through bias.

© The Author(s), under exclusive license to Springer Nature Switzerland AG 2023
P. Luthra and S. L. Muhr, *Leading Through Bias*, Palgrave Executive Essentials, https://doi.org/10.1007/978-3-031-38571-1_4

Intuition Bias

Intuition bias is, as the name implies, when you use your intuition, your gut feeling or your 6th sense, to evaluate another person. We do this constantly, both when we notice it, because we can feel that we react to it (implicit bias), and when we are not aware that our opinions are anything but objective (unconscious bias). In business lingo, intuition bias is often masked as "experience". Experience sounds a lot better and more serious than using the words intuition or gut feeling, but this is exactly what it refers to. When you make a quick judgement based on your experience, you use your gut feeling. And you have to. Particularly in a leadership position, you are required to and even expected to. This is exactly what makes bias so tricky: On the one hand, it overrides rational thinking; on the other hand, it makes us capable of making decisions in the first place.

Another tricky aspect of intuition bias is that it both helps us build strong organisational cultures with belongingness and deeply felt values, and at the same time, makes it difficult to recruit for diversity. If you have ever tried to sit on an interview panel, or if you are an experienced hiring manager, how long would you say it takes before you know if a candidate for a job is recruitable? If your answer is between 2 and 30 seconds, you are in the same range as 99% of the hiring managers we have ever spoken to. If you say between 30 seconds and 2 minutes, you belong to a very small minority, and if you say more than 2 minutes, you'll be the first we know of. This is intuition bias. Your gut tells you if a candidate fits the culture and is a match to the organisation. This might be important in order to build a strong culture, but it has nothing to do with competencies. So, if you want to emphasise competencies and merits in your recruitment processes and other evaluation procedures, you have to be extremely careful with intuition bias.

Of course, we are not saying that you shouldn't hire someone you have a good feeling about. But you should get that feeling tested—particularly up against the criteria that you have set for the position, the promotion or whatever decision you are making.

Intuition bias can, for example, make you change your behaviour in a recruitment situation, when it comes to both your evaluation of the candidates and your personal treatment of them.

> **Making Connections: Poornima & Sara's Experiences**
> Recently, Sara worked with a partner in a consultancy firm. She had just finished a recruitment process, where she had interviewed a young man. She was amazed by his qualifications and really wanted to hire him as she thought he would be a great asset to the firm. So, when she was to make him an offer, she decided that he should start at level 3, thinking that would fit his competencies and make the offer attractive to him. This all sounds very usual and not out of the ordinary, but after a short time, the partner found out that one of this man's female university friends had also recently been hired into the firm—she had been responsible for this process as well and placed the woman at level 1. Luckily, the partner was in the middle of a bias training program and realised that this must be due to an intuition bias. She had such a good gut feeling about the male candidate and hadn't had the same intuitive feeling for the female candidate. But they were equally qualified.

When it comes to behaviour, research shows that when we have a good feeling about and connect with people, we treat them better; we are kinder and more interested in them. This makes a difference in recruitment situations. For example, research shows that if you receive an interview candidate in the reception and walk them to the interview room, you act differently depending on whether you have an immediate good feeling about the candidate or not. If you have a good feeling, you will have a tendency to small talk and walk next to the person on the way to the interviewing room. If you don't have an immediate connection, you are, of course, polite and professional, but you walk in front of the person and don't talk much to them. Which one of these candidates do you think has an advantage?

And here, we always get the question or comment: "yes, that is probably true, but I need to have a good feeling about the person to work with them, they need to fit in". And our reply is always, "yes, that might be true, if you have to work extremely closely with this person all the time and are extremely dependent on your conflict level being very low and that you are best friends". Is this really the case? No, often not. You're not hiring a best friend or looking for a life partner. You are hiring a colleague or an employee whose competencies are what matter the most. Then, of course, they have to fit the culture to a certain degree. But if you are only hiring people who fit really well, you risk overdoing the "cult" part of culture. And is that what you want? Do you want to build a cult, where it's difficult to dissent or an inclusive culture with room for difference? If it is the latter, you have to be careful with that gut feeling, because your gut only wants what makes you feel safe and what is comfortable for you—and that might not be someone who can add something different, something unexpected and something that can make you push the organisation forward.

This is why many organisations are beginning to think in terms of culture "add", rather than culture "fit". Culture fit preserves comfort and familiarity, creating teams with people who are similar to each other. Culture add, on the other hand, seeks employees who align with the organisation's values, but also bring diverse experiences, perspectives and ideas to the workplace that add value to the organisation.

Pause and think about what that would mean in your organisation, but more importantly what that looks like in practice—because intuition bias is the trickiest of them all. To make an explicit link to inclusion that we discussed in Chapter 2, intuition bias is brilliant for belonging, but terrible for the value of uniqueness and diversity. But where on these two extremes lies the sweet spot? How do we fight intuition bias as well as ensure belonging, so we can move towards the desired inclusion square in the matrix we presented in Chapter 2 and not end in assimilation (low uniqueness, high belonging) or differentiation (low belonging, high uniqueness). Unfortunately, there is no easy answer to that question. Only the constant questioning and testing of your decisions.

Similarity Bias

We have a tendency to like people who are similar to us more than people who are different. This similarity bias—sometimes referred to as affinity bias—is also known as the Huey, Dewey and Louie effect, because Huey, Dewey and Louie look exactly the same, think the same and even finish each other's sentences.

We know from research on decision-making that groups with similar people make lower quality decisions compared to diverse groups.[1] Research shows that homogeneous groups tend to not question each other's thinking and thus not activate rational and reflexive System 2 thinking. Instead, they have a tendency of biased and irrational thinking that harms the quality of decision-making. The more we have in common (like age, ethnicity, education, gender, etc.), the greater the tendency for us to view an issue in the same way. Research shows that this results in a greater risk that homogeneous groups will not have addressed an issue thoroughly enough.[2] Homogeneous experiences trap us in a behavioural psychological loop, which the psychologist Irving Janis labelled *groupthink*.[3] Groupthink is a bias related to flock mentality. In groupthink, we are seduced or lulled to sleep by the group because it feels more comfortable to agree with each other than to ask critical questions. However, when we align ourselves with each other, this hurts the quality of our shared knowledge and the decisions made.

In research published in 2015, Cass R. Sunstein and Reid Hastie[4] show us how groupthink distorts decision-making by defining the following four subcategories of bias that affect decision-making processes:

1. Amplifying errors is a tendency for homogeneous groups to not only fail to see errors, but agree so strongly, that errors are reinforced.
2. The cascade effect describes the tendency to follow—or be influenced by—the first speaker. One by one, we build on the initial statement instead of adding new, independent knowledge to the discussion.
3. The polarisation effect denotes the group's tendency to become more firm in its joint position during a meeting. In other words, the in-group bond is strengthened during the meeting, creating even stronger loyalty to a bad decision.
4. The shared information effect shows how we find safety in what we all know in advance, which makes it difficult to listen to new or critical viewpoints that would have improved the quality of our decision-making.

Despite the vast amount of research on the danger of homogeneous groups that has been popularised through books like Irving Janis' *Groupthink* from 1972 or Cass R. Sunstein and Reid Hastie's *Wiser* from 2015, we still gravitate towards people who are similar to ourselves when we choose who we want to work with. And this is not (in most cases at least) because we are megalomanic and in love with our own mirror image. In most cases, it is because it is easier. And it is! It is a lot easier to lead a team of people who are like you, and it takes a lot less of your time. It is much easier to work with someone who speaks the same first language, has been to the same educational institution, lives in the same neighbourhood, dresses similarly and even enjoys the same food, hobbies or sports. We often get this question, when we work with organisations who aim to become more diverse: "But doesn't it take more time, isn't it more difficult?". The simple and true answer is yes! But somewhat provocatively, we might ask if it is even leadership to manage a team of clones or "mini-mes"? We would say a loud and resounding no!

Still, similarity bias is one of the strongest and most consistent of biases that influences who we hire, who we promote and who we assign to which projects. Unless we make a real effort to stop our mind going down the similarity route, we will gravitate towards the ones that mirror ourselves, because it is easier and because it makes us feel safe and comfortable. We may even be excited because we have something in common.

In combination with superficial evaluation bias—which, for instance, leads most people to associate strong leadership with White men—similarity bias strengthens the homogeneity of executive boards and leadership teams, because it reinforces the type of person who is already there. Several studies have documented the effects of similarity bias when it comes to gender and race,[5] where it has been shown how White men pick other White men as their successors. However, similarity bias has also been found in other less visible dimensions of diversity. A US study has, for example, shown that CVs with sports and interests that indicate upper-class backgrounds—like polo, sailing and classical music—give applicants an advantage. The researchers sent out fictitious CVs to 316 offices of 147 top law firms in 14 cities in the US. There were two aspects in which the CVs differed. The candidates were either called Julie or James and they either listed typical upper-class activities or reported being part of scholarship programs, mentoring other first generation college students or indicated a preference for country music. The results showed that the upper-class male candidate received more call backs than the other three candidates combined—even though their academic credentials were exactly the same.[6] In a set of follow-up qualitative questions, the authors found that the reason for this was that the recruiters (mostly White upper-class men) felt that James, who liked sailing, polo and classical music was just a better "fit" with the firm culture and the clients' expectations of a lawyer. As for upper-class Julie, she benefitted from a fit with the culture, but she was deselected, as the hiring partners feared that she would leave; there was no financial need for her to work due to her upper-class background, so why would she? In the case of Julie, superficial evaluation bias and the negative effect of gender bias even trumped similarity bias and the bias of socio-economic class.

Focus Bias

Focus bias is activated when we become fixated on one aspect of a person, either positive or negative, and let that influence how we evaluate the person's other qualities. The variation of this bias in which a positive opinion of a person influences our general perception of the person in a positive direction is probably the best-known type of focus bias. This is also known as the halo effect.[7] This bias occurs when one positive thing about a person makes us overestimate the person's other attributes or accomplishments. Such a glorification of a person can happen because of stereotypes—most of us tend to evaluate White, able-bodied, extrovert men's competencies to be higher compared to others. That is, their social identity alone kick-starts a possible halo effect. But attractiveness has also been found to have this effect. That is, if we find a person attractive, we have a tendency to attribute socially desirable personality traits to them.[8] Similarly, the likeability (that is, how nice we think the person is) also has a halo effect that positively influences our perception of that person's competencies.[9]

The lesser-known focus bias is the related, but negative effect that is triggered when one bad quality of a person overshadows our evaluation of that person—also known as the horns effect. Again, this can stem both from a stereotype and from the person's looks and personality. A negative focus bias can, for example, begin with a gender, race or age stereotype. Since most people evaluate the competencies of White, middle-aged men higher, meeting a young person, an older person, a person of colour or a woman or a non-binary person is very likely to trigger a focus bias, where our biased view of that person's competencies, stemming from the person's diversity thumbprint, is likely to influence our overall assessment of that person's competencies. This also explains why mistakes matter more for women and people of colour, as one mistake by an underrepresented person has a higher risk of leading to a negative overall assessment of that person.[10]

Parenthood is also an interesting example, which has very different effects for men and women. In an experiment, a group of researchers found that mothers were less likely to be offered a job and promoted and were offered a lower salary compared to women without children, whereas fathers were more likely to be hired and promoted, and received a higher starting salary compared to men without children. This very clearly shows a horns effect for women and a halo effect for fathers.[11]

Expectation Bias

Expectation bias materialises when our expectations of a person—high or low—prevent us from not verifying the facts about that person. This bias is particularly prevalent in recruitment processes. If we have high or low expectations of a candidate, we tend to act on our expectations without checking whether those expectations are, indeed, valid. These expectations can be formed because you know the person already, because of rumours or stories you've heard about the person, because of the reference check you made or because of something you noticed in the CV—either positively or negatively. This is often combined with similarity bias as we tend not to verify our expectations of candidates who are similar to us or people we like. This is also tied to superficial evaluation bias, as we transfer our general expectations of, say, men onto the man in front of us in a recruitment process. From research on recruitment, we know that this influences our behaviour in interview situations where we pose less tough questions to the candidates that we have high expectations of, but tend to grill the candidates we are not sure about. This, however, also extends beyond recruitment situations. For example, a recent study found that women economists get more questions, and more hostile questions, than men economists do when they present their work.[12]

Making Connections: Poornima & Sara's Experiences

A couple of years ago, Sara was collaborating with a large international consulting firm. In the process, she encountered an expectation bias that became one of the main reasons that the firm launched an ambitious DEI initiative. After a workshop on bias, one of the partners asked for a private chat and said he had something rather embarrassing to share. In one of their European offices, they had very few female partners (as he said, less than the Danish office we were in at the time, which "boasted" 10%). So, this other office was pressured from the US headquarters to "do something about it". They hired a search firm to identify a number of female candidates. The search firm identified 10 candidates, who were then interviewed and tested by the consulting firm. Pause for a moment and consider how many of these women you think made it to partner in the firm? 1, 2 or 3, perhaps? The answer is 0. As the partner explained, none of them were evaluated as living up to the criteria the firm had set for the new partner. At the time, the partner continued sharing, he had believed this to be true, but what he now realised—after the workshop we had just had—was that he didn't live up to those criteria either. And neither did any of the other male partners in the room. But they were not hired that way; they never had to prove their qualifications but were just expected to have them. When we joined the rest of the group for lunch, they all shared their hiring or promotion stories. All the men in the room were hired and/or promoted through their personal relations to their superiors. Some of them were hired at a golf course and some in a taxi on the way home from dinner. The (very few) female partners, by contrast, were all external hires, recruited through professional channels.

This is also a story about similarity bias and closed networks—our networks often comprise people who are similar to us—but the main point here is how surprised this partner group was when realising their expectation bias. They had not seen the fact that they had never checked the CVs or the credentials as carefully and as widely when they were promoting internally or hiring through their networks as they did when they were actively searching for (female) partners externally. When they hired their good friend or collaborator, they knew he was good, they knew his work and could vouch for him. So, it was not that the male partners weren't great, it was just that the criteria set up for the "new searches" were significantly higher than when they hired someone they knew to be great. When the partners of the firm became aware of their bias, they decided to install internal quotas, as they had very clear evidence that they could not rely on their experience and their gut feeling to make assessments—and—hence, needed a measure that would force them to act differently.

Contrast Bias

Contrast bias refers to the tendency to evaluate a person in comparison with another person instead of evaluating both against a set of criteria. Again, this is highly problematic when we evaluate people's competencies or potential, especially if our point of reference is a homogeneous group. If we compare a potential hire's or a new team member's competencies to people who are already in our team, we will tend to only see the things that the candidate/new person is less good at compared to the people we know. We will not see other important aspects of the candidates/new person that the existing team members might not have mastered yet—or that might supplement the team in ways that defy comparison and evaluation. If we compare, we are less likely to pay attention to these less obvious qualifications.

If we make decisions by comparison, it is difficult to find a person who is better than the people we already know and work with; simply because members of the latter group have proven their worth whereas the new person has not—and might never get a chance to if this is how we decide who to hire. If we compare, we will always be able to find something that those in the current team do better. By comparing, we reinforce our similarity bias and stick to a known type of person with familiar competencies. A US study clearly shows this. The researchers studied a hiring process for a police job that required both education and experience. The pool of candidates consisted of men and women and represented a variation of experience and education. The study showed that the male candidate was chosen when he had more education but less experience than the female candidate *and* when he had more experience but less education. The decision was either explained by the fact that the male candidate had more education, which was a valuable trait of the existing members of the force, or it was reasoned that more experience meant the person could enter the team smoothly, which had also been important in earlier hires.[13] However, this has very little to do with the candidates' actual education or experience. Obviously, similarity bias and superficial evaluation bias also "help" support the recruiter's decision here, but so does contrast bias. Because contrast bias provides a justification for the decision, your brain can use the comparison with the existing staff to justify the other biases.

A 2020 study of a tech company found similar results: Women with the same level of feedback on their performance got lower overall ratings because the final opinion of the person was based on things other than "just" the evaluation data. These "other things" were gendered expectations to behaviour, where women were punished for being too aggressive, as well as gendered views on potential, where women with the same level of feedback on current work tasks were evaluated to not have the same potential for advancement to the next level as the male peers.[14]

Proximity Bias

We prefer people or things closer in space and time compared to what is further away. This means that when we staff projects or when it is time for promotions, we first think of people whom we have recently spent time with. Instead of doing a thorough search, we risk picking the person who is closest at hand. This comes back to the issue of having to make decisions swiftly and of needing shortcuts to do so. If you have been working closely with a junior employee when a new talent program is announced, you will automatically think of this person, even if there is a more qualified candidate in an office just down the hall. If you eat lunch or play golf with the person who staffs the talent program, this person will tend to ask you about good candidates, even if someone else might be in a much better position to have an overview of the talent pool. This becomes much more of an issue in the world of remote working and working on Teams or Zoom. With proximity bias at play, it is more likely that we will think of the people with whom we have greater face-to-face time with, rather than colleagues working remotely.

This is not to say that the candidate closer to you in space and time is not good, but if you don't do a thorough search, you don't know if you are getting the most talented employees. Extending this thought experiment, if most of the organisational power positions are occupied by White men and if similarity bias makes us spend time with and be positively inclined towards people who are like us, who do you think is most likely to be invited to join talent programs?

In other words, the influence of many of the other biases will increase the likelihood that people who resemble you and/or members of your organisation's dominant groups are the ones in closest proximity when you need to pick a person for promotions, talent programs, awards, high prestige projects, etc. Proximity bias makes it more likely that the people at hand are the people you choose.

Confirmation Bias

Confirmation bias is the tendency to process information by looking for, or interpreting, information that is consistent with your existing beliefs. This is due to two common traits of human cognition: First, we like to be right and, second, it is easier to look for confirmation than for alternative explanations.

When it comes to being right, leaders like being right even more than the average person since being right is ingrained in the pathway to senior leadership positions. You move up the hierarchy because you're right—because you have made the right decisions that have secured your organisation's success. Being right feels good to anyone; we experience genuine pleasure—a rush of dopamine—when processing information that supports our beliefs.[15] So, your brain will do everything it can to ensure that feeling of being right, and once you think you're right, you become more confident—and more likely to think that you're right. Hence, if you have been told your entire life that you are bright, make great decisions and will be a great leader one day, there is a great likelihood that you will be even more prone to confirmation bias.[16] You internalise others' opinions of you and if the environment supports the view that you're great, you'll have a higher tendency of thinking that you're great—reinforcing the need to continue to be great and make great decisions—and your brain happily assists you in this to keep you safe in that belief.

This is closely related to the cognitive shortcut of looking for clues that confirm your existing belief rather than for evidence that might falsify it, what is known as the echo chamber effect, which leads to confirmation bias. When it comes to hiring, promoting or staffing projects, this is shown in the way your brain will feed you all the arguments for your favourite candidate—or the one that conveniently, with the help of all the other biases, has been placed in close proximity to you.

To envision confirmation bias, just think of this situation: You are part of a recruitment process and for some reason you have a preference for one of the candidates that has been called for an interview—this can be because you know the person, you have worked with the person, you have heard good things about the person or maybe because there is something in the CV that has caught your attention (golf, perhaps?). How easy is it for you (or rather your brain) to ask questions that make this person excel at the interview, confirming your intuition that this person is a perfect "fit"? We are pretty sure that you will agree this would be very easy. At least that is what the vast majority of the participants in our workshops have said. Now, imagine the opposite situation; there is a candidate that you really don't like (focus bias is helping you with this, making you see only that one thing, which makes the person disagreeable). Again, that could be because you know the person, because you have heard rumours about the person or because you have noticed something you don't like in the CV (in contexts where people add pictures to the CVs, this is a real issue!). How easy is it to make this person fail the interview and confirm your gut feeling? It's very easy!

As you read this, you might think that you've never done this on purpose—and you would probably be right. You might also think that you have at some point done this, but still framed it differently, finding a "real" reason to support your decision. And this is also very likely. No matter how you feel, the point is that confirmation bias has influenced your choices—and those of all of us. We all tend to see what we want to see—and to avoid seeing that which we don't want to. Interestingly, however, we are really good at spotting other people's confirmation bias. Presented with someone else's argument, we're quite adept at spotting the weaknesses. Almost invariably, this is not the case with spotting our own confirmation bias.[17]

In that sense, confirmation bias is the grand finale that confirms all the other selection mechanisms, only based on your excellent judgement of character! Or maybe not. Maybe your brain has been fooling you all the way—by serving you the easy solutions. In a nutshell, leading with clarity means knowing exactly that: how your brain is wired to use bias to take shortcuts—and then investing the time it takes to block the bias and do what is right instead of what is easy or feels good. You have to outsmart your brain, forcing yourself to resist the shortcuts and move up to slow System 2 thinking or at least block problematic biases from influencing your System 1 thinking too much. The next chapter deals with ways you can do this, showing how you can use your conviction and your clarity to lead with accountability. Before that, let us look at the impact of identity-related cognitive and situation-related cognitive bias on organisations and employees.

4.2 The Impact of Bias on Organisations and Employees

As we have seen in Chapter 2, organisations that do not have an inclusive workplace culture—one where bias exists unhindered—are likely to find it challenging to gain positive outcomes from having more diverse representation whether that is better financial performance, innovation and team performance. Bias—unconscious, implicit and explicit; identity and cognitive—all work together to create and uphold biased systems, structures, processes and policies that favour some and not all. We see evidence that these systemic biases exist through the following indicators—employee pay and well-being.

Employee Pay

It is hard to believe that even in 2023, the raw gender pay gap, which looks at the median salary for all men and women regardless of job type or worker seniority is prevalent. In 2023, according to UN Women, women worldwide earn about 77 cents to every dollar earned by men. The US census bureau shows that in 2021, full-time working women earned 83 cents for every dollar earned by men,[18] with Black women earning about 64 cents and Latina women earning 54 cents.[19] While this is an improvement from 2015, when the median salary for men was roughly 26% higher than the median salary for women, it is still far from ideal. In the EU, data from the European Commission showed that in 2019, women earned 16% less, or 84-euro cents for every €1 men earned.[20] While progress is being made, at differing rates across the EU, the gap has only decreased by 1% over the past seven years. The gender pay gap in 2019 stood at 20.8% in the UK, 14.7% in Denmark and 21% in Germany.[21] What is, perhaps, most surprising is that for people with university degrees gender pay gaps begin right after graduation. In the UK, men earned 10% more on average than women 15 months after they left university. Even among graduates with similar qualifications, there remained a wide gap in pay.[22]

What about elsewhere in the world, how do these figures look? While China has witnessed a widening gender pay gap in the past two decades[23] and data is limited, a recruitment website[24] claimed that in 2019, China saw a decrease in the wage gap for the first time, with women earning 77.5% of men's average wage compared to 72.3% in 2016. The main reason stated for this was that more women were moving into management because of stronger work capabilities and greater desire in women to succeed professionally. According to a report by the International Labour Organisation (ILO), the gender pay gap in India stands at 27% as of 2023. This means that, on average, women in India earn 73% of what men earn for doing the same job. This gap is even wider in certain industries, such as the technology sector, where women earn just 60% of what men earn.

Surely things must be better when all compensable factors, such as experience, industry and job level, are accounted for, right? Well, they are not. Even when men and women with the same employment characteristics do similar jobs, women in America earn $0.98 for every dollar earned by an equivalent man. In other words, a woman who is doing the same job as a man, with the exact same qualifications, is still paid 2% less for no attributable reason. This has not changed by any significant amount since 2015. Do things get better at the top? Unfortunately, not. In fact, the pay gap widens as women progress in their career, with women at the executive level making $0.95 to every dollar a man makes when all compensable factors are accounted for, and a shocking $0.69 to every dollar when these factors are not accounted for.[25]

It is easy to assume that this gap must be due to the fact that many women take a career break to have children. Some may look for jobs in industries like health care and education that offer flexibility to manage their family, and those are likely to be of lower pay.[26] This does not fully account for the gap. Neither do differences in education, experience and occupation. Women earn less pay per hour across all sectors and occupations for the same jobs and do a significantly larger share of unpaid work.[27] Women with children also make less than men with children or women without children. This is often called the motherhood penalty.[28] No such penalty exists for men. In fact, the opposite is true, as some researchers have found a father premium, as fathers earn more than men without children.[29]

What about the influence of other dimensions of one's identity on pay? A study that looked at data over a ten-year period from 1998 to 2008 showed that in the US, gay men earned 10% to 32% less than similarly situated heterosexual men.[30] In another study published in 2015, a meta-analysis of 31 studies published between 1995 and 2012 from the US and other developed countries revealed that gay men earned 11% less than heterosexual men.[31] On the other hand, a large-scale study by the World Bank found that lesbians earn an average of 8% more than their heterosexual female colleagues and in some countries, like the US, lesbians were found to earn up to 20% more.[32] The findings from a report in 2021 by McKinsey & Company, "Inclusion and the state of being Transgender in the workplace", showed that cisgender employees earn 32% more than their transgender colleagues.[33]

Graduates from elite universities receive a higher starting pay than those who are not from these institutions.[34] This higher starting pay seems to continue into mid-career as well. If we compare data from the top ten and the bottom ten colleges ranked by US News,[35] at the start of their career, the median salary for graduates of the top ten colleges is 31% higher than the median salary for the bottom ten colleges. By the sixth year, this gap has nearly doubled to 58%.[36] This discrepancy is much higher when looking at colleges below the top 100. In the UK, a graduate from London School of Economics earns an annual median salary of £38,000 while one from Cambridge or Oxford earns about £35,000. This is almost double that of graduates from universities at the bottom of the list.[37] It is also worth noting that university graduates earned about £10,000 more than non-graduates.[38]

Employee Well-Being

When looking at the impact of bias on employees, it is important to note that people internalise bias experiences differently. Our individual experience of an episode of bias is based on the bias itself and also our own diversity thumbprint, our emotions, physical and mental state as well as our prior experiences that get triggered during a bias episode. This is why it is important to not brush aside bias experiences or what is sometimes referred to as "gaslighting". While an instance of bias may seem "minor" to one person, the same instance may feel far more intense to another person.

Employees who experience bias—or fear experiencing bias—practice what is known as "covering"—hiding or downplaying their identities for fear of the bias they may experience. According to the Deloitte University Leadership Center for Inclusion report, Uncovering Talent, 61% of all employees "cover" their identities in some way and a 2020 YouGov study, conducted among 2,000 employees and 500 business leaders, undertaken by Mental Health First Aid (MHFA) England, reveals that almost one in five workers—about 6.5 million people—feels they cannot be their whole self at work, with people of colour reporting this most frequently.[39] Many working mothers feel pressured to leave their motherhood "behind" when they enter the revolving doors of their offices in order to be seen by others as professional and an equal contributor. Underrepresented ethnicities will tell you that they need to leave their cultural background behind and make conscious efforts to "fit in" with the majority's norms of behaviour. A White, single dad might tell you that he feels the pressure of needing to leave fatherhood out of the office to be seen as a team player. A gay man might be technically out, but not display pictures of his partner at work. A straight White man—45% of whom also report covering[40]—might keep quiet about a mental health issue he's facing.

Given that 35% of an employee's emotional investment to their work and 20% of their desire to stay at their organisation are linked to feelings of inclusion,[41] it is fair to say that inclusion is key. Yet, nurturing inclusion remains the biggest challenge for workplaces. A 2020 report by McKinsey & Company found that while people's feelings towards diversity were 52% positive and 3% negative, their feelings towards inclusion were much lower at only 29% positive and 61% negative. This emphasises that even the more diverse companies are still finding it challenging to nurture inclusion. The report states: "Hiring diverse talent isn't enough - it's the experience they have in the workplace that shapes whether they remain and thrive".[42]

Deloitte's 2019 state of inclusion survey of 3000 American professionals found that despite organisations making significant progress in inclusion,

63% witnessed bias at least once a month, 61% experienced bias at least once a month and 83% categorise the bias they experienced in the workplace to be subtle and indirect.[43] What is important for us to bear in mind is that this presence of bias can affect productivity, well-being and employee engagement: 84% of those surveyed said the bias had a negative impact on their happiness, confidence and well-being. A further 70% reported a negative impact on their engagement. Termite biases or microaggressions can have a significant negative impact on the mental health of employees in the form of depression, anxiety and post-traumatic stress disorder.[44]

Overall, the presence of bias in organisations leads to toxic, non-inclusive, unsafe and uncomfortable workplace environments. Becoming more aware of bias and blocking the impact of bias on employees and decision-making is crucial to ensuring a positive workplace culture that prioritises the well-being of employees, offers support at all levels within the organisation and has policies in place that encourage respect, trust, empathy and support. In such an environment, every employee feels engaged, included and in an environment where they can be productive. So, how do we block bias? That is the topic for the next chapter.

Self-Reflection Exercise: My Bias Compass Circle

One of the questions we often get asked is: When it comes to bias and especially implicit and unconscious bias, how do we become aware of something we are unaware of? There may be times when we are unsure if we are being biased or if we are failing to recognise our own bias. Having a trusted, diverse group of colleagues who we are comfortable asking for feedback is extremely beneficial. This group of colleagues becomes our compass as we navigate our own biases. We call this the "*bias compass circle*" and it is within this group that we can determine if our actions and ways of thinking or communicating are biased. This circle can provide us with constructive and motivational feedback. If we are being non-inclusive, our circle can help us understand more about a dimension of diversity we may not yet fully comprehend. This bias compass circle provides a psychologically safe zone to help us become more inclusive. At the same time, giving those in your bias compass circle the mandate to give you feedback implies that they will be more observant themselves and more likely to act as active allies in contexts beyond the circle.

Who would you invite to be part of your bias compass circle? Write down the names of these people in the circle.

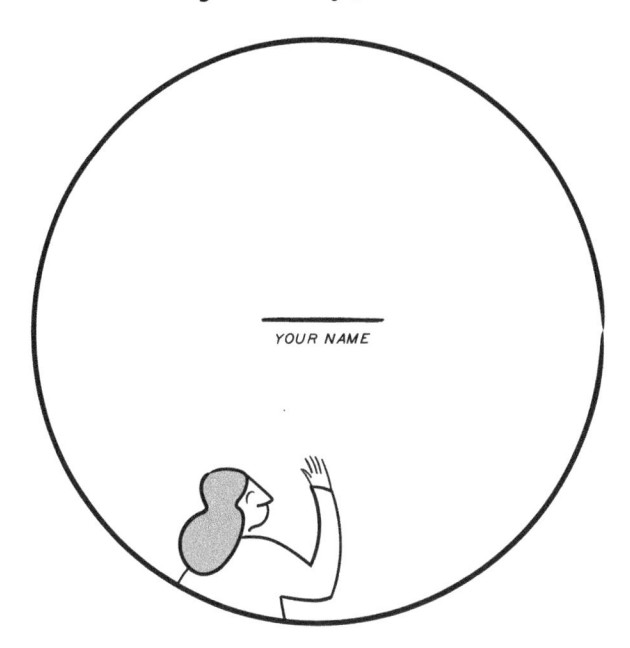

What Can You Do Differently From Today? Leading With Clarity Means:
- Introspecting deeply about where your cognitive biases lie.
- Doing an Implicit Assumption Test (IAT) to identify where your biases may lie.
- Forming a diverse bias compass circle.
- Preparing how you will respond respectfully when you are being biased.
- Addressing bias at work respectfully.

Notes

1. Abatecola, G., Caputo, A., & Cristofaro, M. (2018). Reviewing Cognitive Distortions in Managerial Decision Making: Toward an Integrative Co-Evolutionary Framework. *Journal of Management Development*, 37(5), 409–424.
    Bazerman, M., & Moore, D. A. (2013). *Judgment in Managerial Decision Making*. Hoboken, New Jersey: Wiley.
2. Eckel, C., & Füllbrunn, S. (2015). Thar SHE Blows? Gender, Competition, and Bubbles in Experimental Asset Markets. *American Economic Review*, 105(2), 906–920. Phillips, K. W. (2014). *How Diversity Makes Us Smarter*.

Scientific America. https://www.scientificamerican.com/article/how-diversity-makes-us-smarter/
3. Janis, I. L. (1972). *Victims of Groupthink: A Psychological Study of Foreign-Policy Decisions and Fiascoes*. Houghton Mifflin.
4. Sunstein, C., & Hastie, R. (2015). *Wiser, Getting Beyond Groupthink to Make Groups Smarter*. Harvard Business Review Press.
5. de Kock, F. S., & Hauptfleisch, D. B. (2018). Reducing Racial Similarity Bias in Interviews by Increasing Structure: A Quasi-Experiment Using Multilevel Analysis. *International Perspectives in Psychology*, 7, 137–154. Carlsson, R., & Sinclair, S. (2018). Prototypes and Same-Gender Bias in Perceptions of Hiring Discrimination. *The Journal of Social Psychology*, 158(3), 285–297.
6. Rivera, L. A., & Tilcsik, A. (2016). Class Advantage, Commitment Penalty: The Gendered Effect of Social Class Signals in an Elite Labor Market. *American Sociological Review*, 81(6), 1097–1131.
7. Thorndike, E. L. (1920). A Constant Error in Psychological Ratings. *Journal of Applied Psychology*, 4(1), 25–29.
8. Batres, C., & Shiramizu, V. (2022) *Examining the 'Attractiveness Halo Effect' Across Cultures*. Current Psychology, 42(29), 25515–25519; Olivola, C. Y., & Todorov, A. (2010). Fooled by First Impressions? Reexamining the Diagnostic Value of Appearance-Based Inferences. *Journal of Experimental Social Psychology*, 46(2), 315–324.
9. Fiske, S. T., Cuddy, A. J. C., & Glick, P. (2007). Universal Dimensions of Social Cognition: Warmth and Competence. *Trends in Cognitive Sciences*, 11(2), 77–83.
10. Ryan, M. K., & Haslam, A. (2005). The Glass Cliff: Evidence That Women Are Overrepresented in Precarious Leadership Positions. *British Journal of Management*, 16(2), 81–90. Williams, J. C. (2021). *Bias Interrupted: Creating Inclusion for Real and for Good*. Harvard Business Press.
11. Correll, S. J., Benard, S., & Paik, Getting a Job: Is There a Motherhood Penalty? I. *American journal of sociology, 112*(5): 1297–1339.
12. Dupas, P., et al. (2021). *Gender and the Dynamics of Economics Seminars* (Working Paper 28494). National Bureau of Economic Research.
13. Uhlmann, E. L. & Cohen, G. L. (2005). Constructed Criteria: Redefining Merit to Justify Discrimination. *Psychological Science, 16*(6), 474–480.
14. Corell, S. J., Weisshaar, K. R., Wynn, A. T., & Wehner, J. D. (2020). Inside the Black Box of organisational Life: The Gendered Language of Performance Assessment. *American Sociological Review*, 85(6), 1022–1050.
15. Gorman, S. E. & Gorman, J. M. (2016).*Denying to the Grave: Why We Ignore the Facts that Will Save Us*. Oxford: Oxford University Press; Glaser, J. E. Your Brain is Hooked on Being Right. *Harvard Business Review*: https://hbr.org/2013/02/break-your-addiction-to-being.
16. https://www.newyorker.com/magazine/2017/02/27/why-facts-dont-change-our-minds.

17. Mercier, H. & Sperber, D. (2019). *The Enigma of Reason*. Harvard University Press.
18. https://www.cnbc.com/2022/05/19/women-are-still-paid-83-cents-for-every-dollar-men-earn-heres-why.html.
19. https://19thnews-org.cdn.ampproject.org/c/s/19thnews.org/2023/03/equal-pay-day-2023-charts-gender-pay-gap/?amp.
20. https://commission.europa.eu/strategy-and-policy/policies/justice-and-fundamental-rights/gender-equality/equal-pay/gender-pay-gap-situation-eu_en.
21. https://commission.europa.eu/strategy-and-policy/policies/justice-and-fundamental-rights/gender-equality/equal-pay/gender-pay-gap-situation-eu_en.
22. https://www.theguardian.com/society/2020/jun/18/gender-pay-gap-begins-students-straight-after-university-graduate-data-report-uk.
23. Chi, W., & Li, B. (2014). Trends in China's Gender Employment and Pay Gap: Estimating Gender Pay Gaps with Employment Selection. *Journal of Comparative Economics*, 42, 708–725.
24. Zhipin.com.
25. https://www.payscale.com/data/gender-pay-gap.
26. https://ec.europa.eu/info/policies/justice-and-fundamental-rights/gender-equality/equal-pay/gender-pay-gap-situation-eu_en#why-do-women-earn-less.
27. 6th European Working Conditions Survey, Eurofound, 2015.
28. Correll, S. J., Benard, S., & Paik, I. (2007). Getting a Job: Is There a Motherhood Penalty? *American Journal of Sociology*, 112(5), 1297–1339.
29. Correll, S. J., Benard, S., & Paik, I. (2007). Getting a Job: Is There a Motherhood Penalty? *American Journal of Sociology*, 112(5), 1297–1339.
30. Badgett, M. V. L., Sears, B., Lau, H. & Ho, D. (2009). Bias in the Workplace: Consistent Evidence of Sexual Orientation and Gender Identity Discrimination 1998–2008. *Chicago-Kent Law Review, 84*(2), 559–595.
31. Klawitter, M. (2015). Meta-Analysis of the Effects of Sexual Orientation on Earnings. *Industrial Relations: A Journal of Economy and Society, 54*(1), 4–32.
32. Drydakis, N. (2019). Sexual Orientation and Labor Market Outcomes. *IZA World of Labor*, 111, 1–11.
33. https://www.mckinsey.com/featured-insights/diversity-and-inclusion/being-transgender-at-work.
34. https://www.payscale.com/college-salary-report/bachelors.
35. https://www.usnews.com/best-colleges.
36. https://www.forbes.com/sites/paologaudiano/2018/03/19/recruiting-talent-from-top-schools-is-a-terrible-idea/?sh=2a19a1ed271c.
37. https://www.emolument.com/career_advice/uk_university_salary_2017#gsc.tab=0.
38. https://www.gov.uk/government/news/graduates-continue-to-benefit-with-higher-earnings.
39. https://metro-co-uk.cdn.ampproject.org/c/s/metro.co.uk/2020/09/25/Black-and-ethnic-minority-employees-need-more-mental-health-support-in-the-workplace-13325119/amp/.

40. https://hbr.org/2014/11/help-your-employees-be-themselves-at-work.
41. Travis, D. J., Shaffer, E., & Thorpe-Moscon, J. (2019). *Getting Real About Inclusive Leadership: Why Change Starts With You.* Catalyst: https://www.catalyst.org/research/inclusive-leadership-report/
42. https://www.mckinsey.com/featured-insights/diversity-and-inclusion/diversity-wins-how-inclusion-matters.
43. https://www2.deloitte.com/us/en/pages/about-deloitte/articles/inclusion-insights.html.
44. Nadal, K., Wong, Y., Issa, M.-A., Meterko, V., Leon, J., & Wideman, M. (2011). Sexual Orientation Microaggressions: Processes and Coping Mechanisms for Lesbian, Gay, and Bisexual Individuals. *Journal of LGBT Issues in Counseling*, 5, 21–46.

Leading with accountability

5

Leading With Accountability: Addressing Systemic Bias

5.1 Moving Beyond Conviction and Clarity

Until now, we have taken you through the first two skills of leading through bias—leading with conviction and leading with clarity. Given that you are with us thus far, you have certainly come a long way! You now have a solid understanding of bias and how it impacts our thoughts, words, behaviours and decisions. You have also had the opportunity to reflect on your own attitudes and biases, and you are hopefully feeling better equipped to identify biases in and around you.

But your journey does not end here.

In fact, research shows that if you halt your journey towards leading through bias here, you will not experience much positive and sustainable change. Now don't get us wrong, conviction and clarity are paramount in this journey. Without believing in the purpose of DEI activities, and without having a deep knowledge of bias and how it influences decision-making, you won't be able to make a real difference. Without these skills, your actions would risk being inauthentic or not evidence based—and more likely to fail. However, believing in the value, understanding the purpose and having deep knowledge about the facts are simply not enough. If knowledge and attitudes are not followed up by very concrete behaviours, your newly gained conviction and clarity will stay inside your mind. Given that bias often kicks in automatically, simply knowing that you have bias will not be enough to stop its negative effects.[1] So, the first two leadership skills in this book are essential for you to be able to implement the changes needed and to lead with accountability, a skill that we begin exploring in this chapter.

So, how do we prevent biases from impacting our words, behaviours and decisions? Many companies rely on unconscious bias training, but research has shown that organisational DEI training that relies solely on unconscious bias training could backfire.[2] There is also growing evidence that many unconscious bias training programs do not lead to meaningful changes in behaviour.[3] One of the main challenges is that self-paced unconscious bias training, or a half-day workshop on anti-discrimination, serves as a "check-the-box" item, which perpetuates stereotypes that organisations are trying to fix in the first place. Having a heightened awareness of bias without knowing what to do is like sending someone to the edge of the cliff and asking them to jump without giving them a parachute. The remaining three skills explored in this and the next few chapters form your parachute, and are essential to ensuring sustainable and transformational impact.

Let us first begin with exploring the limitations of bias awareness training.

Limitations of Bias Awareness Training and the Myth of Meritocracy

Many companies—maybe your own—have developed bias awareness training for their employees. However, the sad truth is that these rarely work, and that they sometimes even give rise to backlash and reinforce bias. The reason is twofold. First, you are per definition unaware of unconscious bias, and even when you become aware of them and successfully turn them into implicit bias, this does not stop them from being automatically activated when you are in System 1 thinking—which you are 95% of the time! Second, even though you may become aware of some of your biases, you are most likely to have a lot of others you are not aware of. So, bias awareness training—not followed up by action—risks adding to the illusion of rationality that we explained in Chapter 3 and risks making you think that you now have everything under control. Bias awareness training, therefore, at best addresses explicit bias, educating you to think differently, but is at the same time most likely to suppress the implicit bias down to an unconscious level and to give you a free pass because you think you have control over your biases.

The difficulty of becoming aware of bias is also linked to the myth of meritocracy. Meritocracy, according to the Merriam-Webster dictionary is the term for "a system, organisation, or society in which people are chosen and moved into positions of success, power, and influence on the basis of their demonstrated abilities and merit". We like to think that our organisations are meritocracies, and that the people in charge of them are those best suited for this role and responsibility. However, if we take all the research on bias from Chapters 3 and 4 into consideration, we need to acknowledge that this might not always be the case. Of course, one does not get to the top of an organisation without merits, but sexism, racism, ageism, classism, ableism, neurodiversity bias and heteronormativity, among other identity-related cognitive biases, make us define merit differently in different people, depending on their gender, race, age, socio-economic status, abilities, sexual orientation, etc.

That means that our very decisions on what constitutes merit, and who possesses it, is fundamentally biased.

The myth of meritocracy is further strengthened if we believe that we are doing the right thing, and this is the paradox of meritocracy. When we believe that the world is just, we also tend to believe that inequalities reflect a meritocratic process. This means that we assume that the poorer outcomes for underrepresented groups are due to their inadequate competencies; that inequity and inequality are the result of lack of skills, and not a result of our biased decision-making. This allows us to maintain our belief that we live in a fair world rather than having to actually address the inequities that exist.[4]

Unfortunately, the myth of meritocracy is often strengthened by bias awareness training. If we think we have become more just and fair, having gone through this training, we have a tendency not to see organisational inequalities, or in other words, our biases have become unconscious. They are still there, controlling our decision-making, but we think we have learned to control them. Thus, the problem here is not that we are unable to view merits objectively, it is that we think that merit itself is an objective measure. Several studies have shown that in organisations that perceive themselves as meritocratic, members tend to be more biased than in organisations where people accept the flaws of meritocracy.[5] The learning here is that even though you, by now, know much more about bias and might be much more aware of your own biases, you cannot isolate merit and merit will therefore never itself be an objective merit.

As mentioned in Chapter 3, awareness of bias cannot make you less biased. If bias awareness training programs claim that they can make you "debiased", beware. This is simply not possible, and that is false marketing. Instead, bias awareness training should make you able to identify when and in which situations you are most likely to be biased and find ways to block the biases. In other words, bias awareness training is meant to teach you that there is no way that you can rationally control all of your biases. You need help, and that is what this chapter is about.

So, What Works?

We also have some good news for you. There are things that do work! Research has in the past few years identified the fact that when bias awareness training is combined with concrete actions and habit-breaking interventions, it works.[6] Therefore, training that not only targets awareness and increased knowledge, but also enables change in behaviour has more sustainable effects in increasing diversity, equity and inclusion in organisations. This brings us back to the KAB (Knowledge-Attitude-Behaviour) model of behavioural change. Knowledge and attitude are crucial to behavioural change, but they are not sufficient. Having deep knowledge and the right attitude need to be combined with concrete behaviours to enable change to take place.

This chapter will take you through a number of simple, but impactful behaviours that we, based on Sara's earlier work, call *bias blockers*.[7] *Bias blockers* do not erase bias because, as we know by now, we can't do that, and if we think we have erased them, they will just be unconscious instead of "only" implicit. What we can do very successfully is to block them, preventing them from negatively influencing our words, behaviours and decisions. It is very difficult to avoid triggering bias. Bias activation is automatic, but the effects of bias can be controlled. Therefore, bias blocking is more effective than sensitivity training. As Iris Bohnet, who is professor at Harvard University, famously said in an interview in Harvard Business Review: "It's easier to change your processes than your people".[8]

From our experience, and based on the evidence we have shared in the previous two chapters, it is evident that much of the bias—individual, collective, interpersonal and systemic—in organisations is embedded in all human relations, from a person's very first encounter with an organisation through their job application and the recruitment cycle to retention and development—and even offboarding processes. This is known as the employee life cycle—a process that covers the various stages from when an employee first engages with the organisation to when they leave it. Bias also influences the decisions we make in other organisational processes like designing products and services and marketing those products and services. However, our focus in this book is on the employee life cycle given our expertise in this area, and we believe that learning how to block bias in this area will have a ripple effect on other organisational processes and functions beyond the talent management realm. This chapter is structured as follows. First, we go through what not to do. After establishing these pitfalls and most common mistakes, we move on to what to do. Here, we provide you with several systemic and process-related bias blockers across the entire employee life cycle that will help you lead with accountability.

What Not To Do

During our years of researching and working with a range of different organisations, we have gained a pretty good idea of what works, but also what doesn't work. Unfortunately, some of the things that do not work seem like "easy fixes". However, despite their ease and, thus, attractiveness, these actions also tend to reinforce biases instead of blocking them and reinforce further marginalisation and division of people rather than promoting inclusion. Thus, the "don't dos" that we discuss below have been specifically chosen to help you avoid the "usual" mistakes. Because they are actions, we see leaders take them with the best of intentions in mind, hoping to increase diversity and nurture inclusion in their organisation. They are not done because leaders don't want to make a change; they are chosen because leaders don't know how to make change happen. The list below is not exhaustive, but we hope that the contrast will help you reflect further on how and why the bias blockers that we provide later on actually do work.

Be Careful With Minority Initiatives

One of the most common mistakes is trying to increase representation of certain groups of people by engaging in initiatives for minority groups, such as courses and talent programs targeting those underrepresented groups. These initiatives can take the form of a women's course on strategic thinking, power and politics, salary negotiation or programming, or it might be a training program for refugees or other immigrants. Such targeted minority initiatives face various degrees of backlash and may result in resistance towards DEI efforts in an organisation, as they are seen as unfairly supporting only some groups and excluding others.[9]

Courses for women typically come in two forms:

- Courses to teach women the skills that women are assumed not to have (often STEM-related competencies). This might sound reasonable and like a very good solution to increase women's competencies in this area in order to make them promotable. The problem, here, is that these initiatives reinforce the stereotype that women do not have this competence and often end up being offered to all women, also the ones who do not need a competency-lift in the area. On the other hand, men don't have to take the course, but often rise through the hierarchy even without having to gain those extra competencies. Thus, a skills course is not a bad idea in itself, but offering it only to women might produce backlash. Instead, you

can offer courses to everyone who feels that they need a competency—lift and make active efforts to ensure equal representation or a representation that reflects the gender composition in the organisation.
- Courses that teach women personal competencies. These are usually focused on competencies not typically associated with women, like negotiation skills or learning to be more confident. However, even though these courses are offered with the best of intentions, they tend to be built on biased assumptions about women's personal competencies rather than facts about women's qualifications, and therefore tend to reinforce that bias rather than blocking it. These courses are "fix the women" solutions and detract from addressing the actual systemic biases that exist. So, if we offer a course in salary negotiation to women because we think this can help close the gender pay gap, it tends to have the exact opposite effect, reinforcing the bias that women aren't really cut out for leadership positions, because the course implies that women cannot negotiate. As we will discuss in one of the bias blockers later on, it is much more efficient to ensure equitable and transparent salary negotiation guidelines, processes and policies that apply to everyone.

Trainee programs for immigrants constitute another problematic initiative. Establishing such programs might be seen as a responsible and efficient way for your organisation to help immigrants to find their way into the labour market. But research shows that trainees are rarely given the opportunity to continue into permanent positions. By giving them a special trainee position, something similar to "fixing the women" happens, as those offered the position are viewed as being in need of extra help and not cut out for a permanent position. Researchers refer to this with the metaphor of a "sticky floor".[10] By engaging in special agreements at the bottom of the hierarchy, people often get stuck there, because they are associated with entry-level (or lower!) competencies. This is one of the reasons why so many organisations are ethnically segregated with many underrepresented ethnicities in the bottom of the hierarchy, becoming more and more White towards the top. Again, trainee programs are great, but offer them to a mixed group of people that are representative of the intersectional identities you want represented in your organisation. Then make concrete plans on how to promote these people into permanent positions. If there are not enough permanent positions in your organisation, then you can work actively with outplacement, possibly through external labour market intermediaries to help support these immigrants to find jobs in other organisations.

A final form of minority initiatives, which tends to result in backlash, are female talent programs. Many organisations have, in recent times, set up such programs in order to ensure that women are spotted and included in programs that should advance their career. Again, such programs tend to draw on (and reinforce) stereotypes of women, providing guidance on how to talk, dress and present oneself to appear more confident and powerful. Such programs tend to reinforce the perception in the organisation that the talent programs for women are not as ambitious or "serious" as the "real" talent programs (mostly occupied by men). A much better approach is to make sure that you have equal representation on your regular talent programs. Most of the organisations we have worked with have not managed to secure equal representation here, often because the definition of "talent" is very superficial and has to do with who has "potential". And as should be clear by now, we are not able to view "talent" or "potential" neutrally. Thus, as we will go into detail in this chapter, having clear criteria to access talent programs and directly seeking out women to take part in them is a much better way, than "special" programs for women, which tend to side line them. Similarly, if you send your employees to do a business school MBA, then don't send mainly White men to do an MBA, but make sure the opportunity is given to a diverse group of people.

Avoid a Charitable Narrative

The second most common mistake is communicating DEI efforts and courses for underrepresented groups as efforts to "help" these underrepresented groups. A charitable narrative effectively reinforces the stereotype that these underrepresented groups are not qualified for leadership roles. Let us give examples to illustrate this and how it tends to produce backlash. Often, the courses for underrepresented groups that we discussed in the previous section start with a charitable narrative. One of the companies we worked with offered a course for women in "power and politics" because they found that women needed a gentle push in order to become better at the political game in the organisation. In another organisation, helping to upskill immigrants through a training program was part of their corporate social responsibility (CSR) efforts. In the first company, the CEO gave a speech about the organisation's women's initiatives expressing how he genuinely wants to support women and show them that they are *also* cut out for a leadership role, so that they more proactively would seek these opportunities. In other words, he placed the responsibility for the lack of women leaders on the women themselves and their lack of proactiveness, and explained how he was going to help fix them. As such, the charitable narrative communicates that it is the women who need to be fixed, not the organisation and its processes. Instead, the CEO could have communicated that he has realised that the way the promotion system works is biased and thus discriminatory, and he could have focused on steps to actively change the evaluation system in order to ensure equal access to promotion. This would have been a "fix the system" strategy that is less likely to marginalise women and also less likely to alienate men.

If a certain group tends not to display as much confidence as the other groups, don't offer them help through skills training. Instead, figure out why this is the case. Quite often, it is because they are left out from certain networks, not included in certain decision processes, silenced at meetings, etc. To address this, include the underrepresented groups in all the organisation's processes. Another reason certain groups appear less confident is that we typically have a very narrow definition of what confidence looks and feels like. Challenge yourself to redefine the very definition of confidence in your team and organisation to be more inclusive towards diverse intersectional identities. We will explore this further in Chapter 6 on leading with allyship.

DEI Efforts Need More Than a Good Heart

Although it is paramount to have conviction and believe in the purpose of DEI, it is not enough. The conviction from leaders is extremely important for the success of DEI efforts, but it needs to translate to changed practices and processes. If we draw on the KAB (Knowledge-Attitude-Behaviour) model of behavioural change, DEI needs to be embedded into processes, metrics and compensation systems. We will get back to this in detail later in this chapter. But the fact is that if DEI is only heart and talk, then during times of crisis or when people are busy, DEI is the first to be left behind. Leaders need, as the cliché tells us, to walk the talk.

Similarly, DEI efforts cannot rely on a few individuals invested in the "cause". DEI efforts in organisations are often started by a few passionate individuals—and often individuals who have experienced discrimination themselves or have had moments of epiphany through their relationships with people who have experienced workplace discrimination. Although this might be a powerful and important starting point, DEI efforts must not be limited to the people passionate about it. Why? Because it does not spread to the rest of the organisation, as the passionate people might not hold the formal power to change things systemically or organisation-wide, and also because DEI efforts are rarely seen as career progressing tasks. Analyses show that DEI efforts are among the first that people stop engaging in when they are busy or stressed.[11]

So, although a diversity council or employee resource groups can be very valuable to organisations, as they can be forums for sharing knowledge, moving an agenda forward, organising events and educating advocates, these are not sustainable if they are not well supported, resourced and recognised—neither for the people performing the often voluntary and non-promotable tasks (as DEI tasks outside of HR often are), nor for the organisation's DEI efforts. Instead, such efforts tend to fizzle out once the passionate people leave the organisation or feel burned out. There is, sadly, a growing number of DEI leaders experiencing burnout due to the lack of resources and leadership support, working in silos without a community, a disconnect between the DEI vision and what is actually happening and an excessive focus on the optics of diversity rather than enabling actual change.[12] DEI change cannot rely on unpaid labour and voluntary involvement. It needs to be anchored in senior leadership and in the processes, along with being well resourced and rewarded. We will detail how this can be done, both later in this chapter and in Chapter 6, when we present the concrete bias blockers.

Resist Fake News!

The topic of DEI is not only one of the strategic areas that managers have the least understanding of, it is also the one that most people have an opinion about and *assume* that they have knowledge about. The reason for the former is that it is not (yet) part of general managerial education, like marketing, finance, HR and microeconomics, but something that managers need to proactively seek information and knowledge about (like reading this book). Luckily more and more are, but the fact is still that when we are approached by a group of managers to provide advice on DEI, they often start from a very different starting point compared to if they were revising the company's financial strategy, marketing strategy or employer branding strategy.

However, it is a topic everyone has some experience with and, therefore, also an area that most people have an opinion about. This is why there is nothing as emotional and potentially conflict-prone than discussing and developing an organisation's DEI strategy. Most people have an opinion, very little knowledge and a lot of emotions and feelings associated with this. Hence, it is extremely important that you, as a leader, are able to resist fake news, unwarranted claims and personal opinions.

Let us provide examples of these three sources of misinformation:

- Fake news are facts that are plain wrong and could include statements like: "but there are equal opportunities. DEI efforts are reverse discrimination" or "the explanation for the lack of minorities in management positions is that they lack the competencies". The first is based on a lack of knowledge of history and facts, and much of what we have covered in Chapter 2 (leading with conviction) is meant to debunk this. The second has its roots in the trust in meritocracy, but after reading Chapters 3 and 4 (leading with clarity), you should be able to counter this view as well. Fighting fake news with facts is essential!

- Unwarranted claims are similar to fake news but occur at a more individual level in the form of arguments in a discussion. For example, Sara once conducted a seminar on gender equality in academia where a participant said that "it is natural that there are very few female professors, as it is scientifically proven that men are more intelligent than women". Addressing such unwarranted claims through research-based evidence is key, as it is, in fact, NOT scientifically proven that men are more intelligent than women. The claim is based on studies, which show that historically there are more male "geniuses" (also a problematic term, but we will let that rest for now), than there are female ones. But this has nothing to do with people's actual capacity for intelligence and everything to do with the fact that women have (and still are) denied access to university education and experience far more barriers in certain areas and levels of education compared to men. Again, this should be clear after reading Chapters 2–4 of this book.
- Personal opinions are opinions that are formed based on personal experiences. This would be, for example, when a CEO, who has a stay-at-home wife, has strong opinions about women's ambitions and aspirations based on the conversations he has at home, or when a manager who has two children, where the son happens to be good at math and science while the daughter happens to be good at languages, ends up generalising these personal experiences in a way that confirms gender stereotypes. On a positive note, personal experiences can also act to support DEI efforts, such as when a manager suddenly realises the importance of racial discrimination because her son-in-law is Black and she has heard first-hand stories, from a person she loves about racism, or when the male CEO realises that his daughter does not have the same opportunities in life as his son. When discrimination is felt at an emotional or personal level, it tends to make more of an impact (which is also why we have the A between the K and B in the KAB model).

The variations and examples are many, but the fact is that you must be careful about inaccurate facts and universalised individual beliefs. Organisations tend to know a lot about their technical area or markets, but very little about their people. So, in short, do the groundwork and get your facts straight!

Now that we have warned you about all the things that you have to be careful about (and given you some hints on how to prevent them), it is time to get specific. We anticipate that you, by this point in the book, really want to know what to do. And now that time has come! The rest of this chapter will focus on what you can actually do—things that will result in inclusive and equitable outcomes.

5.2 Blocking Bias in Systems and Processes Across the Entire Employee Life Cycle

In this chapter, we focus on systemic bias blockers that can be set up throughout the entire employee life cycle (Image 5.1). An employee's journey with your organisation—including your own—begins the very second a potential applicant is exposed to your employer brand—the attracting stage. This is then followed by the recruitment and selection stage, which refers to the process and experience of moving from applying for a job to being an employee. This stage includes the organisation's process of sourcing, researching, generating, identifying and building relationships with potential candidates. Once hired, the employee goes through the onboarding stage during which the organisation supports newly hired employees to get acquainted with their team, the organisation and its culture, with the aim of inclusion. This is followed by the retention and development stage during which the organisation aims to keep employees satisfied through rewards, benefits and recognition while also helping them grow in the organisation through a variety of development initiatives. The last stage is that of separation, which refers to the process when an employee leaves the organisation.

Your organisation—like most others—is likely confronted with one or more of the following challenges regarding the pool of candidates ready to fill a vacant position, also known as your talent pipeline:

1. Your organisation has a general talent pipeline problem,
2. Your organisation lacks diversity in your talent pipeline and/or
3. Your organisation has a solid talent pipeline but is unable to raise people from underrepresented groups through the organisational layers.

The recommendations on how to block bias that we present here help address these challenges but are not a one-size-fits-all set of solutions. There are many factors that influence which of these bias blockers work in individual organisations, and we will try to address the various factors along the way. In the following sections, we will look at a number of steps you can take to block bias across the employee life cycle and they are summarised at the end of this chapter for easy reference.

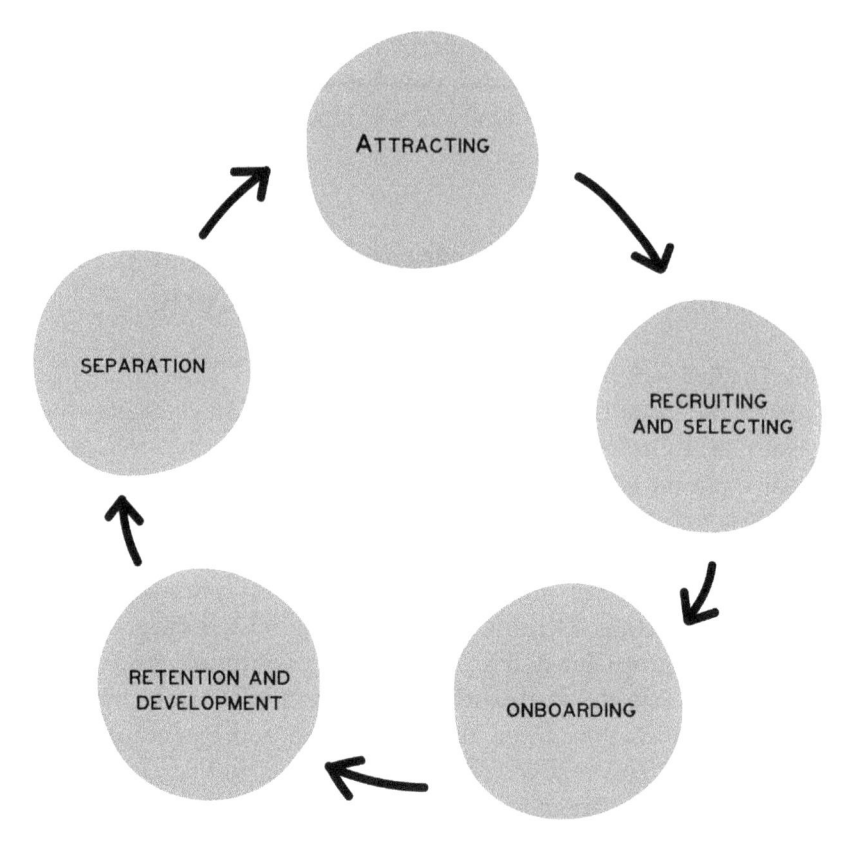

Image 5.1 Employee life cycle

Blocking Bias When Attracting Talent

> *Who is applying to your organisation? Are you attracting a diverse pool of candidates, including those from underrepresented groups?*

Generating the Job Description

Identify the Required Competencies for the Specific Job

This first bias blocker might seem simple and banal, but in our experience, it is the one that most hiring managers skip. Either because they are too busy or because they don't find it important. But this step is pivotal to being able

5 Leading With Accountability: Addressing Systemic Bias

to professionalise—and therefore for the success of—the rest of the employee life cycle processes. Ask yourself this: How many times have you—or other people in your organisation—copy-pasted a job advertisement description? Be honest. If you are anything like the many leaders that we have worked with over the years, the answer is probably "many". You can then extend that mental exercise with the following question: How many standard formulations are there? And with your increased knowledge of bias, how much harm to equity do they do? Copy-pasting job advertisements is a mistake that can have biased consequences further on in the cycle. So, spend half a day, or even a full day, to really think hard about the competencies that you need the candidate to have for the job.

As a first step, think of the professional and personal competencies that are necessary and reflect on how these should be complementary to the team that the person will be a part of. Ask yourself the following questions in this order: (1) Which competencies are necessary to do the job?, (2) which competencies are necessary to be part of the team? and (3) which competencies are necessary to be part of the organisation? With the second and third question, it is very important that you think about culture add rather than culture fit. This means that instead of letting your intuition bias decide who feels right and who "fits" the culture, you activate System 2 thinking and through an analysis of the needed competencies, you get a solid idea of which competencies are most important and which person would add value to the team. This is also where diversity can actually be a competence. The first question is more focused on the professional and personal competencies that are necessary to do the actual work tasks, but in questions 2 and 3, diversity and/or an inclusive mindset can be a competence. If you truly believe in the value of diversity—that is if you lead with conviction—and if you truly understand the way bias works—that is if you lead with clarity—this is your chance to let diversity count as a competence and lead with accountability with a focus on culture add rather than culture fit.

When you list the competencies needed to be part of the team and the organisation, think about the diversity of the team first. Are there perspectives and/or personal competencies that are needed but missing from the team? What is the team's and the organisation's overall diversity challenge? Could you, through this hire, address that? In this way, you begin to block intuition bias from the very beginning. Of course, your gut will be allowed to also have a say, but it shouldn't be the loudest voice. When you can hear your gut "speaking", try to explain the gut feeling using competencies. If you can't, intuition bias, similarity bias or proximity bias might be fooling your brain.

The competencies needed to complete your team and make your organisation diverse should be a priority.

Check Competencies for Similarity to Yourself/Your Favourite Colleagues

As much as we would like to work with people similar to ourselves, giving in to similarity bias is not what is best for the team or the organisation. So, once you have listed all the competencies needed to do the job, check how similar these competencies are to your own. If you have done a thorough job of thinking about culture add, this might already have addressed the bias that this step is designed to block.

> **Making Connections: Poornima & Sara's Experiences**
> We often observe similarity bias in the organisations we work with. For instance, similarity bias surfaced in a one-to-one coaching session that Sara once had with a leader. The leader had been part of a bias training program and was trying to figure out which biases to be careful of and which behaviours he needed to change. One of the tips we always give when we advise organisations about blocking bias in their decision-making process (we will take a deeper look at this in the next chapter) is to be very clear about the criteria and competencies that they are looking for in a new employee. This can, among other things, block the expectation bias, which we will explore in the coming pages. So, this particular leader very proudly announced that he had made a list of criteria and competencies in order to be concrete and professional in the recruitment process. However, as he looked closer at the list, his pride turned to embarrassment. He could just as well strike out all the competencies and just write his own name. The candidate he was looking for was a complete replica of himself! This became a defining moment in his journey towards leading with accountability.

Check if You Have Prioritised Unnecessary Features

Although it varies a lot from industry to industry, there is a great likelihood that your organisation prioritises certain educational or other professional backgrounds when looking for new employees.

This is, of course, sometimes necessary, as specific jobs require specific competencies. However, it is far from always the case. Often, hiring managers request an educational or professional background that is technically not necessary for doing the job in question—and this might prevent potential candidates from applying for the position. To mention a few very different examples from our work with organisations, we see that when looking for top managers, pharmaceutical companies tend to prioritise scientists, universities tend to prioritise professors, military organisations tend to prioritise military trained individuals and hospitals tend to favour doctors. This might be a very reasonable prioritisation if the organisations are searching for a person to be a scientist, a professor, a soldier or a medical doctor. However, do the specific professional profiles automatically make such people the best managers? No, not necessarily. Nevertheless, many organisations transfer the profile/skills needed to work in the machine room of the organisation to managerial and leadership positions. What these organisations miss out on are candidates who may not have expert knowledge (they might have industry experience) but are the best suited for a leadership position exactly because they have general organisational and managerial skills rather than specialised expertise. So, checking for background bias could open up your potential pool of applicants considerably and provide you with a much more diverse pool of candidates.

> **Making Connections: Poornima & Sara's Experiences**
> Poornima was approached to address the lack of innovation and creative ideas in the digital marketing team of a global FMCG. The digital marketing team comprised of about 80 employees from around 60 nationalities with a pretty even (binary) gender mix. Yet, they were struggling with doing things differently. When we looked at the professional backgrounds of the employees, they all came from three organisations—the FMCG itself, and two other competitors within not just the same industry but the same product line. Creative ideas were not flowing because everyone was thinking the same way, based on their experiences. They were simply replicating what had been done before in this or similar companies with some modifications, rather than really being creative about their digital marketing strategy and campaigns.

Define Words Such as "Talent" and "Potential"

Do you use the word "talent" or "potential" when you discuss the competencies of your up-and-coming employees? Yes, you probably do and so have we in this book. But, even though it might be a bit provocative, we would like to claim that when leaders use the words "talent" and "potential", they have no idea what they are talking about. Now, before you write this off as nonsense, give us a chance to explain.

When we perceive someone as a talent or as having potential, it is often because we have a good relationship with them, because they are easy to assign a task to and because they "run with the ball" and get things done. However, this also often means that the people we view as talents are very likely to be similar to ourselves. Moreover, we know that women and people of colour are more often hired based on accomplishments, while White men are hired on potential. Women and people of colour have to prove themselves, or have had a similar position, to get the job, which makes it challenging to demonstrate—and become recognised as—talent. Harvard professor Joan C. Williams calls this a "prove-it-again-bias".[13]

Consider this situation: You have two employees. Employee A is someone who you really connect with and whom you feel very comfortable giving responsibility to. You can't pinpoint what exactly makes this employee so brilliant, but you're ready to give them any task that you can't cover yourself. Employee B is really good at three specific things, which is central to your core business, but you don't really connect with them. Which one are you most likely to see as a talent, as having potential?

We have a tendency to see talent and potential in the people who are similar to ourselves and candidates that we feel the best connection with, but this has very little to do with competence, and this has very little to do with talent. Also, if we combine this with proximity bias, we favour employees and candidates who are spatially close to us, negatively impacting colleagues and candidates working in other locations or remotely.

So, what we propose here is to shift the conversation to competence rather than potential, and you can do this very easily. Every time you use the word "talent" or "potential", check if you know what you mean. WHY is this person a talent? WHY does this person have potential? If you can't be specific, it is probably bias that is fooling your brain (again).

Place Emphasis on the Required—"Must Have"—Competencies Rather Than the Length of the CV

Another common mistake is to be unduly impressed by the length of a person's CV or the number of different competencies that a person has. However, it is not necessarily the length of the CV that makes the best employee, but the one that actually matches the list of required competencies for the job you are hiring for. So, if you have defined a list of needed complementary competencies, you need to stick to these when evaluating candidates. If there are not many candidates from underrepresented groups with similar lengthy CVs and you prioritise the length of the CV, then you risk reinforcing the inequity by limiting access for underrepresented groups. So, keep focused on the actual required competencies that you have defined for this role.

In fact, findings from a Hewlett Packard internal report that has been cited many times showed that men apply for a job when they meet only 60% of the qualifications needed, but women apply only if they meet 100% of them. So how do you ensure that more women apply for the job, consider dividing the competencies into "must-haves" and "nice-to-haves". This can ensure that women—and other underrepresented identities who may not have considered applying for the role—are attracted to do so.

Job Advertisements

Neutralise the Language Used in Job Advertisements

Several studies have shown that wording that is gender biased, words that people implicitly code to be masculine or feminine, creates subtle gender bias in the way that job advertisements are perceived. Danielle Gaucher and colleagues, for example, found that recruiters tend to envision the perfect candidate to be a man if they code the words in the advertisement to be masculine while women tend to not find the job appealing if they code the words to be masculine.[14] Typical words that are coded—often unknowingly—by most people as masculine are words like "active", "ambitious", "individual" and "self-confident" reflecting agentic traits, and words that are typically coded as feminine are words like "collaborative", "empathetic", "responsible" and "trustworthy", reflecting communal traits. This, however, should not be understood to indicate that women are feminine and men are masculine. Rather, because we all have a tendency to internalise this bias, as explained in Chapters 3 and 4, women have a tendency to be less drawn by the masculine wording in job advertisements. Women can be very ambitious and assertive, but still be influenced unconsciously by the masculine worded advertisements. So, if you use masculine words in an advertisement, you might not attract people who ARE actually ambitious and amazing, but those who PERCEIVE themselves to be ambitious and amazing. The words above—and words like capable, excellent, successful, strong, dynamic or experienced—may prevent people who are disabled, young, neurodivergent or from underrepresented ethnic groups from applying.[15]

In a recent study conducted by Danish-based company Develop Diverse and the Danish Association for Managers and Executives, over 11,000 job advertisements published in the Nordics were examined. The analysis showed that agentic-coded language (e.g. "dominant" and "competitive") was more dominant in the job advertisements for middle and senior-level positions compared with entry-level positions.

In addition, not only agentic words, like "ambition, "competitive" and "proactive", or fluffy words, like "talent" and "potential", are problematic. Also, words and competences that are often perceived as "warm" and always desirably like "emotional intelligence" can be problematic. In a LinkedIn post, published in our network recently, a neurodivergent person shared how many neurodivergent people struggle with the word "emotional intelligence" as many neurodivergent individuals find it difficult to understand social clues and may therefore not fit the traditional expectations of emotional intelligence. Again, it is not our point that you should not use this term, but that you should only use it if the job requires emotional intelligence.

If it is only a nice-to-have, it is not beneficial to list it in the add, as it might discourage people with excellent professional competencies from applying.

One of the ways to block this bias is to try to neutralise or remove biased words from any corporate text (not just job advertisements) to make sure that your organisation is appealing to more than simply those who perceive themselves as amazing, and this has a positive impact! A recent analysis by LinkedIn showed that 44% of women and 33% men would be discouraged from applying if the word "aggressive" was part of a job advertisement. It should, however, also be mentioned that you should not simply swap all the masculine-coded words with feminine-coded words and then think that the problem is solved. If you do this, you risk writing an advertisement that is very far from the competencies you are looking for. So, what we recommend is twofold.

First and foremost, go back to the list of competencies that you defined as the very first thing when planning for this new hire, and create a realistic and convincing narrative of the person you see fitting this job. Don't copy and paste text from a previous job advertisement (as we so often hear that organisations do!) but construct it specifically for each job, based on the complementary competencies you identified as necessary. This is important for two reasons: First, if you make an effort to describe the competencies required in detail, it is easier to avoid the words that are associated with masculinity. You don't need words like aggressive, ambitious, proactive, etc., if you have described what the job is about. And second, research also shows that more women and (other) underrepresented identities can see themselves in a job description if the description is precise.[16]

As we have seen earlier, White men tend to think they can do the job if they live up to 60% of the described competencies and they tend to see their competencies reflected in more fluffy words, like ambitious and proactive. Many women and people from (other) underrepresented groups have internalised that this might not be the case, as they have learned that they have to prove themselves to be seen. There is still a tendency that White men overestimate themselves, and women and people with minority ethnic background underestimate themselves when they are asked to compare themselves to a generic type of description that includes words like "ambitious" or "driven". Using this method does not necessarily mean that more women and minorities apply, but that the ones who apply fit the job better as they actually applied for the job and not for a set of generalised buzzwords.

Have you been tempted to use generative AI tools like ChatGPT to help write job advertisements? A study by Danish-based company Develop Diverse analysed 7400 job advertisements and asked ChatGPT to generate job advertisements for those jobs. The study showed that ChatGPT was 40% more biased than when human beings wrote the job posts. The research also showed that the language used in the ChatGPT advertisements were particularly discouraging towards people from underrepresented ethnicities, women, people living with a disability and those who are neurodivergent.[17] While ChatGPT can save us time and effort, beware of the biases embedded in the AI system. So, before an advertisement is published, scan it again for biased words. There are various software options available today through which you can identify biased language, and even get suggestions for neutral word swaps. Use them. Neutral job advertisements tend to be more appealing to not just women, but also men and people with underrepresented intersectional identities, and this is very likely to result in more applications overall.[18]

Include Diversity and Inclusion Skills in the List of (Leadership) Competencies/Personal Values

Let us ask you two questions. (1) Is DEI of strategic importance to the organisation you work in? (2) Think of your organisation's last 10 job postings for new leadership positions. How many of these had diversity management or inclusive leadership listed under required skills? Many of the organisations we work with would answer "yes" to the first question and "none" or "very few" to the second. And this is puzzling. If DEI is truly of strategic importance to your organisation, why is this not an explicitly required leadership skill?

When it comes to hiring practices, diversity enters the picture far too late in the process. Diversity of thought, experience, background and skills should be a part of the early job analysis and description stage and be a key criterion for the roles candidates are being hired for or promoted into. If we only discuss diversity after shortlisting candidates, or hiring a minority or under-represented candidate, we risk the perception of tokenism. That is, no matter what strengths an individual brings to the role, they will be perceived as a token hire.

We sometimes get asked: Shouldn't we be focusing on the best person for the job? Yes, absolutely. Bringing diverse perspectives is a core part of being the best person for the job, and very importantly, those diverse perspectives add value to the team and organisation. So, ask yourself which candidates would add value to the team. Yes, they need to be able to do the job, but do they make the team better?

So, the next time you have an opening for a leadership/managerial position, make sure diversity management, inclusive leadership or something similar is among the required skills for the position. If it is listed in the advertisement, you can ask the candidate in the interview what they envision doing to make their team more diverse and inclusive, and you can include this as a parameter in the candidate evaluation. But more importantly, including it in the job advertisement is a great signal to the organisation, industry and future candidates that you take DEI seriously! That will likely also have a positive impact on the diversity of the candidate pool.

Ask Applicants to Not Include Their Picture and Personal Data in Their CV

Depending on the context, many applicants include picture and personal data in their applications and/or CVs. In some countries, the employer is not allowed to ask for this information, but in other contexts, this is still the norm even if it is illegal to ask. In the Danish context, for example, it is not legal to ask for age, but most people still have age on their CVs, as well as a picture, marital status, whether they have kids, their hobbies, etc. Having read Chapters 3 and 4, you are well aware that you will not be able to neutrally evaluate their competencies if you have all this extra information that you absolutely have no need for in the first round of selecting a short list of candidates.

The easiest thing you can do to address this is to clearly state in the job advertisement that interested applicants should not include their picture or any personal data in their application. This would also be an effort to brand your organisation as an inclusive employer. Do you have a version of the following sentence in your job postings: "we encourage everyone, regardless of gender, race, age and sexual orientation, to apply"? If the answer is yes, you might mean well, but you are also unambitious. What if you instead wrote: "we wish to minimise the influence of bias in the recruitment process, and therefore ask you to not include your picture or any personal data". This would not only broaden the field of applicants but also be extremely good employer branding.

If you do this, you're not only blocking your own bias in the process, but you're also minimising the stress on applicants from underrepresented groups. We have heard several times that an individual, let's say a person of colour or a woman who wears a headscarf (hijab), has been advised not include a picture in their application. However, if they apply for a job in a country where including a picture is the norm, then what happens if they don't? It is likely that the recruiter would find it odd and maybe even wonder what they might have to hide. So, it is NOT the individual's responsibility to not include a picture, it is your responsibility as an inclusive leader to communicate that you are not interested in having a picture and other personal data.

Use an Application Form and Beware of Bias Against Poorly Written Applications

If you want to go "all in" on anonymity, the best thing you can do is to use a job application form. If you do this, you can control the information that the candidates provide. You can also ask directly for job-relevant information and reflections, and you can avoid some of the long stories that are sometimes included in CVs but are not relevant for the job. This also blocks some of the socio-economic and linguistic privileges because some people are gifted in writing given their educational background, and may have a network to help them write applications or can even pay someone to help them, while others do not have that opportunity. If you use an online application form with predefined categories to fill in, you minimise this inequity.

If you have asked people to fill in an application form, you can also request your HR business partner to compile a table of all the candidates indicating whether each candidate has the competencies required for the role based on the information collected in the form. This means that your first screening of the applicants would not be hinged on a gut feeling of the applicant's CV, their picture or their personal hobbies, and would instead be based on the competencies they listed.

Blocking Bias When Recruiting and Selecting Talent

> *How many of the candidates from underrepresented groups who applied made it to the shortlist?*
>
> *Who are you deciding to hire? Are you hiring candidates who are similar to current employees?*

There are three guiding principles for blocking bias in the recruitment and selection process—criteria, anonymity and transparency. These principles guide our recommendations in this section as we explore ways to block bias when recruiting and selecting talent.

Sourcing for Applicants

Depending on which industry you're in, you will have your own unique recruitment challenges. Many of the bias blockers we have explained in the previous section are for organisations that are able to attract a large number of applicants and therefore can focus their efforts on blocking biases in the attraction phase. However, if you are in a situation where you are struggling to get applications and only have a handful of applicants to choose from or if you attract a very homogeneous group of applicants, blocking bias in the attraction process might not be enough. If you're in this situation, you will have to supplement those efforts with blocking bias when sourcing for applicants to ensure that you have a diverse pool of candidates to choose from.

Advertise Positions Externally and Widely

When it comes to job advertisements, make sure that you always post the positions—and post them widely. Too many of the organisations we work with don't post positions but find a candidate internally or through their network. And a large part of the organisations that do post all jobs, do so for legal or moral reasons, which means that it might be because they have to—not because they see the value of it. If that is the case, the job posting will not be distributed widely. Following such a strategy might get you a great internal candidate or someone in your closest network, but it won't give you access to the wealth of talent that might be outside of these closed circles. If you struggle with limited diversity in your team, hiring through your own networks will not change that. In our experience, the reason that many companies hire through closed circles is not that they don't want more diversity, but that they want to save time and other resources. It takes more time to distribute a job advertisement widely—and it is also more expensive. On top of that, if employees are used to seeing job advertisements posted internally first, it might make existing employees feel frustrated or left out if you change this practice.

However, leading with accountability is about not letting the easy or quick decision guide you, but that you—based on your conviction and clarity—make the right choice; the one that increases the number of candidates that will have access to your openings. To address internal nervousness of the change in recruitment practice, clearly communicate the purpose of changing your job posting practices and your commitment to ensuring greater equity.

Search for Talent in New Places

Next, actively search for talent in new places. We often hear this: "but we can't find diverse talent". The question we ask back is: "are you searching for talent in the same places that you have always hired from, or are you looking in new places? Do you always hire only university—graduates? Is a university degree really necessary to do the job? Is it the same universities that you hire from? Is there a pattern in the neighbourhood your applicants come from?".

Having more candidates with diverse backgrounds and intersectional identities apply for a job increases the chance of hiring a candidate that is different from others already employed in a team or function. This search can be concentrated on identifying new geographical locations or specific underrepresented groups. When it comes to geographical location, it can be helpful to conduct an analysis about where your organisation's employees come from. It is often the case that employees tend to come from a rather small geographical area or a cluster of several different small geographical areas that might make the hiring look diverse, but actually isn't when the data is broken down. So, the first step is to do an analysis of where you hire from and identify if there are certain locations you miss out on—either nationally, regionally or internationally. Once you have identified the areas you could target, set up specific targeted employer branding campaigns in those markets to attract new talent.

If the candidate pool you hire from is homogeneous, you could also benefit from targeting candidate sources where potential candidates with backgrounds and intersectional identities different from this homogeneous group congregate. These sources could, for example, be professional certificate institutions and universities that have a larger representation of students from underrepresented communities, a community or network for young women programmers, women in Tech or minority hackathons arranged by minority interest organisations. Targeting these sources directly would make it possible for you to reach individuals who might not otherwise see you as an attractive or even possible employer. This type of employer branding effort can also be expanded into broader CSR activities and thus influence more than "just" recruitment positively. When taking such steps, ensure that these efforts are sincere and consistent and not just a one-off public relations stunt to appear to be recruiting from underrepresented communities.

Build Collaborations With Pipeline Institutions Such as Universities, High Schools and Primary Schools

As a leader, you may have heard or even yourself used the explanation that the talent pool is too homogeneous because the industry as a whole does not attract a wide variety of intersectional identities. A closely related explanation for the lack of diversity might also be that the few candidates who do apply from underrepresented groups lack the same level of experience as those from well-represented groups. You may find it difficult to justify hiring a "less-qualified woman compared to a more-qualified man". Do these excuses sound familiar?

If yes, the question we should be asking ourselves and others when confronted with such explanations for the shortage of diverse talent is, why is there such a dearth of candidates from minority groups in the first place? What are the biases, including systemic biases, that exist in our society, culture and educational systems that are causing this, and how do we help address those issues in partnership with the relevant organisations? One area to look to for inspiration is the Science, Technology, Engineering and Mathematics (STEM) sector. STEM companies, which have recognised that their talent shortage from underrepresented communities is a result of the low number of young people from these communities studying STEM subjects, are working closely with educational partners to nurture a more robust talent pipeline of women and minority ethnic groups by supporting, encouraging and promoting STEM courses in schools and universities. Leaders in these companies from underrepresented groups can act as powerful role models to encourage young talent to pursue careers in this field.

Employer branding efforts should also take a more long-term perspective. Depending on where in your pipeline you begin to experience diversity challenges, this is where you begin. If you are looking to hire university graduates and if the graduates themselves are in fact a heterogeneous group, it might well be your own image as an employer that is the problem. Here, collaborations with and visibility at universities will make you more attractive to graduates. Try to think more creatively than simply giving out flyers. Engage in collaborations that involve guest lectures, live-cases, hackathons and case-competitions, and be present at university events that matter to the students, such as sustainability and DEI events. Although it is a rough generalisation, we know that employees today choose an employer because of their values, not just attractive compensation packages and benefits. So, make sure your presence at universities—and other pipeline institutions—reflects this.

If your pipeline problem starts earlier, you might want to team up with universities, high schools or other educational institutions to change this. Many universities or other higher education institutions face the problem that their students come from a homogeneous group of people—when it comes to both gender and other dimensions of diversity, particularly race/ethnicity and socio-economic background. Universities should also be interested in changing this, so there is a potential for collaboration for you. If there is less than 20% representation of a gender in a class, the drop-out rate is much higher from students in that group.[19] A high drop-out rate is neither good for a university's finances nor for the social climate in the class. Thus, both you and the higher education institutions should be interested in changing this. Also, if you target these groups together, there is a greater chance of success.

You can also extend your effort all the way down to primary schools, as we know that gender biases on career choices form early on, with bias expressed by teachers influencing primary school children of colour and from lower socio-economic backgrounds. Research by the OECD shows that female, Black and Hispanic students believe that they are not good at math and science, because of the low expectations of teachers and family members who perpetuate the myth that they are not good at math.[20] This affects the number of these groups of young people who apply for STEM courses in their secondary education and then at university. EIGE (European Institute for Gender Equality) has shown this through an analysis of the STEM gap of all European countries. Their analysis shows that all the countries experience a significant gap between girls under 14 who have STEM competencies and girls under 14 who can see themselves in a STEM career. That is, even though the young girls are great at it, they don't perceive STEM as something for them. Efforts that you can make here might influence both the children's later educational choices and teachers' bias towards certain lines of work, academic disciplines and students. This is, of course, a long-term strategy and not likely to result in direct immediate recruitment of more diverse groups. However, your presence here can make you a more attractive employer to those already in the job market or already employed in your organisation. So, again, it is important not to see these efforts as isolated matters of recruitment, but part of a much broader employer branding effort, as well as CSR and communications strategy.

Have Referral Bonuses for Referrals of Candidates From Underrepresented Groups

Many organisations use referral bonuses to encourage their employees to act as ambassadors for the organisation. This can help increase application rates dramatically. However, it also presents a risk of similarity bias and through that an increase in homogeneity. If your pool of employees is already homogeneous, referrals will tend to increase homogeneity, as people will often refer their good friends and people in their closest networks. So, what you should do is to give referral bonuses for referrals made to potential candidates from underrepresented groups, or bonuses for referrals made to people who match the exact competencies you are looking for.

Offer Internships or Training Programs to Target Groups, but Be Careful That the Internships Are Not Unpaid and Training Programs Are Not Side-Lined

If certain groups have difficulties entering your organisation because of a lack of education or having a different educational background from the norm in your context, you can benefit from establishing training or internship programs. Let's first talk about internships. They are a great way for younger talent or talent without prior experience in a certain industry or country to gain exposure, experience and build their career. But ensure that your interns are paid. Far too often, we see unpaid internship opportunities and these are exploitative. 43% of internships by for-profit companies are unpaid.[21] Also, unpaid internships perpetuate the lack of diversity, as they limit the pool of applicants who apply for these internships to those who can afford to work for free, excluding and disadvantaging those who are unable to do so. The opportunities are typically only accessible to those from privileged backgrounds with the financial support to take on an unpaid position. Unpaid internships also perpetuate gender inequity. Studies have shown that women are more likely to take on unpaid internships than men and be paid less than men when they enter the workforce.[22] This in turn affects their career prospects and earning potential.

What about training programs? You should be careful with how you target these groups and how you compose the programs. As we have pointed out earlier, offering a program only for women or only for a racial minority group risks reinforcing the bias towards this group and thus marginalises them even further, but it can be very beneficial to ensure their representation in regular courses and programs. So, you need to directly target these groups, but make sure there are other people from the more well-represented groups also represented.

For instance, if you wish to hire more women programmers, but you lack a pipeline of women programmers, you can benefit from establishing a training program, in which individuals—not just women—with programming skills, but no formal education, can take part. In this program, you can make sure that you have at least 50% women on your program, but you also let men who lack formal education in that field into the program. If you currently have a gender composition in the department of 20/80 favouring men, but your training program is composed of 60/40 favouring women, you have the possibility of dramatically increasing the number of women you hire even though you also attract new male talent through this program. Similar efforts can be made if you want to hire employees from underrepresented ethnic groups who may not have the skills needed or skills with credentials from different contexts. You can identify individuals through the methods mentioned above; however, also make sure that you include other groups as well. To put it more simply, the groups that are underrepresented should be overrepresented in your training programs, but not solely represented, as that would reinforce stereotypes and further marginalisation.

Use, but Place Demands on Head-Hunters and Other Labour Market Intermediaries

If your recruitment challenges are experienced higher in the organisational hierarchy, at managerial and leadership levels, you might find it useful to use head-hunters. This can be a very good way of blocking one's own biases. However, you have to remember that head-hunters are just as biased as you are, and on top of that, they also have an economic incentive to find you a "good" candidate. So, when you use head-hunters, you have to place demands on the long and short lists they provide. You can do this by inquiring into how broad and diverse their networks are. Many head-hunters identify the candidates on their short and long lists from their existing networks. If they are to find new candidates outside of these networks, they need to identify new contacts and build trust with them first. It is no wonder that the candidates that they have spent the last many years building a relationship with are more likely to say yes to an interview compared to ones they have just contacted. So, if you have a good relationship with a head-hunter, explain your future needs and that you expect them to build a more diverse network for future hires.

This may mean that you might have to pay more for the service or that you also agree to take some of the risk of new candidates. Again, if your organisation is homogeneous, someone who is different from the employees already hired will take more time to adjust and will require more inclusive leadership from the rest of the leadership team. We will get back to this in more detail in Chapters 6 and 7. For now, it is important to note that you might get the "diverse" candidate from the recruiter, but it is your job to make sure this person is included in the organisation, not side-lined and not just assimilated to the organisation.

An alternative strategy is to seek out the head-hunters (or other labour market intermediaries) who specialise in finding talent from your underrepresented groups and producing more diverse short and long lists. These organisations have already done the preparations and have candidates ready. Finally, across several contexts, grassroots organisations and NGOs are beginning to produce talent lists full of potential candidates from underrepresented groups. The point here is that the excuse, "oh, but I just couldn't find anyone else", is no longer valid, as there now are a lot of different options. You just need to spend a little more time seeking them out. And once you have established these recruitment channels, it is easier to make this the new norm.

Selecting Candidates

Mask CVs: Remove Personal Data and Picture From the First Screening

Should interested candidates add a picture or personal information, make sure to remove it—in fact, mask applications completely. There is software available to assist you in this, and if you don't have access to this software, we bet it will be more cost-effective to hire a student assistant to remove the data (or to do it yourself!) than to limit yourself to a certain group of potential candidates, because of bias.

This personal data is not just limited to picture, age, gender and which educational institution the candidate graduated from. Other information, such as pronouns, marriage, parenthood status or hobbies, also risks biased decision-making. This type of information does not negatively impact candidates that fall within the norm. However, women without children, candidates who are single or LGBTQIA+ candidates tend to be judged very differently compared to Peter, a White man who is 46, married to Julie, 44, with two children aged 12 and 15.

> **Making Connections: Poornima & Sara's Experiences**
> One of the companies that Poornima has worked with, a large global FMCG company, conducted an experiment in their Swedish office. They were undertaking a hiring process and consciously chose to remove the following identifiers—gender, name, age, picture, educational institution and even address. These masked CVs were given to the hiring panel who then created a shortlist of candidates who would proceed to the next round. The corresponding identity markers were then reintroduced to the CVs, and the members of the hiring panel reflected on their choices. What they concluded was that they would have likely not picked some of the shortlisted candidates had the identity markers been part of the CV. Masking CVs is a concrete way of increasing the diversity of your shortlisted candidate pool.

Adopt an HR System to Help You Hide/Leverage Specific Data

Finally, you can also invest in an HR system, where you can—with a few clicks—hide or access desired data. That means that you can begin the first screening process with as little personal data as possible and then get more once you invite the chosen candidates for an interview.

When it comes to masking CVs and applications, we often get two reactions to this bias blocker. The first reaction is that while this is certainly a good practice, the hiring manager wants a "feeling" for the applicant and that is difficult with limited knowledge about the candidate. That is, of course, completely true. However, this is because you have been used to having this data, and not having it makes you feel uncomfortable. But this is a matter of learning new ways of doing things. Try it out a few times and learn to focus only on the candidates' competencies, not on the personal information that automatically and beyond your rational control influences the way you perceive these competencies. As should be very clear from Chapters 3 and 4, you cannot evaluate a candidate's competencies independently of their gender, race, age, socio-economic background, hobbies, looks, etc. The best you can do is to make sure you put yourself in a situation where you don't allow for this information to influence you, that is block their effect. So, remove this data in the beginning of the process and remember that you will get a chance to meet the person later in the process. This is after all only the first screening.

The second reaction we often get is that it is impossible to anonymise CVs and applications completely. Yes, this might also be true. Certain competencies give away other information, like nationality, gender and age. However, if you try, you will end up blocking some of it—you will mask the CV. Here, you also have to remember that the end goal is not only a masked CV, but also learning how to block bias. When reading CVs without personal data, our mind automatically constructs a mental image of the person. If you succeed to at least mask some of the candidates' information, and a different person shows up at an interview than what you expected, this can be a very important learning experience for you—to reflect on the associations you made based on the information that was provided.

> **Making Connections: Poornima & Sara's Experiences**
> Poornima recalls a story that a Black Scottish man had shared about his experience with his name in Denmark. He had a name that many would automatically assume was a White Scottish name, and this worked against him during interviews. While his name meant he would get called in for an interview (when his picture was not on the CV), the reactions once interviewers met him were very different. He described the time he interviewed in a Danish organisation, and as he was led to the meeting room, he noticed people looking at him as he walked by. He noticed that they were all White. When the door to the meeting room opened, he was met with a shocked look from the interviewer, who asked repeatedly if he was, indeed, who he said he was. And what made matters worse was that his first interview question was: "How do you see yourself fitting in with our organisation?". You might have guessed, he did not get the job, and the response he received from the company was "we did not see you fitting in with our organisation".

Interviews

Once you have sourced and selected, it's time for the interviews. And unless you are hiring musicians or other candidates where you are able to successfully mask the interview process and only focus on competencies, interview situations are human interactions and therefore very prone to bias. Luckily, there are also many ways in which you can block bias in interview situations.

Shift Your Attitude Towards the Interview Process; You Are Being Interviewed Too

The first thing you should do is to change your attitude towards the interview process. You might be lucky to operate in a market where you can pick and choose between brilliant candidates, but if that is the case, you are one in a million. Most employers today are fighting for talent. So, remember that it is not only the candidate that is being evaluated—so are you. Since we already have established that DEI values are important to candidates, now more than ever, use the interview situation to make your DEI values visible. Poornima was in an interview for a role. Towards the end of the interview, she asked the interview panel how the organisation would ensure that she felt included. Their response was: "you will have your own office". So, be careful how you respond; be thoughtful and do your homework on this topic before you enter the interview. This is your chance to make a good impression. Whether you end up hiring the person or not, you want them to think well of you and your organisation.

Use a Diverse and Trained Hiring Committee

Once you have shifted your attitude to the interview process, the first thing in the actual process is to set up a diverse hiring committee. Most organisations already take this into consideration, at least when it comes to gender representation, so a candidate never meets an all-male or an all-female interview panel or that a homogeneous group is making the decision on who to hire. However, a diverse hiring committee goes broader than gender. It might be difficult to have checklists and quotas for other diversity parameters than gender. However, try to take race, age, hierarchy and competencies into consideration. Not all interviewers need to be more senior to the new hire; to the contrary, it would be good to also have employee and peer-level voices represented. Similarly, they don't all need to be experts in the new employee's field. Sometimes, an outsider can ask really good questions too.

If your organisation lacks diversity, you have to be careful to not use the same underrepresented individuals in all committees. Being part of a hiring committee or interview panel is a very important task for the organisation, but it is rarely a directly promotable task. Often when organisations focus on composing gender diverse hiring committees, a few selected senior women end up in many committees. It might be great for representation, and for the candidates and potential new employees to meet women in the committee, but it is not necessarily beneficial for the senior women's chances of further advancement. So, first of all use a more broadly diverse hiring committee (e.g. age, hierarchy and skills), as this will take the workload off a few "diverse" individuals and, second, make sure to reward committee work so that it is not a career liability for the ones whose presence is necessary for diverse hiring. In this way, you avoid that individuals from underrepresented groups are overrepresented in these tasks.

In addition to having a diverse hiring committee, ensure that the hiring committee is trained in bias awareness and cultural competency, so that they know how to block bias from their engagement with the candidate, from conversations about the candidates with each other, from the evaluation process of the candidates and from the final decision that they take.

Make Sure That Your First-Round Short List Is Diverse

Once you have made a first (masked) screening of the candidate pool, make three pools of candidates: those you want to interview, those you don't and those you may want to. Next, check for representation, you can move underrepresented individuals from the "maybe" pool to the "invite for interview pool". The chance of hiring a person from an underrepresented group is much higher if there is more than one person from an underrepresented group among the interviewees. More specifically, Joan C. Williams and Sky Mihaylo[23] found that the odds of hiring a woman are 79 times greater if there are at least two women in the finalist pool; for people of colour, the odds are 194 times greater.

If neither your "invite for interview" pool nor your "maybe" pool contains the underrepresented gender or minority group, you need to go back to our sourcing and screening bias blockers or change your strategy from bias blockers to affirmative action/quotas.

Standardise Your Greetings

Your first interaction with a candidate who is being interviewed starts well before the actual interview, and if you do not block bias here, some candidates might already be disadvantaged even before the formal interview begins. When you first meet the candidate—at the reception, perhaps—keep the following two things in mind: (1) Standardise how you greet the interviewees and (2) ask open-ended questions.

Research has shown that if a recruiter feels a connection with the candidate (often based on similarity or intuition bias), they have a tendency to walk next to the candidate and small talk on the way to the interview room. If there is no immediate connection, they have a tendency to walk a polite step ahead of the candidate and lead the way. The second is not inappropriate or offending. However, it gives the candidate with the connection a head start, and confirmation bias might kick in once the interview starts. Standardising one's greetings and conversations between greeting the candidate at the reception to arriving at the interview room can block some of this bias. Also greet the interviewee by their name, making an effort to pronounce their name correctly. Ask the candidate if in doubt. Ensure that all members of the hiring committee learn how to pronounce the candidates' names.

This leads us to the second point, which is to always remember to ask open-ended questions. Some questions might be completely neutral for the majority of your interview candidates but could put others in a very tricky situation. Two such questions are: "where do you come from?" and "so, what does your husband do?". Imagine that in an effort to start a polite conversation with a candidate, you ask them where they come from. If the person is of colour and your organisation is based in a country where the majority are White, this can be a question that triggers a series of memories of subtle (and even overt) discrimination. However, the answer the candidate provides can also trigger socio-economic class or urban/countryside discrimination among others that you don't want influencing the interview. If you happen to come from the same place, similarity bias kicks in (if you like where you grew up!). We have lost count of how many times we have heard the response: "but I was just curious". While this may be so, this type of question can be linked to historical discrimination, so it might trigger something completely different than the casual conversation you were looking for. As an interviewer, your most important role is to make the interviewee feel comfortable, not satisfy your personal curiosity about things that have very little to do with the candidate's competencies.

The other question, "so, what does your husband do", can be a completely acceptable question to a woman who is happily married to a man. But imagine if you, like many of our collaborators, ask this question to a lesbian woman, a single woman or a woman who recently lost her husband or got divorced. The question is in itself reflective of societal norms and heterosexual relationships. It puts the interviewee in a really tricky situation and you in an awkward position. If you want to engage in small talk, then rehearse open questions that anyone can answer as much or as little as they feel comfortable to. You ask open questions like: "Tell us about yourself", which allows the candidate to control what and how much they would like to share about their personal life. Avoid following up with probing questions like "where are you actually from" that reflect your stereotypes and biases about the person.

> **Making Connections: Poornima & Sara's Experiences**
>
> In the DEI workshops we conduct, we often discuss how asking personal questions to initiate casual conversations can lead to unexpected awkwardness. This often creates space for participants to share their personal stories and experiences, providing other participants with an opportunity to reflect on how the people who are different from themselves do in fact live life in a variety of different ways. This challenges us to reflect on how our questions that we think are uncontroversial are actually based on our assumptions about others and could lead to unintended consequences. In these workshops, there is almost always someone in the room, who has either asked a question to an interview candidate or a new colleague assuming partner status, parenthood and/or heterosexuality or someone who has been asked such questions themselves. Think about the heterosexual man who just lost his wife, the asexual man who lives with a lesbian couple, the single woman who doesn't want to be in a relationship, the married woman who never wanted children, the parent who lost a child, the woman who just had a miscarriage, the couple who don't live in the same household, etc.
>
> In all of these instances, a casual question can turn the situation from professional to awkward in a split second. In an interview situation, this can influence the candidate's performance as well as your evaluation of the candidate. Once Sara gave a speech to a group of HR professionals in the Danish pharmaceutical company Novo Nordisk. We discussed the above issue of questions, and a woman named Fatime Selimi said the most brilliant sentence that has forever stuck with Sara. She said: "*One person's casual conversation is another person's confession*". We find this to be a very powerful sentence, as it describes how some personal questions can be part of a very casual conversation to some, and an excellent way of building a relationship and getting a "feel" for the other person. However, this is only the case when the answer falls within the norm. That is, if it is unsurprising and "normal". However, answering the same question can feel like a confession if the person does not live by societal norms. For the person asking the question, it might not be controversial, but for the person who feels like they have to "confess" and face judgement, it can be an extremely difficult situation.

Interview Individually at the First Interview

Now, we come to the actual interview itself. Many candidates meet an interview panel of about 3–5 people the first time they are invited for an interview. However, this is a bad idea, at least if you want to block bias. Bias is contagious and the power dynamics in the interview panel affect the way bias is allowed to influence the process. For instance, it has been demonstrated that people tend to follow the one that speaks first and that we tend to follow the opinions of those with more structural power in the organisation. This groupthink and the echo chamber effect influence the dynamics between people on an interview panel. To avoid this, you can break the interview up into smaller, one-to-one conversations. In this way, every interviewer can get their own impression of the candidates and then you can compare afterwards. The comparison should of course be against the list of competencies you had defined as essential for the job—not according to your gut feeling, because then you just invite bias right back in. If you need to test how the candidates interact with a larger group, you can invite them for a second interview with the whole interview panel. Interviewing individually not only blocks group bias, but it is also more inclusive for introverted, shy or nervous candidates. If you are not looking for an extroverted salesperson, you really don't want to disadvantage introverts at the stage of the first interview.

Use Structured Interview Guides

Research shows that we have a tendency to ask different people different questions in interviews. It has, for example, been found that we tend to ask women closed questions and men more open-ended questions. Open-ended questions generally give the interviewee a better chance to unfold their competencies, compared to closed questions where the interviewee is often left to confirm or defend themselves. However, open-ended questions may also be challenging for neurodivergent candidates who may not know exactly what the interviewer is looking for. When using open-ended questions, focus on asking questions about the competencies needed for the job, and follow up an open-ended question with a more specific question if the candidate did not provide the information you were looking for.

We also know that there is a tendency for the recruiter to ask women more personal questions and men more professional questions. This entails both personal questions about family life and parent status (which in many contexts are illegal to ask, but are asked anyway), and questions about one's personality, whether one "feels ready for the role" or "has what it takes". Women also tend to get more critical questions than men. For instance, a study found that, when presenting research to peers, women economists get more patronising, disruptive, demeaning or hostile questions compared to men.[24] This goes straight back to the bias that makes us doubt women's ability to do the job.

Even though such questions constitute discrimination and the law states that candidates should not be discriminated on the basis of religion or parenthood choices (among other identity dimensions like age, gender, sexual orientation, etc.), they still seem to creep in. There is a very simple way to block this bias and that is to use an interview guide that is structured according to the lists of competencies you defined before the recruitment process began. Neurodivergent candidates may ask for questions to be shared with them in advance. If the candidate requests this, be open to accommodating this request.

Also allow time for the interviewee to ask you questions. Remember the shift in attitude we talked about earlier? When candidates have asked you questions, have you ever thought that they may be "annoying" and dismissed the candidate as not being the right "fit" because the questions made you feel uncomfortable? A good candidate asks questions to learn about the role, the boss and the organisation to assess whether it's the right job, and you should embrace them.[25] So, you as an interviewer and representative of your organisation need to be ready to answer these questions well. After all, you are promoting your organisation to the interviewee as well hoping that they would consider taking the role if you make them an offer.

> **Making Connections: Poornima & Sara's Experiences**
> Poornima recalls three separate incidents shared with her.
>
> In the first situation, a student of Poornima's—a Danish Muslim woman who does not wear a headscarf and has a Pakistani name—shared that in an interview with a large Danish company she was asked how she would fit into the culture of socialising that involved the consumption of alcohol.
>
> In the second situation, as part of a recruitment training exercise conducted by the HR team of a large global alcohol manufacturer, line managers involved in recruitment decisions were asked to provide examples of questions they would use to assess the following in a candidate: (1) if they were the right person for the company; (2) if they were a team player; and (3) if they had resilience. One manager's responses were: (1) ask them if they drink beer; (2) ask them if they played a team sport; and (3) ask them when they cried in the office last. Who do you think this manager was likely to hire? A man who enjoyed drinking beer and playing or just watching football who was not prone to tears? In other words, a man exactly like himself and many others in leadership positions in the company.
>
> Finally, in the last situation, a master's degree student who had a 6-month-old baby was looking for a job in Denmark. She shared how, time and time again, she found recruiters asking her some combination of the following question: "how will you manage work and a young baby, especially when your baby falls sick". Some even probed further: "you look young, so your parents and in-laws must be young and working so who will help you with the baby at those difficult times". Mind you, there was no mention of her husband in these conversations.

Use Skills-Based Testing, Cases and Problem-Solving Activities That Assess Job Competencies

While structured interviews are a common practice in the selection phase, consider supplementing them with skills-based testing, cases and problem-solving activities that test the candidates for the specific competencies that are needed for doing the job. When interviewing, we tend to ask candidates to self-assess. However, based on internalised bias, people self-assess differently. Middle-aged candidates usually rate themselves higher compared to younger or older candidates, men usually rate themselves higher than women, White people rate themselves higher than people of colour, extroverts rate themselves higher than introverts and so on. You are not interested in the candidates' own rating of their competencies; you are interested in knowing what their competencies are and what value they will bring to the team. Furthermore, if you use skills-based testing, you assess competencies, rather than culture fit, as you don't focus on how they answer and relate to you but on their ability to solve relevant tasks.

So, instead of (only) interviewing and asking candidates questions about their competencies, you could ask them to solve a specific problem. For example, rather than asking a candidate how good they are at budgeting, programming or marketing, you can ask them to solve an actual problem that they would face in the job they are applying for. In this way, you would test their skills, not their own opinions about their skills. If the competencies of the job, for example a leadership position, are not very specific, then pose a leadership dilemma that is likely to happen in the organisation and ask the candidate what steps they would take to handle that dilemma. That gives you a much better idea of their ways of thinking, skills and competencies, compared to relying on how they evaluate themselves.

Rate the Candidates

Although it can sound a little instrumental and unpersonal, it can be a very good idea to rate all the candidates after the interviews, using a consistent scale that is developed based on the competencies that you have identified as necessary for the job. You might not get a candidate that excels in all competencies, but if you rank the competencies in order of importance and then rate all the candidates according to those competencies, it will be easier not to let the gut decide in the end. This also helps avoid proximity bias, as you tend to remember the candidate from the most recent interview better than the others. If you use consistent grading rubrics, you can ensure that everyone is assessed according to the same criteria and that you do not apply harsher standards to some candidates and not others. Thus, ratings help block confirmation bias, proximity bias, focus bias and expectation bias, all of which tend to make you treat some groups harsher than others. If you have many interviewees, calibrating meetings along the way, where you test your bias as a team, will also be a good idea. If you are more than one assessor, make sure you rate individually first and then compare ratings. If you do the rating together, you will most likely influence each other, as your internal power dynamic will make a difference.

Redesign the Interview Process

Being on an interview panel is an important and time-consuming role, but it isn't seen as a promotable task in most organisations. The interview process is also stressful, especially for the candidate, and requires candidates to "perform" under that stress, including making eye contact throughout the interview. We have a bias that someone who maintains eye contact is, indeed, someone we can trust to do the job and "be a good colleague". However, for those who may not do well under stress especially when sitting across a panel comprising of 4–5 people, are more introverted, from certain cultural backgrounds where maintaining eye contact is frowned upon or autistic, the traditional interview process requiring eye contact for an extended period of time is daunting at best and may prevent competent candidates from even applying.

What if we could redesign the interview process? We have been inspired by the Danish recruitment company Specialisterne who has helped find jobs for around 10,000 people on the autistic spectrum. They have their own unique interview process in which, rather than having to attend a formal job interview, candidates are asked to construct a robot with Lego blocks. While building the robot, interviewers and the candidates have the opportunity to engage in a conversation in a much less stressful environment that does not have the requirement of formality and maintaining eye contact. This provides the right environment for candidates who would otherwise not apply or not perform well in a traditional interview setting.

Also, when designing the interview process, ensure that it is fully accessible for those with visible and invisible disabilities. As a starting point, ensure that the interview location is fully accessible for disabled candidates and always offer an online interviewing option. Block your bias from evaluating candidates who choose the online option and focus on evaluating the candidates against the competencies required for the job.

Reference Checks and Making the Offer

You have now attracted a broad pool of candidates and from that pool, selected the final few that are all able to do the job and add value to the team and organisation's culture. In this section, let us look at the bias blockers you can apply in the final stages of the hiring process.

Be Careful With References

References—both written references in CVs and applications, and referees that you, as the hiring manager or HR partner, will call to get a better feel for the person you're hiring—are very often central to this final stage. You may want to find out how the person performed in their former job or what their strengths and weaknesses were. While this might sound very reasonable to you, ask yourself what you're really checking for here. You are likely not checking the person's competencies, but the person's relationship with their former boss or colleagues. As we all know, performance is contextual. So, do you really want to rely so heavily on the candidate's personal relationship with a former boss or how much this former boss liked the candidate? Of course, you can call references, and they can give you some important information. However, you should be very aware of the fact that reference checks are extremely prone to similarity bias and focus bias (and the former boss' similarity and focus bias) and your confirmation bias. So, use reference checks with extreme caution.

Ask Yourself—and Others—Flip Questions

When you are discussing the final candidates, you will most likely compare them to each other. Resist this. Be very careful of contrast bias and also of the risk of judging some groups of people differently from others. A way to block bias at this stage could be to ask yourself—and others—flip questions. So, if you are evaluating a Black man, ask yourself the following question: "would I have said the same thing if it was a White woman, a Black woman or a White man?" Similarly, if you are evaluating a homosexual woman, ask yourself if you would have said the same if the person was a heterosexual woman, a homosexual man or a heterosexual man, etc. If you are discussing the final candidates in the recruitment committee, then make sure you ask each other these flip questions.

Use Bias-Buddies to Test Your Decision

Bias buddies are people who know you very well and with whom you have discussed your biases, people who are different from yourself in one way or another and, perhaps most importantly, people who you know will tell you the truth. Use these bias-buddies to test your decisions. Ask them to ask you the tough and critical questions as you walk them through your decision-making process. Reflect on their questions and feedback, and make a conscious effort to block bias in making the final decision.

Think Culture Add, Rather Than Culture Fit

We have already discussed the benefits of thinking of culture add instead of culture fit. And now, at the very end of the hiring process is a great moment to take this up again. If the candidates have made it this far, they must have alignment in terms of their competencies and values. So, at this point, it could be an advantage to think more explicitly about culture add. Compare the candidates and choose the one that adds something of value to your culture—someone who might ask interesting questions, someone who might challenge the culture and make it stronger, and someone who brings different experiences and perspectives to enrich the culture.

Use Soft Quotas

At this final stage, you can also apply soft quotas, such as a threshold quota. A threshold quota is a quota that you only use at the very last stage of the hiring process. For example, if you have three candidates in the final short-list and you know that they are all qualified for the position, you need to be very careful that you don't let your gut decide. If you have defined the required competencies well at the beginning of the process, you also know that all three candidates can do the job. So, at this point in the process, you can let diversity count; hiring someone from an underrepresented group is much more valuable to the team and organisation than the one you—or someone else—feels similar to. It is valuable to hire someone from an underrepresented group as that candidate can have a significant positive impact as a role model, encouraging candidates from other underrepresented groups to apply to your organisation. Also, this person will add value to the team in terms of creativity, innovation and better decision-making (as shown in Chapter 2). Remember that all the candidates at this stage meet the competencies needed and could do the job. Thus, letting diversity count at this stage in the process is not compromising on competencies. To the contrary, NOT letting diversity count would be compromising on competencies, as the value the person would add to the team and organisation must be taken into consideration.

Establish Relationships With Candidates That Might Not Have Been Shortlisted or Chosen for This Role

Finally, if you have managed to source great diverse candidates and advanced them through the entire recruitment process, it would be a shame to lose them just because you can only hire one person for the role. So, make sure that you either stay in contact with them, add them to a database of potential candidates for the next job or, even better, find them a different job in the organisation. Even though it is likely that they would end up getting jobs in other organisations, they will have had a positive impression of your organisation and will spread the word in their network. Again, employer branding, and efforts towards including diverse talent, goes much further than the actual recruitment process and the candidate that finally gets hired. As we wrote in the very beginning, you're not only testing them; they're also testing you.

> **Making Connections: Poornima & Sara's Experiences**
> Sara recently worked with a professional service firm. As is typical for professional service firms, this organisation did not have many women in senior management or among the partners. The CEO had hired Sara to do a series of workshops with them. After the first workshop he came up to her and said, "I am… sorry, but I have just hired a mini-me and I should have used the threshold quota to avoid this". It turned out that he had just hired a CFO. At the very end of the process, after several interviews and tests, they had two candidates left: a man and a woman. They ended up hiring the man, as the employee (a man) who was going to work most closely with him was "most comfortable" with this candidate. Here, the CEO should have insisted on hiring the woman. She would not have gotten this far in the process if she wasn't a good match, and hiring a woman—and a woman CFO even—would have made a huge difference to all the women who wanted to advance in the company but only saw men in the top of the organisation. This was NOT choosing the most competent, this was choosing the most comfortable, the one that looked like the rest.

Block Bias When Onboarding Talent

> *Is every new hire receiving the same level of onboarding support or are there differences? What support is being provided to help new hires understand the culture of the organisation and country? Are new hires satisfied with the onboarding process? How long does it take for new hires to feel included in your team/organisation?*

The onboarding process begins when the person who has been hired signs the contract. The expectation of new hires is usually to be productive and start delivering as fast as possible, but an inclusive and thorough onboarding process is the key to retention. From the point a new hire signs the contract, the employee has various interactions with the HR team of the organisation and the hiring manager that continue during their first year or so of employment. It is crucial that biases are blocked throughout the onboarding process to ensure retention. Often, onboarding is thought of as consisting of the first few days after the new hire joins the organisation or maybe the first few weeks, but research shows that employees go through a honeymoon period before getting hangovers.[26] This means that it can take up to 12 or even 18 months before the employee has adjusted to the new organisation.[27] The hangovers can occur for many reasons, but biases and not feeling a sense of belonging and inclusion are key factors. It is crucial to block bias during onboarding to minimise the hangover effect by standardising the processes and support as well as providing a thorough introduction to the organisation's culture, its people and the societal context in which you are located.

Standardise Administrative Processes and Support

Some of the early onboarding interactions revolve around administrative tasks and standardising these is essential to ensure that all employees receive the same information and are treated in the same way. These early interactions can include signing the contract, going through a session on the terms of employment, getting access to an email account and IT systems, orientation programs, mandatory training programs and so on. They can also include a welcome for all employees on their first day at work. This could be a handwritten note from the person's manager welcoming them at their desk, plus a breakfast session where they meet colleagues. This practice can also be applied in virtual teams as a virtual team breakfast or coffee where the new employee meets other colleagues and is given an opportunity to engage informally to get to know colleagues. This ensures that some employees in some locations are not getting "better treatment" than others.

If you are hiring people from other parts of the world and require them to move to a new location, many organisations provide support for the visa application process, moving their personal goods, finding housing and taking care of children's schooling. Many of these tasks can be outsourced to global mobility companies who specialise in them. However, the experiences vary significantly, even within the same organisation, and some nationalities receive better support than others. Hence, be clear with external vendors that you expect standardised processes.

For employees moving with a partner or spouse, providing support to them—regardless of their identity—can make all the difference. The more comfortable employees and their families feel in the first few months, the easier it will be for them to be engaged and productive at work. Research shows that one of the primary reasons expatriate assignments fail is because of an unhappy spouse/partner or children.[28] This support you provide can take the form of helping the partner/spouse look for a job, paying for global mobility agents to help the partner/spouse with understanding local systems or even providing language classes for both the employee and their family when the local language is not familiar to them. Once again, don't make assumptions about what people may need or not need based on their nationality.

It can be beneficial to assign two buddies to the new employee. An office buddy could be from the same or a different department who would be assigned to take the new employee on an office tour and to help them take care of practicalities like explaining where the printers and toilets are as well as having lunch with them for the first few days. The other person is an onboarding buddy, someone from the HR team providing ongoing support and regular check-ins. These check-ins should continue for up to a year to ensure that the employee has fully adjusted to the organisation and team. These buddies can also help introduce the employee to other colleagues across the organisation, helping them build their network. These buddies should be provided clear guidance on their role and what they need to cover or do to avoid interactions that are biased.

Having standardised and comprehensive processes helps avoid the bias of a hiring or HR manager or buddy from creeping in to the decision of who should get what level of support.

Offer Introductions to Context, Culture and People

In the first few days and weeks of onboarding—or even prior to onboarding, a period known as pre-boarding—employees often have the chance to learn about the organisation's culture and the culture of the country they are moving to, if relevant. In different companies, this can take the form of talks or workshops with leaders in the organisation, pre-recorded videos of employees and leaders sharing their experience of working in the organisation or even documents about the organisation's/country's history and values. Very often, this material establishes a certain perspective on the organisation or country that is shared with new hires. If your organisation is not very diverse in representation at the top, this can create feelings of insecurity about one's role and belonging in the organisation. This is heightened if the new hire has an intersectional identity where they are the first or the first few to be hired. Addressing this upfront and being honest, saying that "we are not where we would like to be", helps highlight that there is work to be done. Share the goals for inclusion as well as the efforts being made in the area of DEI as part of the pre-boarding material.

Leaders should make an effort to share information about the new team member prior to the new hire's first day so that everyone is aware and informed. This communication should include information about the new hire, the role and responsibilities of the new hire, and how this may impact the workload and division of responsibilities in the team. Without this information being shared, leaders unintentionally risk fostering bias about the new hire. Leaders should also organise inclusive social events where the new hire gets to meet their new colleagues, and vice versa. This should be done in the first few days of the new colleague joining the team.

In cross-cultural teams, we are often basing our interactions on stereotypes of colleagues, based on their nationality or ethnicity and leading to biased engagement. It can be very helpful to have workshops in which team members engage in understanding their own cultural frameworks that influence how they communicate, build trust, view time, provide feedback, are motivated, view conflict, make decisions and lead others. Having honest and open discussions of the different cultural frameworks of team members can be very helpful to building a high-performing culturally diverse team. As a leader, knowing the cultural frameworks of your team members can be very helpful to block your own bias and adapt your leadership style to ensure that your team members are performing at their best.

Blocking Bias When Retaining and Developing Talent

> *How do employees rate their experiences of inclusion in employee engagement surveys? How diverse are teams across a range of dimensions of diversity? Is the pay equitable across intersectional identities? Are policies and practices inclusive? Are efforts being made to ensure that everyone is trained in DEI?*

Conduct a Robust Diversity and Inclusion Audit

Leading with accountability requires you to understand the progress of diversity and inclusion in your organisation. Conducting a DEI audit within your team or organisation can be very helpful to get a sense of where bias and discrimination lie and what challenges need to be addressed. This can include a gap analysis to understand where you are now, where you would like to be and to decide on a pathway and areas of focus to help you get there. It can also be helpful to identify key metrics that will help you track your progress. These can include the diversity composition of your team or organisation, employee engagement surveys that ask questions about how valued, appreciated and respected people feel in the organisation and team alongside questions on their sense of belonging. Further, you can look at data on remuneration to assess pay equity in the organisation.

It is important that data is collected in a way that makes participants feel safe. Data protection laws that exist in many parts of the world, including Latin America, Africa and the EU can make collecting data in today's world more challenging. GDPR regulations in the EU mean that collecting data to track DEI progress across dimensions beyond gender can be nearly impossible and even punishable by law. There are, however, ways of working around these barriers. Anonymous and/or voluntary surveys or third-party interviews are effective ways of collecting (some of) this data. For instance, German sportswear manufacturer Adidas has found a way to measure their DEI progress by asking employees to voluntarily share personal data about their ethnicity, nationality, gender identity and sexual orientation as part of their efforts to improve diversity at the organisation. It is important to note that this should be done with caution, in order to be sensitive to people's private lives so that employees do not feel pressured into sharing aspects about their identity to be seen as a part of their organisation and/or the team.

The data collected can help unveil conscious and unconscious biases that exist in your team or organisation, and it can illuminate the impact of those biases on talent and culture. The insights collected can be used to determine what kind of training and learning experiences are needed for yourself and your colleagues to block and address the biases that exist.

Check for Bias in Pay

As we have seen in Chapter 4, there are still considerable pay gaps between men and women, and between racial or ethnic groups—even if these numbers are adjusted for industry, seniority, job type, etc. The most common response to this data is that these groups should be better at salary negotiations. However, it is not as simple as that. Research shows that women who negotiate salary are punished for being too pushy and aggressive. In other words, women face the tightrope bias that we discussed in Chapter 3. Similarly, studies have found that men of colour are 25% less likely than their White peers to get a raise when they ask for one.[29] One way of addressing this is to explicitly state in the job advertisement that the salary is negotiable, as research has shown this will make more women and people of colour negotiate their salary and also reduce the bias associated with that negotiation.[30] In addition, if you define clear salary brackets that are based on competencies and job levels, then a fair salary is also easier to obtain, as different people will have the same point of departure.

So, rather than placing the responsibility with the individual employee, you as a leader should be accountable for ensuring greater pay equity and equality. Pay equity compares the value and pay of different jobs, while pay equality compares the pay of people in similar jobs. Conduct a pay equity/equality analysis in your team and organisation to understand how different salaries fare between men and women and (if possible) between people of colour and White employees, able-bodied employees and disabled employees and so on. Do this analysis annually and set up a pay scorecard to track progress.

> **Making Connections: Poornima & Sara's Experiences**
> Sara worked with the executive directors of a Danish company. After giving them examples of how candidates' self-assessments influence our evaluations of them, one of the directors shared a story. She was conducting interviews for a position and during the second interview, she asked the candidates about their salary expectations. A man with middle Eastern background, who was a perfect match for the job, asked for 20% less than she expected. She didn't think of it back then, but she now recognised this as the prevalent pay gap. She had instead perceived his suggestion as being "not serious enough" and dismissed him as a potential candidate and hired someone else.

Build DEI Into Salary/Bonus Structures

Add DEI measures to all leaders' objectives and link DEI goals to management compensation. If you, as we recommended earlier, listed DEI skills as part of the job description, you can also build this into the person's compensation and benefit package (where relevant, of course). If DEI is a part of the employees' bonus structure from the beginning, they will think of it as an integral part of the job. This can also be added to leaders' yearly objectives so that it is clear that they are expected to increase the diversity of their team and/or increase the team's inclusion ratings. Bonuses and rewards can be tied to these measures. While DEI should come from the actual conviction that it is the right thing to do, it sometimes takes external motivation to keep it on the agenda.

Ensure That Policies and Practices Are Inclusive

Many biases, as we have seen in earlier chapters, are embedded in policies and practices. These policies and practices are often developed or have been developed to fit well-represented groups and individuals, ignoring the (potentially different) needs and desires of the underrepresented. In her book Invisible Women,[31] Caroline Perez makes the case through data and evidence that our world, including our workplaces, has been designed for men, making women invisible. We would go a step further and clarify that our world and workplaces have been designed for cisgendered, heterosexual, abled-bodied White men. Block the bias by revising and revamping your policies and practices so that they are more inclusive to a range of intersectional identities across gender, sexual orientation, age, physical abilities, neurodiversity, parenthood choices, etc.

Here are some policies and practices that you should consider revising or implementing to be more inclusive:

- Inclusive and comprehensive parental/eldercare leave policies
- Comprehensive childcare/dependent care support
- Healthcare policies for different stages of life and circumstances (e.g. mental health, menopause and menstrual leave and support, pregnancy, trauma/PTSD support, trans-health support)
- Comprehensive whistle-blower and anti-discrimination policy to create a safe path to address overt bias and discrimination
- Well-communicated and comprehensive flexible working options for all employees, not just women with children
- Gender neutral toilets
- Hygiene products in workplace toilets
- Inclusive dress codes

Be Respectful of People's Time

Who do you think is considered to be an ideal employee? Is it someone who is deeply committed? And what might commitment look like? You may be thinking of someone who sacrifices personal priorities and family responsibilities to further their career. This likely involves working late nights and weekends or attending to work demands when the need arises, even dropping personal commitments to make that happen. In most contexts, such expectations will favour men over women, as women are assumed to be primary care givers to children and to elderly family members. This is biased against women who have personal responsibilities but also against men who would like to be more actively involved in their families. To block this bias and challenge the assumptions about gender roles at home and work, schedule meetings during work hours and respect people's personal time. While there can be emergencies and urgent work that requires you to engage with work-related matters outside of working hours, the default should be respectful of people's time.

Have Clear Procedures for Raising Concerns About Bias

A student of ours once shared that at one of the big 4 accounting firms in Paris, issues raised about sexism were brushed aside as "that is just the way it is" by HR personnel. Having clear procedures—including whistle-blower policies—to address such serious issues, along with people who are trained to address them, is crucial. It is paramount that the fate of a raised concern is not dependent on one person, and their personal assessment of the nature and severity of the issue. There should also be an accompanying policy that assures employees that their concerns will not just be heard but addressed, with appropriate action taken. At the same time, it is important that action is only taken at the victim or reporter's will. It can be extremely vulnerable to raise a concern and sometimes organisational action will just put further pressure on this person and in many cases even hurt their career or cause exclusion from their team, colleagues or managers. These policies and their supporting procedures should be well communicated across the organisation; much too often they are posted somewhere on an intranet where it can be very difficult to find/locate?

Use Standardised Measures When Evaluating Performance

Similar to evaluations of candidates in the recruitment process, performance evaluations are also prone to bias. As we have seen in Chapter 3, there is plenty of research to show us that people's performance is rated differently depending on their intersectional identities. Given this knowledge, standardised measures are extremely important to blocking biases. For example, one study found that 66% of women's reviews contained comments about their personalities, but only 1% of men's reviews did.[32] One way to block bias is to have clear evaluation criteria that focus on the competencies required to perform the job in question, not on personality or potential. Also, because of similarity bias and proximity bias, relying solely on the line manager's subjective evaluation is extremely prone to bias. In addition to the line manager's view, performance should be evaluated using more data-driven performance measures. It is also valuable to collect 360-degree feedback on a person's performance from other people who work closely with the person, again based on clear evaluation criteria. Finally, written evaluations should be checked for biased language, preferably by using one of the many biased-language detection software options out there.

Offer Continuous Training and Learning Opportunities

Our biases have become ingrained through decades of cognitive priming and social training; it will take time and effort for us to become aware of them and be able to block them in our behaviours and decisions. We have argued that a one-off bias awareness training does very little to ensure long-term and sustainable shifts in behaviour. Much like building a new habit to go to the gym every morning requires us to wake up early for between 21 and 60 days before it becomes part of our daily routine, so too with inclusive behaviours and bias-blocking efforts.

Research has shown that training that is ongoing and scaffolded helps commit new knowledge to memory, facilitate retrieval and maximise retention. Leading through bias requires you to engage in DEI training and micro-training activities that are ongoing and that regularly reflect on biases and their impact, just as you must continuously reflect upon what you actually do to block bias. In addition, only DEI training that is intersectional can help you understand the depth and breadth of biases.

Blocking termite biases should be a key focus and not be forgotten. Training should also cover cultural competency, developing skills to work across cultures. You should spend time reflecting on your own awareness of and ability to block bias, assessing your affective, cognitive and behavioural change. As an organisation, you should assess if these trainings are having a cultural impact on inclusion levels through employee engagement surveys.

Make Social Activities Inclusive

Many of our social activities tend to revolve around alcohol and often take place in the evening after work. These practices mean that those who do not drink alcohol or who have other responsibilities (e.g. children, parents or pets) would be excluded from participating. Whether for religious, health or personal reasons, employees may choose not to consume alcohol or to consume it in limited quantities. Yet, many workplace social events often centre around the consumption of alcohol. An after-work drink at the local pub or bar is often the default means to socialise and network with others.

Though these efforts to socialise with colleagues are usually well intentioned, they may leave employees who don't drink feeling excluded, or worse, feeling forced to attend to avoid missing out on valuable team building or networking opportunities. Even when they do attend, these colleagues are often battered with micro-aggressive questions about why they do not drink. Men who don't drink have told us that people make the assumption that they "must be driving", while women who don't consume alcohol often face questions and assumptions regarding pregnancy. Those employees who choose not to attend social events because of the emphasis on alcohol may feel left out of the "morning after" banter.

In addition to the exclusionary effect, alcohol consumption at company events also increases the risk of sexual harassment. This has led many of the organisations we work with to not include hard liquor at company events or to limit the amount served. It still, however, is a social context where many women feel they have to be extra careful not to be misunderstood, make collective strategies about who to avoid or strategies about how to protect each other and constantly make sure they are not left alone. We probably don't have to say that such strategies are emotionally taxing, sometimes leading women to feel that it is easier not to take part in the events, something that is often misinterpreted as "women are not good at networking".

> **Making Connections: Poornima & Sara's Experiences**
> Sara worked with a team of executive directors. There was one woman in the team of 7. They often met to have dinner or went for a drink together to socialise and bond. Sara had a 1:1 session with each of them. The first session was with the CEO. In this session, he expressed a concern that the woman director in his team did not take part in the social gatherings and very rarely joined the others at the bar. He was worried that this would negatively affect her status and influence in the team, and wanted her to network more and place greater priority on these informal events. However, when Sara talked to the woman, she had a very different story. The woman said that she would love to be part of the fun at the bar or the dinners, but being the only woman made it very difficult for her. Throughout her career, she had heard things like "women use their sexuality and gender to get close to the CEO and to get promoted". She was, therefore, extremely careful to ensure that no one got that impression, and that people only valued her for her competencies. As she explained: "one of the other directors can go to the CEO in the bar, put his arm on his shoulder and that would just be a "lad-like camaraderie". I cannot do that. I am so afraid that that I will be misunderstood. I have learned that it is easier to go to bed early and be prepared for the next day". This woman ended up leaving that organisation for another where she wasn't the only woman in the leadership team.

These social events are also often not inclusive to people's food choices. There are many reasons why people choose not to consume certain foods. The reasons could be religious, health or sustainability driven. Colleagues adopting food practices different from the norm are forced to continuously justify themselves because they are unable to find options at lunch or during workplace social events. We have heard leaders of SMEs (small and medium-sized enterprises) in the pork-loving Nordics jokingly share that the real reason that they do not want to hire more diverse talent is because they may need to alter the menu at the annual Christmas lunches to accommodate dietary needs. Providing multiple options at lunch and work-related events is a simple way to ensure everyone feels included and block bias against people's food choices. Also reconsider lunch-time events during the Muslim fasting month of Ramadan to be sensitive to colleagues who are fasting.

Finally, there are other informal social activities involving colleagues—like playing golf, road or trail biking or going to the sauna—that exclude those who are not already part of the close-knit group of participants and/or do not feel comfortable in joining the activities. These groups are accessible to a particular gender identity (i.e. men) and are difficult to gain access to for men who have a different background from those already in the group, let alone women. While you can't prevent people from forming these informal social groups, ensuring that no decisions are made on the golf course or in the sauna is key to blocking biased decision-making.

> **Making Connections: Poornima & Sara's Experiences**
> During a bias awareness workshop for a large FMCG company, a participant shared his reflection with Poornima. At the end of the workday, he often asked colleagues to join him for a drink at the pub. While this came from a place of wanting to socialise and get to know each other better, the session made him realise it was excluding some colleagues who don't drink alcohol and those who have to pick up their children or care for their elderly parents. At that session, he committed to making an effort to be more inclusive. Since then, he has organised hikes, brunches/dinners and walking tours of the city at different times and days of the week to cater for the diversity of his colleagues. So, make a conscious effort to redefine what social activities look like to be more inclusive to people's different lifestyle choices.

Blocking Bias When Separating

> *Who is leaving your team/organisation? What does that data tell you? Are there some intersectional identities who are leaving sooner than others? Do you know why that is?*

Collect Data About Who Is Leaving

The final stage of the employee life cycle is separation. There are many reasons why this occurs. It could be due to retirement, finding a new job outside the team but within the organisation, finding a job at another organisation, taking time off to follow personal pursuits, being asked to leave due to underperformance, restructuring or even a merger/acquisition. While there are many reasons why people leave, take a look at the data to see if there are any trends about who is leaving your team or organisation. Is it primarily women? Is it people of colour? Is it women of colour? Is it younger employees? This data can be very helpful indicator of possible biases at play and can provide insights into the focus areas for bias blockers.

Conduct Exit Interviews to Assess the Role of Bias

While there are usually mixed feelings during this stage, in both the manager and the employee leaving, it is also an opportunity to collect insights into why someone is leaving, especially when the choice is their own. Keeping your own personal biases aside, conducting exit interviews using a standardised exit interview question guide to block bias can be a great source of very valuable information about the person's experience as an employee. The employee is leaving the organisation and has less to lose by being honest and candid about their experiences. This is an opportunity to ask questions about any biases and discrimination they have felt, and how inclusive the culture of the organisation is as well as positive aspects of their time as an employee. This is also an opportunity to thank them for their service to the organisation. After all, people who have left have the possibility to act as ambassadors for your organisation, and exit interviews can act as a form of employer branding.

On occasion, you may need to take the difficult decision to let go of an employee who was simply not willing to be inclusive to the diversity in the organisation. This person may be someone who is good at their job, and they may be someone you hired or could even be a good friend at work. While it may be hard, it is important to have the courage to block your own bias and let go of everyone who is not willing to change their mindset towards inclusion. This is also a powerful lesson when considering who to recruit as a replacement for that person. We have worked with a number of organisations where employees were not willing to or uncomfortable working with women, homosexual people or transpeople or where someone continued a harassing or bullying behaviour towards (members of) minority groups. All too often these people were kept on because of their value to the organisation, their unique skillset or their powerful status in the organisation. However, what people tend to forget when prioritising the harasser is that they also produce significant harm on others causing them to not thrive, feel excluded and not be able perform at their best. Ask yourself, who do you want to keep, the one high performer who is hurting the performance of others or the many that this person harms?

Summary of Bias Blockers

In the table below, we provide a summary of the bias-blocking actions that we have discussed in this chapter.

Employee life cycle stage	Bias Blockers
Attracting	**Generating the Job Description**: *Identify the required competencies for the specific job* *Check competencies for similarity to yourself/your favourite colleagues* *Check if you have prioritised unnecessary features.* *Define words such as "talent" and "potential"* *Place emphasis on the required—"must have"—competencies rather than the length of the CV.* **Job Advertisements**: *Neutralise the language used in the job advertisements* *Include diversity and inclusion skills in the list of (leadership) competencies/personal values* *Ask applicants to not include their picture and personal data in their CV* *Use an application form and beware of bias against poorly written applications*

(continued)

(continued)

Employee life cycle stage	Bias Blockers
Recruiting and Selecting	**Sourcing for Applicants**: *Advertise positions externally and widely* *Search for talent in new places* *Build collaborations with pipeline institutions such as universities, high schools and primary schools* *Have referral bonuses for referrals to candidates from underrepresented groups* *Offer internships or training programs to target groups, but be careful that the internships are not unpaid and training programs are not side-lined* *Use, but place demands on, head-hunters and other labour market intermediaries* **Selecting Candidates**: *Mask CVs: remove personal data and picture from the first screening* *Adopt an HR system to help you hide/leverage specific data* **Interviews**: *Shift your attitude towards the interview process; you are being interviewed too* *Use a diverse and trained hiring committee* *Make sure that your first-round short list is diverse* *Interview individually at the first interview* *Standardise your greetings* *Use structured interview guides* *Use skills-based testing, cases and problem-solving activities that assess job competencies* *Rate the candidates* *Redesign the interview process* **Reference Checks and Making the Offer**: *Be careful with references* *Ask yourself—and others—flip questions* *Use bias-buddies to test your decision* *Think culture add, rather than culture fit* *Use soft quotas* *Establish relationships with candidates that might not have been shortlisted or chosen for this role*
Onboarding	*Standardise administrative processes and support* *Offer introductions to context, culture and people*

(continued)

(continued)

Employee life cycle stage	Bias Blockers
Retention and Development	*Conduct a robust diversity and inclusion audits* *Check for bias in pay* *Build DEI into salary/bonus structures* *Ensure that policies and practices are inclusive* *Be respectful of people's time* *Have clear procedures for raising concerns about bias* *Use standardised measures when evaluating performance* *Offer continuous training and learning opportunities* *Make social activities inclusive*
Separation	*Collect data about who is leaving* *Conduct exit interviews to assess the role of bias*

Self-Reflection Exercise: Which Bias Blockers Work for Your Organisation?

In this chapter, we have presented a number of bias blockers across the entire employee life cycle. Choose a minimum of three bias blockers and complete the below action plan for each of them.

Bias blocker: _____

1. Why did you choose this bias blocker? Which bias is it meant to block?

2. Who is the target of this bias blocker? That is, whose biased actions is it supposed to block and who is supposed to benefit from it?

3. Who needs to be involved in the implementation of this bias blocker? Who do you need on board?

4. How long will it take to implement this bias blocker? What are the key milestones?

5. What are the intended results? How will you know that this bias blocker has been a success?

Self-Reflection Exercise: Bias in Other Organisational Processes

In this chapter, we have focused on the many bias blockers that you can implement across the employee life cycle. However, this is not the only organisational process in which biases exist. Which other organisational processes (e.g. product or service design, marketing) are prone to be biased in your organisation? What bias blockers—inspired by the ones provided here— could you use to block the bias in these processes? Use the blank space here to make notes:

5.3 Blocking Bias Metrics

Below are a set of metrics that help you track and trace your efforts to block bias through the employee life cycle. These are by no means exhaustive but should help you reflect on data that may be helpful to collect and track to assess progress.

Employee life cycle stage and Objectives	Key results
Overall employee composition *Increased representation of underrepresented groups at various levels in the organisation*	Identify key underrepresented groups to focus bias-blocking efforts on and decide on the corresponding demographic data that you can/want to focus on (depending on local data protection laws): gender/sexual orientation/age/disabilities/educational qualifications/neurodivergence/nationality/ethnicity/religion/marriage status/parenthood status/location/others relevant to your organisation or industry Collect this data periodically (every 6 months or year) to track progress Map employees by function/job level/tenure against demographic data Map employee status (full-time/part-time/contractor) against demographic data Map representation in management (incl. executives/board) against demographic data
Attracting *Increased diversity in applicants* *Increased brand recognition in underrepresented communities*	Run all your job advertisements through biased-language detection software to see how many biased words or phrases are used. Track this across function/job level and conduct this exercise regularly to assess progress Collect data on new outlets for posting the job advertisement and how many candidates applied across all the outlets, including existing ones
Recruiting and Selecting *Increased diversity of candidates shortlisted and presented to the hiring manager*	Map the number and percentage of job applicants against demographic data and application stage (e.g. CV drop, first round interview, final round interview)

(continued)

5 Leading With Accountability: Addressing Systemic Bias

(continued)

	Track the number of candidates who have come through referrals against demographic data
	Run experiments across function/job level to observe if removing identity markers and personal data (including photographs) helps increase the diversity of the candidates shortlisted through the first round
	Map the number and percentage of candidates and interns hired by role/level/function against demographic data
Onboarding *Increased satisfaction of new hires*	Collect and analyse survey data on new employees' onboarding experience to identify themes around bias through the process. Track satisfaction ratings and time from entry to feeling included in the organisation
Retention and Development *Increased percentage of candidates from underrepresented groups who are being promoted and/or identified as high potential talent and successors* *Improved performance ratings/evaluations for underrepresented groups* *Improved pay equity* *Increased satisfaction in employee engagement survey* *Reduction in bias-related complaints and time to resolve*	Map the number and percentage of employees promoted by level across demographic data Map the tenure in the previous role and at the organisation before promotion across demographic data Map performance ratings/evaluations across demographic data by level/manager/function/tenure in company/tenure in current role Reflect on correlations between performance scores and promotions across demographic data Analyse qualitative data on performance (e.g. write-ups—analyse language used and length of write-ups to see if there is language that is biased) Analyse the number and percentage of employees across demographic data selected for developmental programs (e.g. leadership trainings, high-potential development track) Analyse nominations, invitations to participate, and eventual attendance/participation across demographic data

(continued)

(continued)

	Analyse the number and percentage of candidates across demographic data named in succession and talent plans (i.e. leadership pipeline across demographic data)
	Analyse work/project assignment across demographic data
	Analyse the number and percentage of employees across demographic data participating in mentorship/sponsorship programs
	Correlate the above data points to career outcomes like promotions
	Analyse compensation across and type of pay (base salary, stock awards, equity grants, performance bonuses) across demographic data
	Identify and report pay gaps (pay equity and pay equality) across demographic data within jobs, between jobs and departments/functions. Pay equity compares the value and pay of different jobs, while pay equality compares the pay of similar jobs
	To calculate the gender pay gap: Take the mean hourly pay for men and subtract the mean hourly pay for women. Divide the result by the mean hourly pay for men and multiply the result by 100. This gives you the mean gender pay gap in hourly pay as a percentage of men's pay
	Analyse starting pay for new hires in the organisation, controlling for level, function, tenure, education, office, etc., across demographic data
	Analyse employee satisfaction/engagement scores and survey results across demographic data
	Analyse internal and external complaints (e.g. discrimination, bias, harassment) and resolution status across demographic data

(continued)

(continued)

Separation *Reduced turnover of high potential talent from underrepresented groups due to bias-related issues*	Analyse the number and percentage of employees leaving the organisation by level/function/performance history/tenure at organisation at time of exit across demographic data Analyse voluntary and involuntary exits separately across demographic data Analyse exit interview responses across demographic data

> **What Can You Do Differently From Today? Leading With Accountability Means:**
> - Conducting an analysis of your employee life cycle and assessing at which points your organisation or your team is most prone to bias.
> - Committing to blocking bias at all points in the employee life cycle. It does not help to put all your resources into blocking bias in the beginning of the cycle, if bias nullifies the positive impact later on.
> - Experimenting with bias blocking. Some of the bias blockers may seem banal but try them out and observe the impact.
> - Realising that you don't have to implement all of the bias blockers to make a difference, start with a few across different points of the employee life cycle, observe the changes they result in and then continue to implement more.
> - Accepting that bias blocking is a continuous process. Once some biases are blocked, others might pop up. So, continuously assess your employee life cycle. The best way to keep track is to talk to people about their experiences and conduct regular diversity and inclusion audits.

Notes

1. Dobbin, F., & Kalev, A. (2016, July–August). Why Diversity Programs Fail. And What Works Better. *Harvard Business Review*, 1–10. Dobbin, F., & Kalev, A. (2018). Why Doesn't Diversity Training Work? The Challenge for Industry and Academia. *Anthropology Now*, 10(2), 48–55.
2. https://hbr.org/2019/07/does-diversity-training-work-the-way-its-supposed-to.

3. https://www.scientificamerican.com/article/the-problem-with-implicit-bias-training/.
4. Konrad, A. M., Richard, O. C., & Yang, Y. (2021). Both Diversity and Meritocracy: Managing the Diversity-Meritocracy Paradox with Organizational Ambidexterity. *Journal of Management Studies, 58*(8), 2180–2206. Mijs, J. J. B. (2021). The Paradox of Inequality: Income Inequality and Belief in Meritocracy Go Hand in Hand. *Socio-Economic Review*, 19(1), 7–35.
5. Castilla, E. J., & Benard, S. (2015). The Paradox of Meritocracy in Organizations. *Administrative Science Quarterly*, 55, 543–576.
6. Devine, P. G., Forscher, P. S., Austin, A. J. & Cox, W. T. L. (2012). Long-Term Reduction in Implicit Race Bias: A Prejudice Habit-Breaking Intervention. *Journal of Experimental Psychology*, 48, 1267–1278. Devine, P. G., Forscher, P. S., Cox, W. T. L. , Kaatz, A., Sheridan, J., Carnes, M. (2017). A Gender Bias Habit-Breaking Intervention Led to Increased Hiring of Female Faculty in STEMM Departments. *Journal of Experimental Social Psychology*, 73, 211–215.
7. Muhr, S. L. (2019). *Ledelse af Køn*. DJØF Forlag.
8. https://hbr.org/2016/07/designing-a-bias-free-organization.
9. Flood, M., Dragiewicz, M., & Pease, B. (2021). Resistance and Backlash to Gender equality. *Australian Journal of Social Issues*, 56(3), 393–408.
10. Still, L. (1997). *Glass Ceilings, Glass Walls and Sticky Floors: Barriers to Career Progress for Women in the Finance Industry*. Edith Cowan University.
11. https://www.nature.com/articles/d41586-023-00633-w.
12. https://www.forbes.com/sites/forbescoachescouncil/2022/08/16/the-root-cause-of-diversity-equity-and-inclusion-burnout-and-how-to-fight-it/?sh=338a296b268c.
13. Williams, J. C. (2021). *Bias Interrupted: Creating Inclusion for Real and for Good*. Harvard Business Press.
14. Gaucher, D., Friesen, J., & Kay, A. C. (2011). Evidence That Gendered Wording in Job Advertisements Exists and Sustains Gender Inequality. *Journal of Personality and Social Psychology*, 101(1), 109–128.
15. https://www.developdiverse.com/.
16. Liebbrandt, A., & List, J. A. (2014). Do Women Avoid Salary Negotiations? Evidence from a Large-Scale Natural Field Experiment. *Management Science*, 61(9), 2016–2024.
17. https://bootstrapping.dk/ny-forskning-drop-chatgpt-hvis-i-bekymrer-jer-om-inklusion/.
18. Williams, J. C. (2021). *Bias Interrupted: Creating Inclusion for Real and for Good*. Harvard Business Press.
19. https://eige.europa.eu/sites/default/files/garcia_working_paper_5_academic_careers_gender_inequality.pdf.
20. Copur-Gencturk, Y., Cimpian, J. R., Lubienski, S. T., & Thacker, I. (2020). Teachers' Bias Against the Mathematical Ability of Female, Black, and Hispanic Students. *Educational Researcher*, 49(1), 30–43.

21. https://hbr.org/2021/05/its-time-to-officially-end-unpaid-internships.
22. Zilvinskis, J., Gillis, J., & Smith, K. K. (2020). Unpaid Versus Paid Internships: Group Membership Makes the Difference. *Journal of College Student Development*, 61(4), 510–516.
23. Williams, J. C., & Mihaylo, S. (2019, November–December). How the Best Bosses Interrupt Bias on their Teams: Strategies to Foster Equity and Inclusion in SearchWorks Articles. *Harvard Business Review*, 151–156.
24. Dupas, P., et al. (2021). *Gender and the Dynamics of Economics Seminars* (Working Paper 28494). National Bureau of Economic Research; Levashina, J., Hartwell, C. J., Morgeson, F. P., & Campion, M. A. (2014). The Structured Employment Interview: Narrative and Quantitative Review of the Research Literature. *Personnel Psychology*, 67(1) (Spring), 241–293; Dana, J., Dawes, R., & Peterson, N. (2013). Belief in the Unstructured Interview: The Persistence of an Illusion. *Judgment and Decision Making*, 8(5), 512–520.
25. https://hbr.org/2019/03/stop-eliminating-perfectly-good-candidates-by-asking-them-the-wrong-questions?utm_medium=social&utm_campaign=hbr&utm_source=facebook&tpcc=orgsocial_edit&fbclid=IwAR17laVQaLX1uaH2odfbpLqlouj9IFQaVd5MmKIxELXCk8tSOWcZZq8kqOI.
26. Boswell, W., Boudreau, J., & Tichy, J. (2005). The Relationship Between Employee Job Change and Job Satisfaction: The Honeymoon-Hangover Effect. *The Journal of Applied Psychology*, 90, 882–892.
27. Gibson, R. (2021). *Bridge the Culture Gaps*. Boston, MA: Nicholas Brealey.
28. Gupta, R., Banerjee, P., & Gaur, J. (2012). Exploring the Role of the Spouse in Expatriate Failure: A Grounded Theory-Based Investigation of Expatriate' Spouse Adjustment Issues from India. *International Journal of Human Resource Management*, 23, 1–19.
29. Williams, J. C., & Mihaylo, S. (2019, November–December). How the Best Bosses Interrupt Bias on Their Teams: Strategies to Foster Equity and Inclusion in SearchWorks Articles. *Harvard Business Review*, 151–156.
30. Liebbrandt, A., & List, J. A. (2014). Do Women Avoid Salary Negotiations? Evidence from a Large-Scale Natural Field Experiment. *Management Science*, 61(9), 2016–2024.
31. Perez, C. (2019). *Invisible Women: Data Bias in a World Designed for Men*. London: Penguin Books.
32. Cecchi-Dimeglio. P. (2017). How Gender Bias Corrupts Performance Reviews, and What to Do About It. *Harvard Business Review*. https://hbr.org/2017/04/how-gender-bias-corrupts-performance-reviews-and-what-to-do-about-it.

Leading with allyship

6

Leading With Allyship: Moving Beyond Tolerance and Obligation

Leading with allyship involves blocking biases in our interpersonal relationships with colleagues, managers and employees to nurture inclusion at work. Inclusion is not felt in grand strategies or visions of DEI; inclusion is felt in our day-to-day interactions with others—by the coffee machine, at lunch and during meetings. Allyship is key to being able to nurture an inclusive culture, a culture where everyone feels valued, respected, heard, seen and can build a sense of belonging.

One of our pet peeves is when we hear leaders say that engaging in DEI is their obligation and describe inclusion as "being tolerant". We want to set the story straight. Being inclusive to people who are different from yourself is not about being tolerant, nor is it an obligation. Tolerance can be thought of as the ability or willingness to put up with—to tolerate—the existence of opinions or behaviours that one dislikes or disagrees with.[1] If one is tolerant, then one is actually opposed to inclusion, equity and equality but simply "puts up" with it. If you lead with conviction, clarity and accountability, then engaging in DEI moves you well and truly beyond the stage of tolerance and obligation. Allyship will empower you to take your journey as an inclusive leader to the next level in focusing on your relationship with people. While Chapter 5 gave you the tools to block bias in organisational processes, this chapter will give you the tools to block bias in and lift others through everyday inclusive practices.

6.1 What Is Allyship?

Within the context of DEI, an ally refers to "a person who is not a member of a marginalised or mistreated group but who expresses or gives support to that group",[2] and allyship describes the extent to which an ally cultivates relationships with others who look different, think different and/or have different backgrounds and life experiences from them, with the conscious intention of nurturing inclusion.

Though the word first appeared in English-language sources as far back as the 1840s, its use within the DEI realm can be dated to the late 1960s when cisgender heterosexual individuals stood up—as allies—for the rights of the LGBTQ+ community in the Stonewall Inn riots in the US. In 2021, the word made its way into the Oxford English Dictionary and was later named "Word of the Year". This spike in interest in and usage of allyship came in response to the murder of George Floyd in the US and the global racial justice protests which followed. Here, the focus was on allyship across racial divides. While the term is relatively well known in the US, awareness and use of it are still somewhat limited in other parts of the world, though that is quickly changing. We hope that this chapter on allyship will show how everyone can become an ally. The journey towards more active allyship can be a fruitful and rewarding DEI effort.

It should be noted, however, that the title of "ally" is not a title you can give yourself. You can't call yourself an ally. The title has to be earned through frequent and consistent behaviours and given by members of underrepresented, marginalised or discriminated groups. Also, it is possible for us to be an ally to one (or several, perhaps intersecting) underrepresented, marginalised or discriminated group(s) while also being a part of another underrepresented, marginalised or discriminated group ourselves.

Allyship can be defined both as a noun and as a verb. As a noun, it refers to the state of being an ally. Drawing on Poornima's earlier work on allyship, we adopt the view of allyship being a verb, and define the term as "a lifelong process of building and nurturing supportive relationships with underrepresented, marginalised or discriminated individuals or groups with the aim of advancing inclusion".[3] It is important to note here that allyship is a process and never something that can be achieved as a fixed status. It demands constant focus and constant attention to your everyday actions.

Allyship is[4]:

- Made up of frequent and consistent behaviours.
- Not a "mere" performance or to be seen as something to showcase to others.
- About supporting others in a way that is comfortable for them.
- Not only focused on the behaviours performed by the ally but also the impact those behaviours have on others, whether they make others feel included or not.
- Not about fixing others but about supporting them.

Allyship should not be staged. Staged allyship refers to the set of actions or behaviours that are performed to demonstrate support for underrepresented groups but that do not result in any meaningful change of or challenge to systemic bias. Such behaviours can give the illusion that progress towards inclusion is being made in your organisation when in reality, that is not the case. It can include posting on your organisation's social media channels like Yammer or Slack about gender, racial and social justice issues without taking any concrete action, or when leaders make empty promises to support these causes without following up with action. Those who engage in staged allyship are most concerned about their own personal image and reputation rather than the needs and concerns of underrepresented others. This chapter will provide you with not only a deeper understanding of allyship but also the concrete tools and exercises needed for you to be an active ally.

6.2   Phases of Allyship

Allyship is about what we do, our behaviours, and consists of phases from denial—not engaging in allyship behaviours—to active—engaging in frequent and consistent behaviours. In between those extremes are a range of passive behaviours. We will describe and discuss the phases below.[5]

Denial: Someone in the denial stage does not see the need for diversity, equity and inclusion, and does not believe that bias and discrimination need to be addressed. At this stage of allyship, this person prefers to stay in their comfort zone, interacting with those who look and think in similar ways to them or with whom they share life experiences and backgrounds. Such a person is usually uncomfortable around those who are different from themselves.

Passive: Someone in the passive stage understands the need for (and benefits of) diversity and acknowledges that lack of equity and inclusion is a problem to be addressed. At this stage of allyship, this person is in environments where they interact with people who look and think differently from themselves and can identify bias around them, but they do not make any concrete efforts to nurture an inclusive environment.

Active: Someone in the active stage keeps themselves well informed about the latest happenings in the areas of diversity, equity and inclusion, believes that being inclusive is the right thing to do and is certain of the value that diversity brings. At this stage of allyship, this person is very aware of their own biases and makes concrete, frequent and consistent efforts to nurture an inclusive environment.

Self-Reflection: What Stage of Allyship Am I at?

Based on your career so far, which stage of allyship would you believe you are currently at—active, passive or denial? Importantly, it should be noted that as allyship is a process, you can engage in allyship at different stages with different people. You can also move back and forth, depending on the context within which you engage in allyship.

6.3 Moving From Passive to Active

The vast majority of us are passive allies. We are good people who understand the need for DEI, but we don't know what to say or do. If we want to work in truly diverse and inclusive workplaces, we need each and every one of us to become active allies. Simply saying "I am not racist or sexist" is not enough. We need to be anti-racist, anti-sexist and more generally anti-discrimination of any form. Many of us are far too passive. We might be fearful of doing or saying the wrong thing; fearful of confrontation on issues we may not know enough about. However, when we are bystanders, we become an accomplice and co-conspirator—even if that is not our intention—permitting discrimination and bias to continue to exist and even thrive.

If we want to see real change and progress in DEI, we need every human being to stand up and be an *active ally*. This cannot be an issue for the minorities to deal with. It isn't an issue for women, it isn't an issue for minority ethnic groups or the communities of LGBTQ+, disabled or neurodivergent people to deal with—this is a human issue for all human beings to resolve. Individuals from well-represented and underrepresented groups alike need to actively stand up in organisations as well as societies to make real change happen.

To be effective, active allyship should take place at four levels—individual, interpersonal, team and organisational.

Being an active ally begins with ourselves as individuals in nurturing an inclusive mindset. This self-work is crucial and is the foundation for active allyship at the other three levels. At the interpersonal level, active allyship refers to efforts in our interactions with others. At the team level, active allyship refers to allyship within team or group interactions, such as meetings and gatherings with three or more members. Finally, at the organisational level, active allyship involves addressing more systemic issues that impact interactions between larger groups of people in the organisation.

Initially, being an active ally can feel like we are walking on eggshells, fearful of our biases being called out and hesitating to address the biases of others. At times, we may get it right. At other times, we may fumble and find ourselves making mistakes. This is OK. In fact, it is healthy and demonstrates movement in the right direction. We need to get uncomfortable first as we understand and make sense of our own biases, and how they impact others and the decisions we make.

Make no mistake, leading through allyship is challenging. We need to train our "brain muscles" to think and act differently than we have been used to. This means that there will be moments of discomfort. There will be moments of frustration. There will be times you will get things wrong, and other times when you succeed. This is not easy but essential to moving forward as a leader who leads through bias.

6.4 Foundations of Active Allyship

Leading with allyship involves adopting a set of behaviours as we interact with others to help move the needle further and faster towards inclusion. In this section, we provide a set of behaviours that will empower you to be able to lead effectively through allyship; these form the foundation of your active allyship efforts.

Nurture Psychological Safety to Be Able to Have Honest and Open Conversations

To nurture inclusion, we need to have open and honest, and occasionally difficult or uncomfortable, conversations about bias. For this, we need psychological safety. Professor Amy Edmondson from Harvard Business School defines psychological safety as "a belief that one will not be punished or humiliated for speaking up with ideas, questions, concerns or mistakes, and that the team is safe for interpersonal risk-taking".[6]

Psychological safety has two aspects. The first aspect is safe spaces where everyone can share their ideas, questions, concerns and even mistakes without being fearful of punishment or humiliation. The second aspect has to do with risk-taking. The two are connected, as creating safe spaces is also about creating spaces where employees feel safe to take risks. Psychological safety, across both aspects, is crucial to ensuring that we are able to engage in the difficult conversations in the area of DEI—and there are many such conversations. For those of us who are more conflict-averse, psychological safety is key to ensuring that we are able to have open and honest conversations about discrimination, bias, inequality and inequity. In the previous chapter, we looked at how we can block bias in organisational processes. To be able to do this sustainably requires psychological safety among the people implementing the bias blockers.

To enable psychological safety, it is crucial that we approach conversations from a place of deep understanding that everyone is biased and that we are on a journey towards being active allies. These conversations about DEI should never become a "shame, blame and guilt" game. When engaging in these conversations, there is a danger of gaslighting someone's experiences of bias. Gaslighting is the "psychological manipulation of a person usually over an extended period of time that causes the victim to question the validity of their own thoughts, perception of reality, or memories and typically leads to confusion, loss of confidence and self-esteem, uncertainty of one's emotional or mental stability, and a dependency on the perpetrator".[7] Hence, gaslighting is a form of social control whereby the lived experiences of marginalised groups are consciously and/or unconsciously rejected and explained away by those in the majority to protect their dominant and taken-for-granted worldviews.[8] Ultimately, gaslighting protects the status quo while at the same time confusing and delegitimising those who struggle to fit in. Within a workplace context, gaslighting occurs when a colleague or manager manipulates a person to the point that they begin to question their own sanity, memory or perceptions. The gaslighter can do this by denying past events, downplaying the person's emotions or retelling events so that the person takes the blame and not them.[9]

Fostering psychological safety and avoiding gaslighting means NOT doing the following:

- denying a colleague's recollection of events
- dismissing or belittling a colleague's experience
- casting doubts over a colleague's feelings, behaviour and state of mind
- openly shaming a colleague in meetings or in front of clients
- retelling events or twisting facts to shift the blame to a colleague
- insisting that you are right and refusing to consider a colleague's facts or perspective or
- insisting that your colleague said or did things that they didn't do[10]

Within teams, Amy Edmondson defines psychological safety as "a shared belief held by members of a team that the team is safe for interpersonal risk taking".[11] Psychological safety is not about being nice or soft, or a ticket to whine or not get the job done. It does not mean that we will get support for everything we say and do. Edmondson suggests that to nurture psychological safety, leaders need to set the stage and explain the current situation transparently, proactively invite engagement, questions or concerns, making it hard for someone to remain silent, and finally to respond in a future-oriented and appreciative way. To nurture psychological safety in your team, prioritise engaging in honest and open conversations about DEI, encourage a feedback culture, focus on learning and having a growth mindset as a team, have an "open door" policy for team members to come to you to raise issues they are facing, establish team norms on addressing bias, engage in continuous bias awareness interventions and set aside time to have honest and open conversations.[12]

Be Aware of Your Privilege and Use It to Lift Others

Leading through bias means listening to others' experiences of bias and discrimination, and remembering that just because you haven't experienced something yourself does not make someone else's experience invalid or untrue. Resist the urge to gaslight others' experiences. If an employee is sharing something with you that you've never personally gone through, and you're not sure how to respond, thank them for taking the time to share their experiences, and let them know that you will be getting back to them with the actions you're going to take. Take the time to reflect on what they shared, on your own privilege in relation to not having had that experience and on how to use your privilege to help address the biases they are experiencing. Refer back to the self-reflection exercise in Chapter 2 on your own sources of privilege.

While you may not have chosen many of the privileges or advantages that were afforded to you in your life, you do get to choose how you will use them. You can make a conscious choice to level the playing field for others. After all, your privilege has power. So, consider using your privilege for the benefit of all, rather than to benefit yourself or others like you.

Self-Reflection Exercise: Using My Privilege to Lift Others?

Referring back to the self-reflection exercise in Chapter 2 where you identified your sources of privilege, consider how you can harness your privilege and list three concrete ways in which you can lift others at work who are less privileged than you. Not sure what you can do? Read the rest of this chapter and come back and complete this. There are plenty of ideas coming up.

How can I use my privilege to lift others at work?

1._____

2.

3.

6.5 How Do I Become an Active Ally?

By now, you have a good understanding of the importance of active allyship and how active allyship depends on your ability to foster psychological safety within your own spheres of influence along with your ability to identify and use your privilege to lift others. However, much like our argument in Chapters 3–5 that identifying and understanding one's bias does not make them go away, knowing and understanding active allyship does not make you an active ally. To become an active ally, and not just a passive one, we again emphasise the importance of the KAB (Knowledge-Attitude-Behaviour) framework. For change to happen, you need to engage in concrete behaviours frequently, even daily. The behaviours laid out here provide a guide for you to further harness your privilege to lift others.

These behaviours are divided according to the four levels of active allyship introduced earlier—individual, interpersonal, team and organisational. Individual behaviours are behaviours you engage in to become more reflexive; interpersonal behaviours concern the way you interact with other individuals or groups; team behaviours address group dynamics and the culture of team meetings; and finally, organisational behaviours are behaviours that impact broader groups of employees at the organisational level. Of course, as with most classifications, the levels overlap. Hence, they are not meant as strict divisions, but as a means to help us make sense of active allyship and give you an overview of the tools that you can use at each level. No matter how interconnected the levels are, however, becoming an active ally begins with you.

Behaviours That Nurture an Inclusive Mindset

> *These behaviours enable you to develop an inclusive mindset in yourself; this mindset is crucial for active allyship.*

Expand Your Network

With the influence of similarity bias and confirmation bias that we described in Chapter 3, we have a tendency to stay within our comfort zone and surround ourselves with people who are similar to us. In Chapter 5, we saw that we tend to reach out to those in our network when a new role becomes available in our team. If our network is homogeneous, then we reach out to people who are like us—those who have been to the same school or university, live in the same area or enjoy the same activities, like mountain biking or golf. However, this can limit your ability to think out of the box and be creative, as you are not being stimulated and inspired by different ideas. It can also limit your development of empathy towards others, as you are not challenging your ability to view an issue from another person's perspective.

A very simple way of starting your journey towards being an active ally is to be more aware of your network by asking yourself these questions: Who do you surround yourself with? Who do you get inspired by? And who helps you grow as a person?

Challenge yourself to expand your own network beyond those who are most similar to you, be that people from the same organisation, industry, nationality, educational institution, race, gender, age, etc. Think of professional networks in your country, region or even globally that you are not yet a part of. Seek out networks that attract members from different backgrounds than yourself. Attend their networking events and connect with those you meet on LinkedIn to follow their work. You can even consider broadening your social networks at work and outside work. Who do you have lunch with? Are they colleagues who are similar to you? Try and have lunch with colleagues who you don't usually socialise with at work. Maybe invite a colleague who has a different background from you for coffee to understand their role in the organisation. If you only have friends who are similar to you, seek out opportunities to meet people who are different from you. This could be through a sport, hobby or even the parents of your children's friends at school. In making a conscious effort to build a more diverse network, you benefit from new ideas and solutions—and a wider and more diverse candidate pool when recruiting.

Self-Reflection Exercise: How Diverse Is My Professional Network?

Think about the people within your professional network. You could think about the 5 people that are closest to you, professionally. How similar are they to yourself? Scroll through your LinkedIn level 1 contacts or your email lists. How similar are they to you? How different are they from you?

Use the Image 6.1 from Chapter 2 to help you identify the dimensions in which you have similarities with your network and the dimensions in which you have differences. Are there any intersectional identities missing from your professional network? Reflect on why that is and what you can do about it. Remember that the more diverse our network is, the more we are able to tap

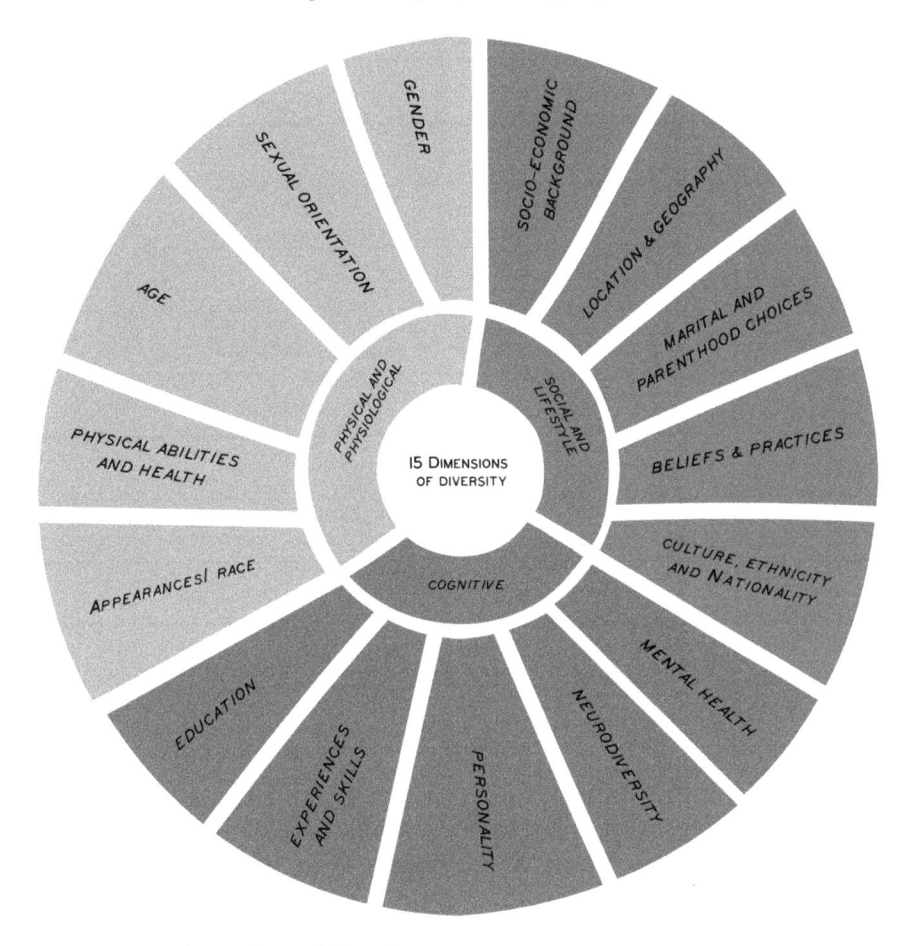

Image 6.1 15 dimensions of diversity

into this network to seek different perspectives and even hire more diversely than we have in the past.

Seek Advice From People You Don't Usually Ask Advice From, Especially People You Know Will Disagree With You

Ask yourself this: Who are the five people that you go to for workplace advice? If these five people come from the same team or function, or are people who are similar to you, it may be time to expand and seek advice from others. If you approach people who are similar to you in terms of their diversity thumbprint and intersectional identity, there is a higher chance that they have similar life experiences as you and will likely be unable to give you perspectives on an issue that you wouldn't have thought about yourself.

Business literature is full of examples of how ideas, campaigns and products are developed when the team lacks diversity. Think of how seat belts were constructed to protect male-sized bodies, how electronic soap dispensers in the beginning could only register White hands or think of Volkswagen's embarrassing campaign where a big White hand flicked a little Black man into a café called Petit Colon.[13] In 2018, Heineken had to withdraw their 30-second advertisement "Sometimes Lighter is Better". The advertisement featured a bartender sliding a bottle of Heineken Light towards a White woman. The bottle passed several men and women of colour before it reached her, at which point the slogan "Sometimes Lighter is Better" appeared. In a campaign for Indian mattress company Kurl-on, a sequence of cartoon images depicted Pakistani activist and Nobel Peace Prize winner Malala Yousafzai getting shot in the face point-blank, tumbling downward onto a mattress and then bouncing back up to win the Nobel Peace Prize with the slogan "Bounce Back". [14] Turns out, the graphic was created by a South American illustration firm who lacked the cultural know-how to understand the insensitivity.

These situations—and many more—could possibly have been avoided if there had been more diverse representation in the teams involved in the entire development process. People with different diversity thumbprints and intersectional identities experience the world differently, not because of their diversity thumbprint per se, but because of the way people react to them because of their intersectional identities—and because of how their physical bodies interact in spaces and with equipment/tools around them.

If the ones that you ask for advice have a similar background, education and ways of thinking as you, while it might be an amazing and engaging opportunity to discuss a new project with this person, your conversation may not be all that innovative. Imagine the following scenario. You have a new idea, and you go to your good colleague and "partner in crime" to discuss it. They get super excited about your project, and you both share plenty of ideas. You are both ecstatic and full of energy with a strong desire to get this project underway. It feels great! But pause and think. Have you received new perspectives on the project that you wouldn't have reached on your own. Probably not.

> **Making Connections: Poornima & Sara's Experiences**
> Sara had an interesting conversation with a leader who was, among other things, responsible for buildings and sites. He asked if there was something tangible and visible that he could do to show his support for gender equality. She told him that he could place hygiene products in the bathrooms. At first, he looked puzzled but then came to understand that employees who are menstruating often find themselves in a situation where they start bleeding, sometimes quite heavily and unexpectedly, during workhours. So, instead of having to go back to their office to find sanitary products or ask colleagues about them, the sanitary products could simply be available in the bathrooms. The leader now felt embarrassed and said: "I should have seen this". But how could he if he had never experienced this himself nor had peer-level colleagues (it was an all-male leadership team) who could have shared the experience? Asking people, whose experiences are different because of their diversity thumbprint, will expand your view on the world.

Asking people that are similar to yourself feels good, but asking people that are different from yourself challenges you to think and consider your choices much more. So, challenge yourself and ask different people for advice. Ask people with different life experiences and ask people you know will disagree with you.

Construct a Diverse Personal Advisory Board

You can even formalise this by defining your own diverse personal advisory board. This is a group of people who you trust and have established psychological safety with. But they are also different from you in one or more of the diversity dimensions: different ways of thinking, different educational background, different colour of their skin and different gender identity, etc. Make it a new habit to regularly check in on these people and ask for advice and opinions on your work. When you define such a board, then think also of which issues people can help you with. Some people might be great at challenging you in certain areas, but not others.

> **Making Connections: Poornima & Sara's Experiences**
> Let's share our own situation, as Poornima and Sara. Our diversity thumbprints and intersectional identities are very different from each other. We only have a few dimensions in common, and even those we have in common are influenced by the intersectionality of our other dimensions. To illustrate this, we can take the dimension of gender. We are both women; however, Poornima's experience as a woman of colour and Sara's experience as a lesbian woman mean our experiences of womanhood are extremely different. However, we think very much alike and have the same intellectual passions. So, we rely on each other a lot when it comes to qualifying other people's ideas and perspectives; for instance, discussing how to bring research into this book. But if one of us has a new, exciting project idea, we can assume that the other will also be excited and use each other to get energised and enthusiastic. If we want other perspectives on the idea, we need to ask colleagues who will be more critical of our ideas and ask the questions that we wouldn't think of ourselves. So, we are definitely in each other's diverse advisory boards, but only for certain questions and challenges. For others, we have other people we go to.

Have a Neutral Observer in Meetings

It can be very difficult to know how your own behaviour and body language influence others and whether you interact differently with different people. You can get very good feedback on this if you assign a neutral observer in a selection of meetings, interviews or other gatherings. An observer is, of course, never 100% neutral and their mere presence will be disruptive, but they can still be useful. By "neutral" we mean someone who is not directly working with any person in the team, including you. This can be someone from HR, a co-leader from a different division or someone from outside the organisation, either a consultant or a student collecting data for a thesis. The observer should sit quietly in a corner, observe and make notes. The point is to write as much down as possible to enable subsequent reflections. As the observer is not taking part in the activities in the meeting, they can spend all of their energy on paying attention to what goes on.

> **Making Connections: Poornima & Sara's Experiences**
> Recently, Sara worked with an organisation, which assigned a neutral observer to recruitment interviews. Here, the observer found out that the otherwise very DEI concerned manager posed slightly different questions to male and female candidates. The manager had a tendency to ask more personal questions to female candidates and more professional questions to male candidates. After the manager found out, she employed a standardised interview guide.
>
> Similarly, in another organisation we worked with, they had a neutral observer in the group meetings of the leadership team. Here, each member got feedback on their behaviour. One of the managers was told that he was always leaning forward and speaking very loudly. Being tall and enthusiastic, this had an overpowering effect that resulted in other team members keeping quiet or even stopping in the middle of a sentence when he leaned forward. At the next meeting, his body language had completely changed, and he made an active effort to lean back and wait to speak. This changed the dynamic in the team and provided a much more inclusive atmosphere, where people felt safer to speak.

Ask Flip Questions to Change Your Perceptions

As bias is often unconscious or at least implicit, and therefore kicks in to influence automatically and without us noticing, it can be a great help to check your thinking and evaluation of others with a very simple visualisation exercise, using flip questions. If this sounds familiar to you, it is because we suggested using flip questions when deciding on which candidate to select in a hiring process. Asking flip questions can be extended to nurturing your own inclusive mindset. So, if you are engaging in a light humorous conversation at lunch with colleagues, ask yourself flip questions like: "would I have thought/said the same if we were talking this way or saying this about a man, not a woman/a person in their 30s and not their 50s/a White person, not a person of colour/a straight person, not an LGBTQIA+ person?". These flip questions will help you check for biases.

Asking flip questions can also become a standard practice of your team. This can be especially important in discussions where people are being evaluated for jobs, projects, promotions, talent programs, etc. You can make it a habit to ask each other and check whether you would have made the same decision or drawn the same conclusion if the person in question had been a person with a different diversity thumbprint and intersectional identity.

> **Making Connections: Poornima & Sara's Experiences**
> Sara recently conducted a workshop, where the female CEO celebrated another CEO—a White, straight man—for being active in the DEI agenda. In the middle of the sentence, she stopped to ask herself if she would have applauded him if he was a woman. The answer was no, she would have expected it.
>
> Another example, which illustrates a recurrent experience, was shared by a Danish Black man, working in a Danish organisation. Often, when he meets a new person in a professional context, people assume he does not speak Danish and they address him in English. It is most likely always out of politeness, but the problem here is the assumption that Danes are White. Similarly, in Norway, a White British man shared that people address him in Norwegian at work but address his Brown Norwegian colleague in English. Again, assumptions about who is considered to be Norwegian are at play. Of course, this would occur less frequently if the company had an all-English policy and everyone is addressed in English.

Ask Open-Ended Questions

All too often we assume certain things about people because of their visible identity without even thinking about it. For instance, we have a tendency to assume that people are heterosexual, that people have a partner, that women have or want to have children and that people of colour come from "somewhere else" (if we are located in a majority White context). Making such assumptions can get us into embarrassing situations, and, what is worse, it can cause others to feel excluded. Although these situations cannot be completely avoided, they can be reduced in frequency and severity by asking open-ended questions.

The best part is that open-ended questions are not only inclusive to people who have personal circumstances that don't follow the norm, and they are also inclusive to people who may not feel comfortable about sharing personal information in the first place. This can be because of personal choice, their personality or due to power asymmetry in the conversation. It is often a lot easier for a leader to share personal information than for a junior employee to do the same. There is much more at risk for the junior employee.

Let's use homosexuality as an example here. As we wrote in Chapter 2, 40% of LGBTQ employees are closeted at work, while 54% of employees who are out at work remain closeted to their clients and customers.[15] In our interactions with leaders, we often hear that they don't really understand why this statistic is a problem as sexual orientation is not something to be discussed at work. To make the privilege of heterosexuality visible, we ask the participants how many times a day they think a heterosexual person comes out (by talking about their sexual orientation) at work. In most cases, we get three responses, in the same order. The first response is a sound (like huh?) implying that people don't understand the question. The second response is "zero" or "never" (because they assume we don't talk about sexual orientation at work or that only homosexuals "come out", making everyone straight by default) and the third—and correct answer—is "all the time".

Let us explain why. Imagine the following conversation between two women at a company social event:

Colleague 1: "What is your plan for the weekend?"
Colleague 2: "We have an amazing weekend planned! My husband and I are going to our summer house—without the kids!"

In this conversation, colleague 2 does not only come out as heterosexual, but also as in a relationship, a mother and of a certain class/income group with the personal finances to own a second home. So, without knowing it, this type of information displays a lot of information about us and is a lot easier to share if we follow the norm.

Open questions like the above allow the individual to choose what information they want to provide. The conversation can then continue from the information given and become more specific if both partners want to continue the conversation. But if you ask the question, "What does your husband do?" before knowing if the other colleague is married (and to a man), you assume both heterosexuality and marriage and could end up in an awkward situation if she has to correct you or hide her sexual orientation (if she has a wife, has just gotten divorced, is happily or involuntarily single, etc.).

Another example of where things can go very wrong is asking the follow-up question: "Where are you actually from?". While the question, "Where are you from?", can come from a place of genuine curiosity (though one could argue that even that question assumes that the person is not from the local context), the follow-up question, "Where are you actually from?", is (even more) damaging. The latter signals that you are not convinced by the answer the person gave. So, if you do ask the question, "Where are you from?", believe the answer you are given and let the person responding control the information they want to share. Alternatively, ask open-ended questions like, "Tell me about yourself".

> **Making Connections: Poornima & Sara's Experiences**
> Poornima was at a networking event in Oslo where someone she had just met asked her, "So, where are you from?". She answered, "from Denmark" to which he replied, "No, you aren't from Denmark, where are you *actually* from?". To him, she certainly did not fit the profile of a Danish woman—she is not White, blonde haired, or tall enough to qualify as a "typical" Dane. So, she responded saying, "Well, I am originally from Singapore", hoping that would appease him. It did not. He looked puzzled as she did not fit the image of what he thought would be a woman from that region—perhaps someone East Asian looking, which she is not. Before he could repeat his question Poornima said, "I am ethnically Indian". Now clearly *this* was what he expected and was hoping to hear, given his response, "I thought so, you are Indian." While Poornima is ethnically Indian, she left India as a baby and grew up in the UK before moving to Singapore at the age of four. Poornima holds a Singaporean passport but has lived in Denmark for over eight years. While the specific conversation referenced here played out in Norway, Poornima has experienced variations of it in many other countries. Sara, on the other hand, never gets any follow-up fuzz. She can reply, "I am from Denmark", and everyone accepts that. Although being born in Denmark, Sara holds an Austrian passport, but no-one has ever questioned her "Danishness".

Prepare How You Will Respond Respectfully When People Point Out Your Bias

Once your organisation or team has nurtured a psychologically safe culture where you can address bias respectfully, you will need to prepare for one of the hardest aspects of your journey to become a more inclusive leader—when other people catch you being biased. It could be a biased action, joke or evaluation of another person. This usually occurs when you least expect it. Because once you are well aware of bias and have learned in which situations you need to be in reflexive System 2 thinking, you would likely not say something biased. However, you are more likely to say something biased when you're stressed, busy, pushed into a corner and are relying on your System 1 thinking to make fast and efficient decisions. This is where you slip up, as your biases are making the choices for you. And believe us, you will. We still do, despite the amount of training we have. So, we are quite sure you will also revert to bias at some point. Usually when this happens, we have a tendency to start justifying what we said or did, and how we didn't mean it. This does not help. Instead of justifying yourself, try the following when *your* bias is being pointed out:

- Listen intently to gain greater clarity and understanding. Don't interrupt. Ask for clarifications only when needed or after the person has finished saying what they wanted to.
- When someone points out your bias, the best response is trying not to get defensive, dismissing the other person or making excuses for your action. Rather, assume positive intent and use their feedback as an opportunity to learn.
- Apologise but don't over-apologise.
- Respond in a way that shows that you are willing to reflect and take their feedback into account. You could respond with a variation of "I am sorry, I didn't mean it, it must be my biases speaking and I will have to think about why this was my gut-reaction and how to change it" or "Good catch, thanks for pointing out my bias. I will reflect and do better next time".
- Take time afterwards to introspect honestly and deeply. Reflect on how what you said or did had an effect of non-inclusion on the other person.

Understand Your Own Culture in Relation to Others

Each one of us has our own unique cultural lens[16] that reflects our individual cultural identity through which we interact with others. It is a reflection of your life's influences and experiences, and it is some combination of the cultural backgrounds of your parents, the national culture you grew up in, the education systems you were educated in, your personality, your religious or spiritual beliefs and values, the cultural background of your partner or spouse, which countries you have lived in, the culture of the companies you have worked for, etc. These life experiences influence many of our behaviours. Ask yourself the following questions:

- *How do I communicate with others?*
- *What is my attitude to time?*
- *How do I build trust with others?*
- *How do I manage disagreement?*
- *How do I provide negative feedback?*
- *How do I persuade others?*
- *How do I lead others?*
- *What motivates me?*
- *How do I make decisions?*

Understanding your cultural lens can help you reflect on how the way you interact with your colleagues, team members and leaders differs from the interactions of others. This can build an appreciation for the differences and value that each person adds to the team and organisation.

Behaviours That Nurture Inclusive Interpersonal Interactions

> *These interpersonal behaviours enable you to be an active ally in the ways in which you interact with other individuals or groups of people.*

Use Inclusive Communication

The words we use—written or spoken—have an impact on others. Words matter. Some of the words and phrases we use favour some groups over others. Active allies make conscious efforts to have an inclusive communication style. This includes using audience-centred language—where active allies analyse their audience to determine the content, language usage and listener expectations—which demonstrates a deep understanding of DEI and goes a long way in showing not only that they care, but that they are determined to create an inclusive culture.

Here are some ways in which we can be more inclusive in our language[17]:

- Avoid using language that is gender biased. For example, using phrases like "hey guys", "run like a girl" or "she's got balls", or "man-up". Also try to use gender-neutral occupational titles, such as "chair/chairperson", rather than "chairman", "police officer" instead of "police man", "cabin personnel" instead of "stewardess".
- Use your pronouns (he/him; she/her; they/them…) in your email signature or any place in which your name occurs and when you introduce yourself to others at work. While this may not be significant for you, it signals that others who would like to share their pronouns can do so as well. So, the next time you introduce yourself, you could say: "Hi, I am (your name) and my pronouns are …."
- To be inclusive of people who are visually impaired, it is a good practice to include image descriptions in slide decks and documents. These days, most software have accessibility checks that you can use to ensure that your document is accessible for all. Also, include a description of yourself and surroundings, especially when doing virtual calls. So, you could say: "I am a (describe your surface level identity and what colours of clothing you are wearing) and I am in my (describe your surroundings)". Also, use Camel Case (a way to separate the words in a phrase by making the first letter of each word capitalised and not using spaces) for hashtags to ensure screen readers can read it. For example, #LeadingThroughBias.
- Engage in topics of conversation with and ask questions that you would of anyone, not just people who identify with certain dimensions of diversity. As a general rule of thumb, avoid asking any questions that you would not feel comfortable being asked yourself. Ask yourself: "Would I be comfortable if someone asked me this?"
- Avoid conversations that highlight differences. For example: If you are someone who does not wear a hijab/turban, avoid asking questions like

"Why do you wear a hijab/turban?" to someone who does. Quench your deep curiosity through reading credible external sources that will provide you with the answer to such questions. Engage in topics of conversation that do not put the other person in the spotlight by having to justify their life choices, who they are or where they come from.

- When asking a question, let the other person be in control of how they choose to answer. Avoid follow-up questions that question their response. As mentioned, following up the response to the question "Where are you from?" with "Where are you actually from?" is a particularly problematic example of this.
- Beware of termite bias that get embedded in casual comments, humour and compliments.
- Avoid interrupting others, taking credit for someone else's ideas and resist the temptation to assume others don't understand something, requiring you to explain things to them.
- Avoid tone policing. Tone policing can silence the voice of those from underrepresented groups and move the focus away from the issues at hand.
- Avoid communicating surprise when someone acts or speaks in a way that you were not expecting them to. Instead, when you notice that surprised thought, make a mental note to challenge your own stereotypes and prejudices.
- Be aware of your body language when speaking with others. When engaging with other colleagues by the coffee machine, always have an "opening" in the circle for others to join in. Gesture to others around to join the conversation. At lunch, be mindful of the way you are seated to avoid creating "body walls" (with your back to an open seat next to you) that prevent others from joining in the conversation.

Address Stereotypes and Biased Behaviour

Once you begin to educate people about bias and nurture psychological safety in the organisation, you will undoubtedly experience that many more people will begin to raise and address biased behaviour in the workplace. Things that they have not noticed before will suddenly become much more visible. Here, it is important to have tools and strategies of how to address biases respectfully, but also clearly. There are six strategies that we find effective in addressing biases: humour, questioning, reasoning, correction, disciplinary and political.

- Humour can be a way of pointing out that something was not right, without introducing too much discomfort into the room. Even though we have repeated several times throughout this book that discomfort is important to be able to move from *knowing* that something must be done to *feeling* the necessity to do it, discomfort can also be too disturbing and create too much disruption in a group. Here, humour can be a strategy to address biased behaviour in a way that it is effective and through which the discomfort can quickly be released through laughter.
- Sometimes answering a question by asking a question back can make the person reflect on why they said what they said without you having to be direct. You can even play a little naïve and say "Oh, I am sorry, I don't get why that is funny, can you explain that to me" or simply ask "Why do you say that?".
- Reasoning is the strategy to use when you need to explain why the behaviour is inappropriate or discriminating. If the person engaging in the biased behaviour does not know why their behaviour is biased and discriminating, humour might not work, and a rational explanation is necessary. Respectfully highlight that the behaviour might hurt or exclude certain intersectional identities, explain why this is the case and what consequences the biased behaviour has for others.
- Correction is an extension of rationalisation. In a situation where a biased behaviour or comment is plain incorrect, such as statements about women not being ambitious or a particular racial group being lazy, the bias should be corrected, preferably using data or evidence.
- The disciplinary strategy is necessary when something that is said or done clearly is deeply hurtful towards other people in the room. As a leader who outranks the person saying it, you have the responsibility to ensure an inclusive and collaborative environment in the team. This is where you, as an inclusive leader, need to step up to show what is acceptable and what is not acceptable behaviour by respectfully, but firmly, establishing the fact that that type of language and/or behaviour is simply not tolerated at this workplace.
- The final strategy is the political strategy. This is used in situations where you can't act in the moment, either because it will make the situation worse or because you have frozen in shock. And just to be clear. Many people freeze. The most important thing here is not to blame yourself for doing so. Regardless of whether you freeze or actively decide to hold back, this will give you the possibility to think the situation through and then find a better and more effectual time to address the bias to the person/people involved. It is never too late to go back to the person and address the bias.

Sometimes, the effect is even greater, as the person has had time to think about it too.

> **Making Connections: Poornima & Sara's Experiences**
> Sara had a conversation recently with a White male leader who shared this experience: He was at a reception and had a conversation with one of his middle managers and some colleagues. The middle manager was a White man like the leader and the majority of the colleagues. One colleague was an Asian woman. The Asian woman left the conversation after a little while to talk to other people, and the middle manager uttered, "I didn't know that we employed au pairs in the company now". The leader was shocked and froze and had no idea how to react. He usually has no problem reacting, but also knows that he usually gets too angry, so has been trying to control his outbursts. He, however, regretted deeply that he didn't say anything at the time and felt bad about it all weekend. So, on Monday morning, he called the middle manager up. He answered the phone with, "I know what you are going to say, it was not okay. I could see it in your face". They had a really good conversation about why the sentence was potentially detrimental for the woman's ability to function in the workplace and how to prevent anything like that from ever happening again.

All of the six strategies can also be used when you overhear someone being treated in a biased manner or when bias is not directed at anyone in particular, but still feels unjust. The important thing to remember is to never leave the target of the biased behaviour alone to address the bias. An active ally addresses bias.

> **Making Connections: Poornima & Sara's Experiences**
> Consider the following example told to us by a C-suite leader. His team was in the middle of a DEI program, consisting of both leadership training and 1:1 coaching sessions for the management team. He was at a potential client's office where they were gathered to bid on a project. The room consisted of about 90% men and the male presenter adopted a humorous and informal tone. At one point, his jokes got more explicitly sexist, and the C-suite leader felt really uncomfortable. He felt the mood change in the room and many of the others also shifted in their seats with discomfort. He thought about how weird it must be for the women present but he didn't do anything, as he didn't want to embarrass the man in front of everyone else. He was also worried that it would just lead to an argument or the presenter answering back in a way that would make it even worse for the women present. So, he didn't do anything, but he kept feeling really bad about it. The following Monday, he called up the presenter and said that he probably wouldn't have done anything earlier, both out of (misunderstood) politeness and fear of losing the contract, but now as his company was going through this DEI training program, he had to act. The presenter was surprised by the call, but also very much appreciated it. He had also felt the atmosphere of the room change, but hadn't been able to understand why. They then had a conversation about boundaries during workplace interactions.

Practise Active Listening

Listening is a skill that is challenging to practise, but extremely crucial to inclusive leadership—both to gain new insights and to ensure your employees feel heard. Active listening is listening to both verbal and non-verbal communication with all your senses. It requires you to listen attentively to the other person with the intention to understand what they are saying and to reflect on what is being said, to provide appropriate feedback while retaining the information for recall at a later time. Through this practice of active listening, we build trust and greater understanding. With active listening, you are listening to understand and not respond, to ensure that the other person is heard, validated and inspired with ideas to address their concerns or challenges.

Our ability to listen actively is influenced by our personality and the power dynamics between the people involved in the conversation. Being extroverted tends to make people uncomfortable with silence, while being introverted tends to make people need a few seconds to think before speaking. If this is combined with other personality traits such as shyness or boldness, it has a huge influence on how you engage in conversations. How would you engage in conversations if you are extroverted, comfortable with speaking in front of large groups, bold and adventurous, curious while in a leadership position? Remember that these traits are quite likely what got you the leadership role in the first place, as we have discussed in Chapter 3 under personality biases.

Imagine that you are at lunch or by the coffee machine and you meet a colleague who is reporting to you. You know that you should ask open questions in order to make the other person feel included and you are also genuinely interested in other people. Your colleague tells you a story, which immediately resonates with you, so you reply, "Yes, that is SUPER interesting, that reminds me of…" What happened here is that the conversation, which was about the other person, becomes about you. The other person might not have felt excluded as such, but you end up gaining no new insights about that person and perhaps your colleague may not know how or feel able to re-enter the conversation due to their cultural background and/or the power dynamics. Extroverted people—particularly those in positions of power—should actively think about how to include the other person in the conversation.

When we speak to people with different personality types or different ways of thinking from ourselves, active listening becomes tricky. Conversations with people who are similar to ourselves flow more easily, making balancing speaking time between the parties involved much easier. Active listening requires you to be aware of the situation and your own behaviour and attentive to your conversation partner. In turn, what you stand to gain are new insights from people with different perspectives than yourself. Active listening is challenging and needs conscious, frequent and consistent effort. It involves letting go of the space you occupy in order to provide a basis for psychological safety while at the same time making sure that the other person is included in the conversation.

Support ERG Groups

An active ally participates in and sponsors Employee Resource Groups (ERGs). Choose to be part of ERGs that support those who are different from you, those with whom you share only few dimensions of diversity. At the ERG events, listen intently and support actively. Encourage participation from colleagues. If you are in a position of decision-making power, advocating for adequate financial resources and talent to run the ERGs can be a tangible way of demonstrating this support. Also, make efforts to meet regularly with

ERG leads to set collective goals that you and others in decision-making roles are held accountable for.

Be an Active Sponsor, Not Just a Mentor

Active allyship also means mentoring those who are from underrepresented, marginalised and discriminated groups (known as mentees) inside or outside your organisation by providing advice, guidance and support to help them achieve their career aspirations. Mentorship focuses on providing guidance, advice, feedback on skills and coaching but mentorship is not enough.

If you are in a position where you have responsibilities over resources and decisions, being an active ally involves sponsoring colleagues from underrepresented, marginalised and discriminated groups. Sponsorship entails externally facing support, such as advocacy, visibility, promotion and connections. Sponsorship can be understood as a "form of intermediated impression management, where sponsors act as brand managers and publicists for their protégés".[18]

A sponsor is someone who makes efforts, often behind the scenes, to ensure that high-potential employees from underrepresented, marginalised or discriminated groups are given opportunities for career growth and development. Sponsorship is different from mentorship, as a mentor will tell their mentee what to do and how to do it, while a sponsor will connect their protégés to people they may never otherwise meet and lift their protégés into spaces that they may otherwise never get access to. Without sponsors, members of underrepresented, marginalised and discriminated groups may never increase their opportunities for career advancement. A study by the Center for Talent Innovation, now known as Coqual, found that employees who have sponsors are more likely to feel satisfied with their career advancement, earn more money and be promoted faster than those without sponsors.[19]

So, what does sponsorship entail? Rosalind Chow shares what you need to do as a sponsor through these A-B-C-Ds of sponsorship[20]:

- *Amplifying*: Sponsors share protégés' accomplishments with others with the intention of creating or increasing an audience's positive impressions of them.
- *Boosting*: Sponsors boost their protégés by underwriting their reputation and providing a guarantee for the protégé's future success. Boosting can take the form of recommending a protégé for roles and positions in which they would thrive and add value.

- *Connecting*: Sponsors actively facilitate new relationships for protégés, giving them access to people that they wouldn't otherwise be able to be connected with. These connections are seen to be beneficial for the protégé's career growth and individual development. This could take the form of a sponsor inviting a protégé to an exclusive meeting with key decision-makers to increase their visibility.
- *Defending*: Sponsors challenge the status quo to support those who others may consider a "risky candidate". When a sponsor defends, they address an audience who is sceptical or even dislikes or dismisses the protégé and works to persuade them to change their opinion.

Practise Reverse Mentoring

More recently, companies are introducing DEI reverse mentoring programs as a means of enabling well-represented leaders to be mentored by employees from underrepresented groups in the organisation, the point being to challenge leaders to look at things from a perspective that is very different from their own. Through these reverse mentoring experiences, leaders have the opportunity to unlearn and learn, contributing to their own leadership development to be active allies.

However, reverse mentoring might not be as easy as it sounds. You need to have established psychological safety before an employee from an underrepresented group feels comfortable enough to open up to you. Maybe you have tried to persuade your employees that "your door is always open" and that you are "genuinely interested in feedback". This might be how you see it, but from the other person's standpoint, there is a much more visible power dynamics at play that can very easily result in fear and doubt in the employee. They are likely to be concerned about the consequences of sharing openly with you on their career progress.

As we usually say to leaders when we work with them on establishing psychological safety, power looks so much different when looked at from below. If an employee depends on you, there is a very visible power distance to them that might not be visible for you. So, if you engage in reverse mentoring, a few starting tips might come in handy. First, you could try to get a mentor you don't have direct leadership responsibility over, but one who still knows you and interacts with you. Start the conversation by establishing the fact that you are here because there are things you don't know and experiences of the world you don't have access to. Actively acknowledge your privilege. Then start by giving something of yourself. Share some of your own insecurities about the topic and why it might be difficult to talk about. Start with questions that are not directly about you and end with questions directly about you. These could include:

- What is your understanding of DEI, what does it mean to you and why is it important?
- How do you think we, as an organisation, handle DEI, what could we do better?
- Tell me about your career experiences in your life so far. Do you have any experiences where you or others have felt excluded at work?
- How do you think I behave as a leader? Am I inclusive? How can I become a more inclusive leader?

Behaviours That Nurture Inclusive Group Dynamics

> *This set of active allyship behaviours are behaviours that can help you make group/team processes more inclusive. Most of them are focused on meetings because meetings are excellent contexts in which you can change the dynamics with positive impact. However, they can also be applied to other more informal group settings.*

Schedule Meetings During Work Hours, at the Office or in a Professional Setting

Always schedule meetings during work hours and in professional settings. The timing of meetings is important to people with care responsibilities, hobbies or volunteer work, so avoid scheduling meetings at times when your employees are not expected to be working. The location and setting of meetings also matter. Often, it is a really good idea to take sensitive meetings outside the office premises because it can be easier to leave power dynamics aside, and because it is easier to focus on collaborative tasks and not get distracted with other more individual or operational tasks. However, you have to be careful when choosing both the location and the activities that you will engage in as a team to be as inclusive as possible. We have both worked with organisations where leadership training took place at a military training centre, the golf course, with an iron man instructor or similar. It is, of course, not that you can't have fun and, honestly, it is probably impossible to arrange a team-building session that includes absolutely everyone. But you could try to be as inclusive as possible and also try to rotate the activity from time to time to allow greater participation and inclusion. In addition to the choice of time, space and activities, also think of how to best facilitate the team-building sessions to avoid the risk that egos and competitiveness take over. You can get an external facilitator or someone from your talent development function to facilitate the team-building sessions.

> **Making Connections: Poornima & Sara's Experiences**
> During a DEI training Sara conducted, an organisation that did its leadership training at a military centre reflected on their social activities and whether those activities were biased. One of the directors reflected upon the fact that it was almost always a woman coming in last on these military training courses. He realised that it probably influenced his view on women and their leadership skills. He had not, until that day, thought about this and reflected that the skills they needed on the military training course had very little to do with the skills they needed for their leadership tasks.

Change the Seating at Meetings/Lunch

We tend to sit at the same seat and next to the same people every time we walk into a known room—at lunch and in meeting rooms. This means that we don't get to talk to new people; we make new employees feel left out and also increase the risk of whispering or gossiping during meetings while people speak. At lunch, we often sit with people like us who hold views and ideas on topics that are similar to our own. The easiest solution to blocking this similarity and confirmation bias is to make sure that we make the effort to sit next to new or different people at meetings and at lunch. During a long meeting, it can also be beneficial to get up and find a new person to sit next to or ask people to change seats after a break.

Set Up a Rotation for Meeting Chair and Minutes Taker, Don't Ask for Volunteers

It takes very little to break a fixed routine at meetings and get new voices and ideas to the table. It is usually the highest-ranking manager who is the meeting chair. But being the meeting chair—especially if you present the points and your opinion to the others first—can have a huge (negative) effect on who will (dare to) say something. Try to delegate the role of the meeting chair and see what happens. Try to ask your team to discuss a topic and leave the room. Your presence can have an immense effect on people. You can also rotate the role of meeting chair.

In addition to this, assigning the minute taker is always a sensitive topic (unless there is a designated person for this). It is always awkward to ask those in the room for a volunteer to do the task and it is always the same—or the same type of—person who volunteers. So never ask for volunteers but set up a rotation. Also, reframe the role. Think about how powerful that role actually is—the minute taker has the power to write sentences like "We agreed on ….". It is interesting that it is seen as a mundane task when it is actually a really powerful one.

Ask Yourself and Others: "Whose Voices and Perspectives Are Missing From the Discussion?"

An active ally constantly asks: Who is missing from the table? Who isn't in the room who should be there, because they bring a perspective and experience that adds value? Whose voice isn't being heard enough? As you think of your meetings, ask yourself whose voice and perspectives tend not to be represented at the meeting. Both in relation to whether there are groups of employees not represented at important meetings and whether there are people who are present at the meetings whose voice and ideas are not heard. For the first issue, increasing representation is ideal, but this can be difficult over a short period of time, so try to invite people from underrepresented groups to take part and give their perspectives at management meetings. When it comes to including the silent voices in the room, we have several ideas below.

Write Before Talking to Reduce Group Conformity

One of the most common ways of running a meeting is for the manager to present a point and then ask if there are any comments. Does this happen at your team's meetings? And is it always the same people who speak first (and loudest and most often)? If yes, your organisation runs meetings like most others. In many companies, it is often said that 80% of the conversations during meetings happen from 20% of the people in the room.

To change this, you can use one of our favourite tricks—which we both use in our classrooms and at the meetings we chair. Create moments of silence for people in the room to write down statements or gather their thoughts before discussing them. You could present a point as neutrally as possible and then ask people to write down their ideas, comments, solutions or reflections on post-it notes and put them on the wall. Then read them out loud, one by one. You do not need to ask who wrote it, but ask people for comments and feedback, which would completely remove any potential bias linked to who wrote it (that is, if it's not too obvious!).

If this is not possible due to time constraints, you can choose to just write notes on the post-it and let people explain and elaborate themselves. That way, everyone has an equal chance to be heard and are picked in a random order. Also, to get greater engagement, ask participants to discuss with the person next to them, which gives everyone a chance to formulate their thoughts and be better prepared to speak up.

Respectfully Redirect Stolen Credit Back to the Rightful Contributor

Women, people of colour and women of colour, in particular, tend to be talked over in meetings. As we have seen earlier in the book, appropriating occurs when a member of a dominant group takes credit for an idea shared by someone from an underrepresented group. Research even shows that these groups experience that the ideas they voiced, which weren't heard, are repeated by someone else and then suddenly applauded as a great idea.[21] As it can be very difficult for the individual to make people aware of this themselves, they need your help. So, pay attention to stolen ideas and learn to point them out respectfully. Say, for example: "I also liked Maya's point, and I'm glad you did too. Let's develop Maya's ideas further, shall we?" or "That sounds a lot like what Aisha said earlier, Aisha, could you tell us more about your ideas?".

Respectfully Disrupt Interruptions

Did you know that women are interrupted 33% more frequently than men during meetings and panel discussions?[22] These interruptions usually take place by a member of a dominant group who unnecessarily cuts off someone from an underrepresented group during a meeting or group discussion session. Introverted people, women, people of colour and, particularly, women of colour experience being interrupted or "talked over" at meetings by people who are more confident and louder.[23] This means that their voices are not heard.

To be inclusive, your team needs to work on patience to get everyone's voice heard. We can all practice disrupting interruptions—respectfully—by paying particular attention to when this occurs and making sure that we include the voices that otherwise easily get erased from the conversation. If you notice interrupting happening, have a phrase ready. Something like: "I really liked Mark's point, I would like to hear the rest of it" or "Hang on Raghav, Smita had not finished her point. We will come back to you when Smita is done sharing her thoughts". In doing this, you establish new team norms of what is considered to be acceptable behaviour. You can also adopt this when you are being interrupted and say, "Hang on a moment, let me finish what I wanted to say".

Invite People to the Conversation

You probably spend as much time in meetings as we do, but how do you assess if a meeting has been a good one? Usually, people think they have had a good meeting, if they made decisions, reached consensus on issues, there were no heated disagreements and the meeting even wrapped up on or before the scheduled time. However, this form of meeting does not foster inclusion nor creative thinking.

If your team is like most others, you will have team members who speak more and team members who speak less. If the team has psychological safety, you can actively work at inviting various people into the conversation. Rather than asking who has any comments, seek people out actively and invite them to comment on matters where you think they have expertise that would benefit the discussion. If you are the leader of a team and know each member's expertise, you can say: "Julie, this is your area of expertise. What is your opinion on this? What do you think our options are here?".

Check In on Your Quieter Team Members Before a Meeting

If a person in your team comes from a culture in which they have been conditioned to "think before speaking" or if they are more introverted or shy, then their voice may be overshadowed by those who come from cultures where speaking is more spontaneous and continuous as well as more extroverted people.[24] If you have such a quiet team member or colleague, they probably would not like to be called out on the spot, but you can check in with them before a meeting. You can ask them how you can support them in contributing more at the meeting. You can agree on the fact that if you invite them into the conversation, you will make sure that they are not interrupted and that you will be the first to support their idea. If they know that you have their back, they might be more comfortable sharing their views.

Many leaders that we have worked with find this aspect of active allyship very difficult—at least if they are extroverted themselves. Many have said to us that if someone wants to be in their team and rise in the ranks, then they must have the guts to speak up. However, you risk excluding a lot of great talents this way. So, if you feel annoyed or impatient after reading this, the risk is that you only nurture extroverted and outgoing talent. That not only cuts you off from a lot of highly competent people and their ideas, it also risks creating a group dynamic in which the ones that speak the loudest win the battle.

Consequentially, it might foster a tense and competitive work environment, instead of one where there is psychological safety, where everyone, regardless of personality, cultural background, ways of thinking, gender or race feels comfortable speaking up, feels appreciated, included and listened to. Yes, the meetings might take a little longer and you might have to work actively in the beginning to break old habits of interruptions and dominance of team members, but give it a try and see what happens when the conversation slows down. You may be pleasantly surprised.

Behaviours That Nurture Inclusive Organisations

> *The behaviours at the organisational level are those that need to be implemented within organisational processes and procedures, beyond the employee life cycle. Some of them require more effort and coordination, but they also have greater impact, given their broader reach.*

Ensure Representation on Panels and Among the Speakers Invited to the Organisation

Make sure you never arrange an all-male or all-White panel or all-female panel and ensure that intersectional identities are represented. The combination of intuition bias and proximity bias often results in panels ending up consisting of a majority of White men. This is not only embarrassing for an organisation that engages in DEI, but also not good for the richness of the discussion. Also, invite different people as experts and speakers to provide inspiration and different perspectives. Sometimes you have to spend a little more time finding them, if they are not part of your immediate network, but the effort is necessary and rewarding. Finally, make sure that you don't take part in homogeneous panels. Tell the organisers that you will only take part if the panel is mixed. The only exception to this rule is if the panel is discussing a particular group's experiences. You wouldn't want a woman on a panel, discussing what it is like to be a man or a straight person on a panel, discussing homosexuality.

Identify High- and Low-Profile Tasks

Tasks and projects in organisations tend to be divided into high-profile or low-profile ones. Low-profile tasks or projects are those which don't get much attention, might not have external traction or might not involve important clients or markets. The reasons why they are high- or low-profile are many, but most commonly, low-profile tasks do not lead to promotion in the same way that high-profile tasks do, even though the success and performance of your organisation depend as much on these tasks as it does on the high-profile tasks.

On top of this, research shows that women, people of colour and, particularly, women of colour are much more likely to end up with the low-profile and non-promotable tasks and projects. To work towards greater equity, it is very important that you have an overview of which tasks are high or low profile and which are completed by each of your employees. Then find out if certain groups are over- or underrepresented in each type of task and make sure to even this out.

As we all tend to see competency differently in people depending on their diversity thumbprint and intersectional identity, there is a risk that your organisation—without knowing it—gives the high-profile and promotable tasks to White men. Make sure this is evened out by using a competence approach to staffing projects. An active ally makes sure that underrepresented groups get tasks that will enable them to perform well and be in the organisational spotlight.

Set Up a Rotation for Office Housework

Closely related to high- and low-profile tasks and projects is the concept of office housework. Office housework includes all the work that employees do outside the scope of their job description. Office housework falls into three main categories: social housework, emotional housework and actual housework. Social housework can include arranging company parties, team buildings and off-site retreats as well as DEI work, such as organising the company's Pride parade or International Women's Day event, running an employee resource group or sitting on the organisation's DEI advisory council. Emotional housework includes being the person people come to if they have personal problems or just need to talk. Actual housework includes baking Friday cake, cleaning up the kitchen and making coffee. All these tasks are extremely important for the organisation, but they tend to be performed voluntarily by women or underrepresented groups with personal investment in the task—and they tend not to lead to promotions, just like the low-profile tasks.

To work actively for equity means understanding and dividing office housework between people or including it actively in people's job descriptions. Start by making a list of all the office housework that your organisation requires to be done in order to function well. Next, divide it up equally, set up a rotation or write it into people's job descriptions. If it is important, then reward it! A great example of the latter is the amount of time various underrepresented employees spend on DEI activities. This is highly important for many organisations and is of great (employer) brand value, and it should be recognised, rewarded and lead to promotions, just like any other important strategic initiative. Just because your employees care, doesn't mean they shouldn't get rewarded.

So, an important part of being an active ally is recognising that it is not the responsibility of women and underrepresented employees to say no to office housework, it is your responsibility to not expect them to lift the burden alone—and, more, to distribute the burden equally on the team. Again, active allyship takes the responsibility from the individual and actively works to not place the person in that position in the first place.

Have a Quiet Space

A very tangible way to make your organisation feel more inclusive to people is to make sure that your office building has quiet, private rooms that can be booked for meditation, praying, lactation/breast feeding, concentration, etc. Different people have needs for a private space for many different reasons, and as it is impossible for you as a leader to be aware of them all. Simply, having multi-purpose rooms that serve all these needs will make the organisation much more flexible and inclusive. You could perhaps put an idea box in the room for employees to voice their ideas for the usage of the room: What resources do they need to be able to use the room for their individual needs?

Provide Sanitary Products and Menstrual Leave

If you are working towards gender equality in your organisation, chances are that a large percentage of your employees will be menstruating once a month. It would be a great help for your menstruating employees, if the bathrooms carried sanitary products. This would save them from having to make it back to their desk or purse or to ask people for products and hurry back before any "accidents" happen.

The pain that comes with mensuration is real and debilitating for many. Yet, Spain is the only European country to introduce paid menstrual leave, joining Japan, Taiwan, Indonesia, South Korea and Zambia. Regardless of whether the country you operate in has such legislation or not, consider establishing an organisational policy on menstrual leave.

Formulate a Language Policy

If your organisation is placed in a non-English-speaking country and if you have non-locals hired, formulate a language policy. In many of the organisations we have worked with in Europe, English is the corporate language. However, most social gatherings, lunch conversations and coffee machine talks occur in the local language. Always pay attention, not only to who is in the room, but also who (might) enter the room. As a rule, speak English, also when non-locals are not around, to make it easier to join a conversation. However, many of the organisations we have worked with also have staff who are not comfortable speaking English and who might not even understand English very well. If this is so, you would need a language policy that accommodates both groups. This of course needs to be adjusted to your specific context, but it could be worth considering if you should appoint a couple of language ambassadors. These are employees, who are comfortable in both languages and at events can translate and ask questions in the local language. You can also make sure to have online/video options available for talks, so that they can have subtitles—or have the presentation/slide deck in both languages. In a French organisation Poornima worked with, they hired a translator to translate her talk in real time. When you ask for involvement or group work, the groups can also be composed in a way that makes sure that each group has a language ambassador or that the groups are composed based on their language of preference. On a more practical level, you should, of course, also offer language courses, but the option of learning both the local language and English.

Cater to Team Members' Food Habits

Most organisations now provide vegetarian or vegan options. But there is still a stigma associated with it, which can be felt whenever someone calls out "Who ordered the vegan option?". To be more inclusive to various food needs, you could go vegan by default and then add vegetarian, meat or fish as extra options. It would not exclude people who really want their meat, but it would probably nudge many to not choose it as an extra and thus both be inclusive of food habits and serve as part of a sustainability policy, which is becoming more and more important as well. Also, have all food options labelled in English and the local language.

> **Making Connections: Poornima & Sara's Experiences**
> Sara recently worked with the Danish office of a large international consulting firm. They did have vegetarian options in the cafeteria, but the signs were in Danish, which meant that international colleagues who were vegetarians and or had specific dietary requirements often ended up taking the safe choice, which was salad.
> As someone who follows a plant-based diet for health and sustainability reasons, Poornima is often left eating a salad or grilled vegetables at company or networking events. When Poornima joined Copenhagen Business School, she was pleasantly surprised to see that the default setting at all department events was vegan meals, to which employees could add seafood as an option.

Make Sure That Various Festivals Are Taken Into Account and Respected

Many European and American organisations give their employees a day off on national and religious holidays. These are, however, most often the Christian Holidays. It is probably difficult to embrace all religious holidays and festivals, but it would mean a lot to your employees if everyone could get time off for major festivals that are important to their beliefs. Encourage HR to include "festival holiday leave" of one or two days where people have the flexibility to pick when to take leave, just like other leave arrangements are individual.

Celebrating religious events and festivals can also be used to educate your employees and widen their horizon. Ensure that you are not only celebrating Christian festivals but also other festivals of the various employee groups in the organisation. Be consistent in how you communicate greetings for festivals. Alternatively, some organisations choose to adopt a religious-neutral approach and do not celebrate festivals at an organisational level but leave employees to celebrate festivals within their teams.

> **Making Connections: Poornima & Sara's Experiences**
> Sara recently worked with an organisation, where some of the Muslim employees invited anyone interested to Ramadan dinner at sun-down to celebrate the breaking of the fast. The dinners were set up as conversations, where people could ask questions about the hosts' culture and religion. In this way, there was a defined space for questions, which otherwise might be either awkward to ask or not appropriate.
>
> In another organisation that Poornima worked with, celebrating festivals was encouraged at the grassroots level and employees were encouraged within their teams to organise breakfast team sessions where they organised food and shared information about a festival important to them.

Engage in Shadow Coaching

Shadow coaching involves teaming up with a co-leader, preferably someone from a different organisation. If you are part of a leadership network, this is an excellent way to initiate shadow coaching. You team up with someone you can trust and find two days—one where you can visit your co-leader and one where they can visit you. You spend the day observing the other. The observer does not speak but takes notes of everything that goes on and all the interactions they observe. Before the visit you can have a conversation with each other about what you both would like feedback on. After the visit, each of you writes up the notes and also writes a short synopsis as feedback, where you emphasise your main findings, what you particularly noted or if there were any patterns or surprises. You can also extend this with a section in which you reflect on how observing the other person made you think about your own context and your own leadership. What differences did you notice and how did this make you think differently about the way you perform leadership and engage with your employees, colleagues and managers? This is excellent data to improve your relational leadership skills.

Summary of Active Allyship Behaviours

Level	Active allyship behaviours
Individual: *Behaviours that nurture an inclusive mind-set*	Expand your network Seek advice from people you don't usually ask advice from, especially people you know will disagree with you Construct a diverse personal advisory board Have a neutral observer in meetings Ask flip questions to change your perceptions Ask open-ended questions Prepare how you will respond respectfully when people point out your bias Understand your own culture in relation to others
Interpersonal: *Behaviours that nurture inclusive interpersonal interactions*	Use inclusive communication Address stereotypes and biased behaviour Practise active listening Support ERG groups Be an active sponsor, not just a mentor Practise reverse mentoring
Team/Group: *Behaviours that nurture inclusive group-dynamics*	Schedule meetings during work hours, at the office or in a professional setting Change the seating at meetings/lunch Set up a rotation for meeting chair and minutes taker, don't ask for volunteers Ask yourself and others: "Whose voices and perspectives are missing from the discussion?" Write before talking to reduce group conformity Respectfully redirect stolen credit back to their rightful contributor Respectfully disrupt interruptions Invite people to the conversation Check in on your quieter team members before a meeting

(continued)

(continued)

Level	Active allyship behaviours
Organisational: *Behaviours that nurture inclusive organisations*	Ensure representation on panels and the speakers invited to the organisation Identify high- and low-profile tasks Set up a rotation for office housework Have a quiet space Provide sanitary products and menstrual leave Formulate a language policy Cater to team members' food habits Make sure that various festivals are taken into account and respected Engage in shadow coaching

6.6 Celebrate Active Allyship

To lead through bias requires leaders to not just implement a DEI strategy, make public statements of support or set and monitor quotas. Leaders need to not only "talk the talk" but "walk the talk"—and to not just repeat that slogan but to actually practise it. They must be active allies themselves: holding themselves accountable, actively demonstrating inclusive behaviours, building safety to address biased behaviours, making concrete efforts towards eliminating systemic bias in hiring and promotion processes, correcting flaws in organisational systems to make them equitable for all and nurturing a truly inclusive organisational culture for all employees.

Active allyship means challenging the status quo and questioning the "ways in which things have always been done" to expose the bias that exists. Active allyship also means making an effort to recruit beyond the usual channels and your existing network to ensure that talent from underrepresented backgrounds is given a fair chance in our workplaces. Active allyship requires us to challenge what is considered "normal", "professional" and a "good fit".

An active ally understands their responsibility to make workplaces inclusive for all. An ally across intersectional dimensions of diversity, not just an ally for some and not others. An active ally ensures that underrepresented groups are included in all organisational processes. An active ally ensures that every meeting, committee and task force that is set up has adequate representation, and that every person has a voice. An active ally makes a conscious effort to create space for underrepresented to have time to share their perspectives.

For us to normalise being an active ally, we need to celebrate active allyship. We need to recognise our colleagues who are demonstrating the kind of behaviours that are representative of being an active ally. This will, in turn, provide the needed motivation to move those who are passive allies to becoming active allies. While we may celebrate the grand gestures of active allyship, we should, in fact, be focused on smaller gestures and actions, inspiring those who are hesitant to become active.

Self-Reflection Exercise: My Allyship Journey Thus Far—Who Have I Been an Ally to?

Based on your understanding of allyship so far, who do you think you have been an ally to? What evidence do you have that would suggest that you have been an ally to that person or group. You can choose to keep the person's identity anonymous but be specific in how you believe you were an ally to them.

Self-Reflection Exercise: How Can I Be an Active Ally?

Reflecting on the behaviours of active allyship, which behaviours would you like to focus on in the near term and what would do you plan to do to demonstrate active allyship behaviours in that area? Write down concrete ways in which you can adopt these behaviours in your daily work-life. Remember to cover actions across the individual-interpersonal-group/team-organisation levels.

What Can You Do Differently From Today? Leading With Allyship Means:
- Understanding what it takes to be an active ally.
- Being clear about what active allyship is and is not, and why active allyship is needed.
- Reflecting on the current phase of your allyship (denial, passive and active) and pushing yourself towards consistent active allyship.
- Reflecting on the three components of allyship—knowledge, attitude and behaviour—and knowing where you stand with each of them.
- Making a commitment being an active ally and being clear about specific behaviours to engage in to demonstrate frequent and consistent active allyship including acknowledging and using your privilege to lift others.

Notes

1. Oxford Languages, https://languages.oup.com/google-dictionary-en/.
2. https://www.merriam-webster.com/dictionary/ally.
3. Luthra, P. (2022). *The Art of Active Allyship*. København: TalentED.
4. Luthra, P. (2022). *The Art of Active Allyship*. København: TalentED.
5. Luthra, P. (2022). *The Art of Active Allyship*. København: TalentED.
6. https://amycedmondson.com/.
7. https://www.merriam-webster.com/dictionary/gaslighting.
8. Sweet, P. L. (2019). The Sociology of Gaslighting. *American Sociological Review*, 84(5), 851–875.
9. Storm, K. & Muhr, S. L. (2022). Work-Life Balance as Gaslighting: Exploring Repressive Care in Female Accountants' Careers. *Critical Perspectives on Accounting*, 95, Article 102484.
10. Luthra, P. (2022). *The Art of Active Allyship*. København: TalentED.
11. Edmondson, A. (1999). Psychological Safety and Learning Behavior in Teams. *Administrative Science Quarterly*, 44, 250–282.
12. Luthra, P. (2022). *The Art of Active Allyship*. København: TalentED.
13. *Financial Times*. (2020, June). Volkswagen Blames Lack of Staff Diversity for Racist Ad.
14. https://www.businessinsider.com/kurl-on-indian-mattress-ad-uses-malala-cartoon-2014-5.
15. https://www.bcg.com/publications/2020/inclusive-cultures-must-follow-new-lgbtq-workforce.
16. Luthra, P. (2021). Diversifying Diversity. København: TalentED.
17. Luthra, P. (2022). *The Art of Active Allyship*. København: TalentED.

18. https://hbr.org/2021/06/dont-just-mentor-women-and-people-of-color-sponsor-them.
19. https://coqual.org/our-research/.
20. https://hbr.org/2021/06/dont-just-mentor-women-and-people-of-color-sponsor-them.
21. Williams, J. C. (2021). *Bias Interrupted: Creating Inclusion for Real and for Good*. Harvard Business Press.
22. Hancock, A & Rubin, B (2014). Influence of Communication Partner's Gender on Language. *Journal of language and Social Psychology*, 34, 46–64.
23. Williams, J. C. (2021). *Bias Interrupted: Creating Inclusion for Real and for Good*. Harvard Business Press.
24. Luthra, P. (2021). Diversifying Diversity. København: TalentED.

Leading with strength

7

Leading With Strength: Showing Vulnerability

Leading through bias is not easy. In fact, it might be the most challenging aspect of your leadership and career development journey. It is also the most important and impactful aspect. Leading through bias has the potential to transform the lives of so many people that are within your sphere of influence, and to address the rampant injustice and inequity that continues to exist in our workplaces—as well as elevating the performance of your team and organisation. This journey is certainly not easy, and it requires you to lead with strength.

Leading with strength, in turn, requires you to engage vulnerably and openly with all things related to DEI, not just topics and issues within your comfort zone. The very mention of the word vulnerability can make some of us feel uncomfortable. Vulnerability is the discomfort we feel when we are open to the influence of others. In her book, *Daring Greatly*, Brené Brown defines vulnerability as "uncertainty, risk, and emotional exposure". However, she also goes on to say, "But vulnerability is not weakness; it's our most accurate measure of courage".[1]

We adopt this view of vulnerability—as the strength you need to be able to stand up for what is right. At the same time, we would also like to flip it around and add that vulnerability also has the potential to make you stronger by improving your capacity to relate to the people around you and respond to their emotions in an inclusive way. In other words, vulnerability prepares you for the difficult conversations—and the learning that comes with them.

Vulnerability is often misunderstood as a sign of insecurity and weakness. To be viewed as a strength, vulnerability requires psychological safety. For people to be vulnerable and derive strength from it, we must build environments in which people feel safe, where they do not have to worry about being punished or humiliated if they voice opinions and new ideas, questions or concerns. As Amy Edmondson stresses, your team needs to be a safe space for interpersonal risk-taking.[2] She cautions that this does not mean that everyone is nice to each other, that conflict and disagreement don't exist or that your idea will always prevail. In a psychologically safe environment, people feel safe to share their thoughts and ideas, to share their voice knowing that they won't be ridiculed. Psychological safety is crucial for us to be able to engage in honest and open conversations about topics, issues and situations with DEI that can be uncomfortable. In such a psychologically safe environment, people feel safe to address bias in a spirit of doing better and being more inclusive, and people see these moments as opportunities for growth rather than reasons to get defensive.

Engaging in DEI can be very uncomfortable for some, less so for others. Leaders are often "trained" on the job to be comfortable within a certain degree of discomfort. Many leaders will tell you that they lean into being in that zone of discomfort because that is where transformation, change and innovation occur. But believe us when we say that being inclusive and leading through bias require you to step into a zone of discomfort like never before. You will need to face your fears, unlearn and learn anew before growing. Through all of this, you will have to get uncomfortable with the reality of the biases you hold, and the bias all around you—in people, structures, processes and systems. You will need to engage in tough conversations about colonialism and slavery, misogyny and gender violence, and their continued influence on the interpersonal and systemic biases that exist today.

On this journey, being as challenging as it is, mistakes will be made, and obstacles will be met. In the world we live in today, with its cancel and call-out culture, where those who are deemed to have acted or spoken in an unacceptable manner are ostracised, boycotted or shunned, it can be daunting to be vulnerable. However, stepping into this zone of discomfort, tension and paradox is also potentially the greatest learning opportunities leaders can engage in. Learning to lead through bias is a continuous process, not a one-time reflection. It is not simply about learning about tools, and it is not even simply learning new aspects of yourself. It is an awareness—and use—of your vulnerability as a tool to create more inclusive organisations. Having the strength to persevere through those difficult moments of vulnerability will be key to nurturing an inclusive workplace—and key to leading through bias.

But it is also key to grow as a person, as a leader and as an organisation. Are you ready to lead with strength?

7.1 Vulnerability, Authenticity and Strength

Throughout our lives, we have been told to be strong, sit out, endure, persevere, strive for perfection and become a better version of ourselves. You might even have an inspirational self-help book on your bookshelf with one or more of these messages. These mantras have been held as being particularly relevant for leaders or people who aspire to be leaders. The popular leadership literature is full of books to guide you on how to become a strong and excellent leader.

However, what recent research on the psychology of leadership has shown is that leading in this way tends to numb us from our emotions and feelings. We end up pretending that we are in control of all situations—even when it would be best for everyone to accept that we are not, in fact, in control. We trouper on, until we break…

We need to lead differently. We need to unlearn that strength is about not showing weakness and always knowing what to do, even though it seems easier for many leaders to put on an armour to appear strong and self-confident rather than being vulnerable. We need to unlearn that what we have been taught and conditioned to believe as the only path to strong leadership is to endure, control and predict.[3] Instead, what we need is to embrace the role of vulnerability as essential to strong leadership. Vulnerability is not weakness, it is rather, as Brené Brown explains so forcefully, the birthplace of innovation, creativity and change.[4]

In fighting to be strong, we create an armour around our emotions that numbs our ability to be empathetic. This cuts us off from the world we live in. We need to be brave enough to shed the armour and tap into our feelings. Only by losing the armour can we connect with others, connect with the people we want to inspire, influence and lead.

Through vulnerability, you build strength as you learn from your emotional reactions and interactions. Not engaging with your emotions will make you feel like you are operating from a rational mindset (and, as we learned in Chapter 3, that is misleading). Connecting with our emotions is what moves us from the K to the A in the KAB (Knowledge-Attitude-Behaviour) framework (Image 7.1). It is one thing to know what to do, but it is not until you feel it too that it changes your attitude. When your attitude changes, this is when your behaviour changes at a deep level, not just at the surface. Vulnerability, in other words, helps us to get to know ourselves better, and in turn, we operate as leaders from that place of understanding.

Vulnerability is also deeply connected with the idea of authenticity. The armour of predict and control makes it very difficult for others to get a sense of who you really are and what you believe in or stand for. This means you do not come across as authentic. Thus, vulnerability is the only way to begin to show authenticity. It enables us to understand our privilege and draw on who we are in a way that makes us connect with others.

This does not give you the license to say anything you want to anyone on the basis of being your "true authentic self". What this does mean is that you can lay down your armour and open up for the possibility to be emotionally and intellectually moved and influenced by others. It means that you are ready to embrace others' differences. It does not mean that you have a free pass to impose your views on them. It is the courage to be imperfect, yes, but at the same time also comes with the obligation to embrace others' differences in a respectful and responsible way. It is about letting yourself be seen—not on the stage and in the spotlight—but as a whole human being with emotions and flaws as well as ideas and a vision.

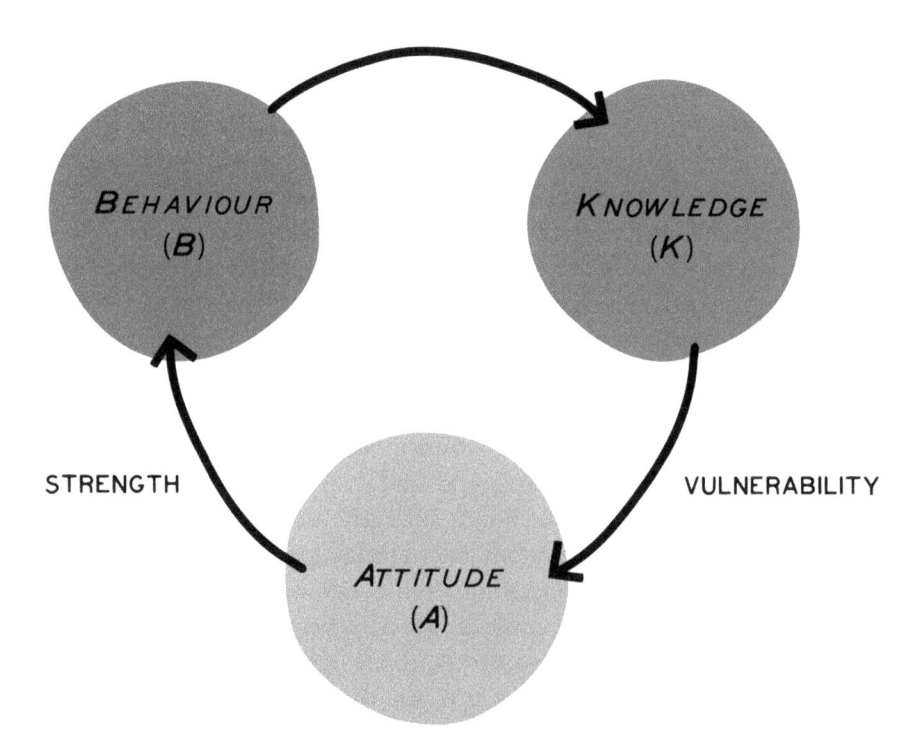

Image 7.1 Knowledge (K)—Attitude (A)—Behaviour (B) approach including vulnerability and strength

So, just to be clear, encouraging the co-existence of vulnerability and authenticity is not about showing every aspect of your emotional state at all times. It is about being in touch with yourself and your emotions; being able to show this to people in a way that makes them feel psychologically safe to open up as well. Being authentic is about connecting with others and building relationships with others in a genuine way, rather than showing them the glittery perfect armour that will make them feel subjugated and unable to be themselves around you. This is leading with strength.

7.2 Relational Leadership

Leading with strength through vulnerability is foundational for relational leadership. Over the past 20 years, leadership theory has moved away from theories on the traits and behaviours needed for effective leadership towards leadership theories that focus on effective leadership through relationships and processes. Where leadership was earlier seen as stemming from the unique characteristics of people who were seen as effective leaders, we now see leadership as the process through which leaders build relationships with their followers.[5]

If you are an experienced leader (and if you're not, you probably recognise this in others), you may have experienced performing the exact same leadership behaviours in different contexts—with different results. It is quite likely that in some contexts you were successful at building a trusting relationship with your followers. In other contexts, you may have failed miserably and never managed to gain the trust of your followers, despite all your efforts to communicate that your door was always open and you were ready for feedback.

The good news is that this difference was likely not because of a lack of leadership skills or professional knowledge on your part. As D. Scott DeRue and Susan J. Ashford say, leadership needs to be both claimed and granted.[6] If you claim leadership, but your followers don't grant it to you, there is no leadership. On the other hand, if your followers grant you leadership and really want you to lead them, but you don't claim it, there is also no leadership present. Leadership is relational and dynamic; it flows back and forth between a leader and their followers. This also means that leadership can disappear in a heartbeat if your followers loose trust in you, but also arise in a heartbeat if something occurs that makes them grant you leadership—and you claim it.

As American professor Mary Uhl-Bien has established, relational leadership is based on an understanding of leadership as a social process of influence through which coordination and change are constructed and produced[7] and where relationships—and not authority, control and dominance—are central to the materialisation of leadership.[8] The meaning ascribed to leadership is never finalised nor does it ever reach a finished form. Further, leadership does not have any ultimate source of origin; that is, it does not come from any one place—not from you, not from your followers, not from titles or organisational structures. Rather, leadership is continuously evolving through the relationships between leaders and followers. A relational view of leadership, therefore, does not focus on identifying attributes of leaders, but rather on how leadership is constructed within the social context of leaders and followers. This way of looking at leadership puts much more emphasis on followers and their role in leadership. This changes our view of followers from being passive to highly agentic co-constructers of leadership. If nobody follows your ideas, leadership does not exist. Even if you do have the formal role or title of a leader but nobody follows you, once again, *leadership* does not exist. You need followers to follow you to ensure that leadership exists, and for this, you need to earn their trust and handle it responsibly.[9] Similarly, you don't need a formal leadership title for leadership to exist. If people follow your ideas and if you influence others, that is leadership.

Defining leadership as relational—and seeing followers and followership not just as an outcome of leadership but as its very condition—implies that leadership is not just about exerting power or dominance downwards in an organisational hierarchy. All too often, leadership is thought of as a process in which ideas, directions and power are shared from people with formal authority to their employees. Of course, this can be the case. However, leadership is also an upward and lateral flow of ideas and power. Reflect on your own role. You probably regularly influence your own managers and leaders, both because you have knowledge and expertise that they need in order to make decisions, and because you have requirements and needs that they need to listen to and take into consideration for you and your employees to thrive. You also regularly influence your peers. This could be when you play the role of a sparring partner and bounce ideas with colleagues or when you discuss common challenges with people at the same leadership level as you in different functions in the organisation. In addition, you also influence people outside of your own organisation when engaging with stakeholders like clients, customers, policymakers, grassroots organisations or unions. Your organisation does not operate in a vacuum and its success is dependent on the way you and all other organisational members extend your influence outside of the organisation, whether this is more formal discussions with your organisation's stakeholders or through more informal conversations with friends and family through which you try to influence their opinion of what you and the organisation do. And finally, you constantly have to lead yourself. Today, most people are, to a certain degree, managing their own career and leadership. Whether you have a flexible work schedule or not (which most people tend to think of when they think of self-management), you must—on a daily basis—manage your time, energy, priorities, passions and what you say yes and no to.

It is extremely rare—we would go so far as to say impossible—that leadership only occurs in the exertion of power and leadership from a leader to an employee. Regardless of the formal position you hold or don't hold, you exercise leadership. Leadership exists in all directions and is constantly being granted and claimed in all directions (Image 7.2).

It is essential to leading through bias that you draw on this relational concept of leadership and embrace leadership, no matter what your formal role is—particularly in DEI efforts, which are so heavily dependent on allies to make change happen. Changing an organisational culture to become more inclusive cannot come from top management only, it needs to be rooted in a deep organisation-wide belief in the purpose of DEI. Don't get us wrong, the commitment of top management is crucial. Change does not happen without

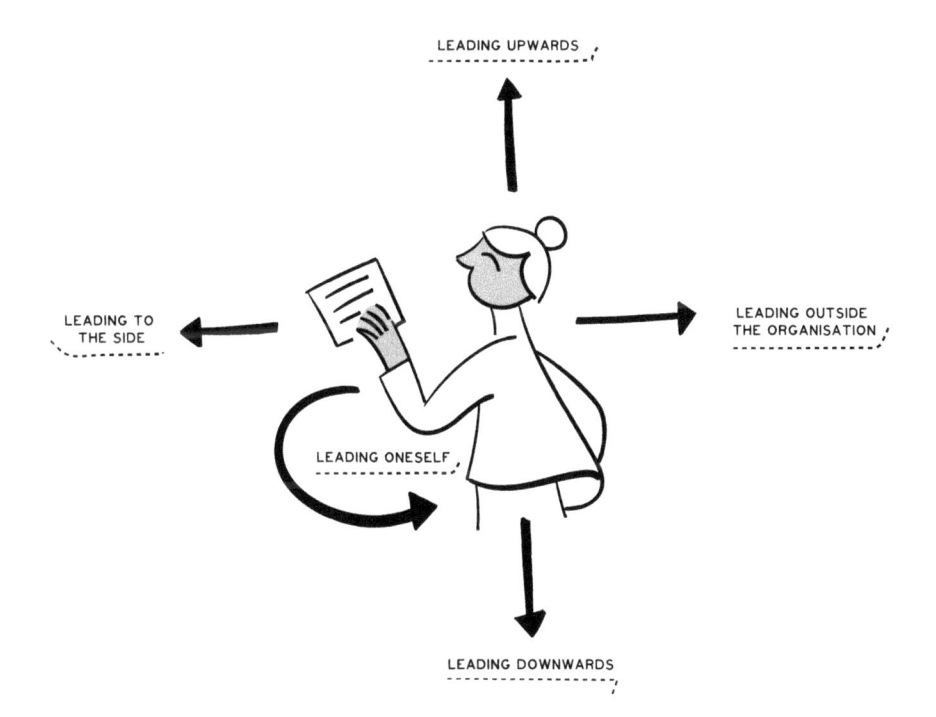

Image 7.2 Multi-directional leadership

the commitment of top management. But it is not enough. For an organisational culture to change towards inclusivity, it takes the effort of everyone. Building a diverse, equitable and inclusive organisation is a leadership responsibility of everyone. It might start with—or at least require—top management engagement, but it is up to everyone in the organisation to make it happen. Everyone is a potential change agent when it comes to inclusion. So, no matter where you are placed in your organisation, know that you can make a difference. Everyone has a sphere of influence, we just need the strength to define it, use it and extend it.

Self-Reflection Exercise: Extending My Sphere of Influence

To nurture inclusion, we all must define our sphere of influence, as you have done in Chapter 1. If you are convinced, have clarity and know what your organisation needs to block bias, then the next step is reflection on who you are influencing to be inclusive. This exercise will help you to extend your current sphere of influence by considering the people or stakeholders that you don't yet have an influence on, but who you would like to influence. Try to fill in names of individuals and/or institutions that you have the possibility to—or want to—influence in your DEI work. Remember to think about all directions: downwards to your employees, to the side to your colleagues, outside of the organisation to stakeholders, upwards towards your leadership—and inwards, towards what you want to change in yourself.

Here are some guiding questions as you reflect on this:

- Who do you want to influence?
- Who will you be able to reach if you practise leadership with conviction, clarity, accountability, allyship and strength?
- In which directions does your leadership extend?
- Who is your most important target group?
- Who are your closest allies in this process? And who do you need to be an ally to?
- How will you keep influencing and blocking bias yourself? (Image 7.3)

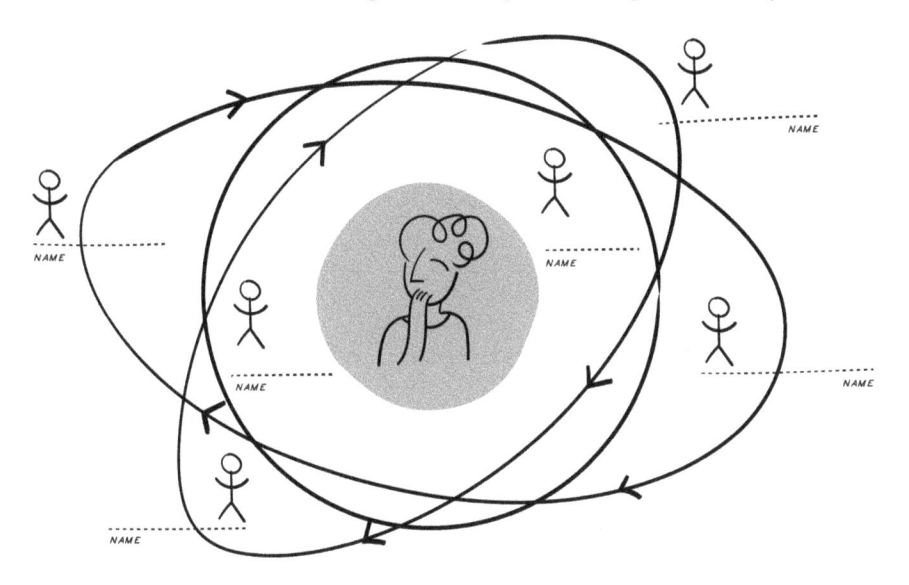

Image 7.3 Extending my sphere of influence

7.3 Stages of Developing Strength

In being able to lead with strength, there are four stages: (1) identifying fear, (2) unlearning, (3) learning and (4) growing. Throughout these stages, there will be moments of discomfort and comfort, with discomfort becoming comfort over time. Whenever you reach a stage of comfort for too long, nudge yourself to find other areas of bias and DEI that you need to work on and get back into the discomfort zone.

Also, these stages should be sequential, but one can easily go back to previous stages when further work is needed in that stage before proceeding to the next one. For example, after having gone through the stages of acknowledging fear and unlearning, you may be in the stage of learning when you come across information about a bias that made you fearful, or you found yourself in a bias-related situation where you knew that fear was present. You may not have identified that aspect of fear before or that bias in you or others, so you should go back to the first stage of identifying fear, working through that before moving to the unlearning stage. Or as you learn, you may discover that further unlearning is needed so you may need to go back to that stage before moving forward (Image 7.4).

Image 7.4 Stages of developing strength

Identifying Fear

Fear arises when we perceive a danger or threat. In leading through bias, this threat of danger comes from needing to acknowledge the hard truths that we are all biased, that our bias impacts our ability to be rational leaders and that leading through bias involves vulnerability. This makes us uncomfortable and holds us back from moving forward, from progressing towards inclusive leadership. The fear of facing discomfort can even be debilitating, preventing us from stepping up to make the changes needed to address bias. In fact, it is this very fear that causes us to remain bystanders or passive allies, accomplices in allowing bias to continue to propagate in our workplaces and society. Fear prevents us from becoming active allies.

Fear can look and feel different depending on whose perspective we take. Those who are well represented are fearful of getting uncomfortable, fearful of needing to let go of the power and privilege they have enjoyed and fearful of saying and doing the wrong thing. On the other hand, those from marginalised, discriminated and underrepresented groups are also fearful—fearful of being perceived as the token hire, fearful of addressing bias and discrimination and fearful of the impact of doing so on their careers.[10]

Identifying fear involves, first, acknowledging that you are fearful of leading through bias and, second, identifying where your fear lies. Without knowing the causes of our fear, it is very difficult for us to address it. But having identified your fear, you are ready to move to the next stage of unlearning.

Self-Reflection: Am I Fearful and What Am I Fearful of?

Let us first begin with an honest reflection. Do you feel fearful of leading through bias, of being an inclusive leader, of addressing existing bias?

☐ No: I am not fearful of leading through bias and am ready to be an inclusive leader.
☐ Yes, but slightly: I am slightly fearful of leading through bias but excited about the positive impact of leading through bias.
☐ Yes: I am quite fearful of leading through bias. It makes me uncomfortable.
☐ Maybe: I am not sure if I am fearful or not. I need more time to reflect on this.

If you ticked yes or maybe, take a look at the list below and tick the sources of fear for yourself within the topic of DEI and bias. These sources of fear relate to the Knowledge-Attitude-Behaviour (KAB) framework and arise because of:

- a lack of knowledge about the topic and how to address bias (K)
- the discomfort that comes with reflecting on our attitudes and bias, and facing the attitudes of others (A)
- not knowing what actions to take that are appropriate and helpful to nurturing inclusion (B)

You are welcome to add in any other sources of fear that are not listed below.

☐ Fear of not knowing the right words and phrases.
☐ Fear of not knowing enough about the DEI topic.
☐ Fear of the discomfort of addressing your own bias.
☐ Fear of the discomfort of needing to discuss difficult topics about DEI and bias with others.

☐ Fear of addressing the bias that you witness or experience, and the conflict situations that may arise from doing so.
☐ Fear of being perceived as the token hire.
☐ Fear of the impact of addressing bias on how others perceive you and the impact on your career.
☐ Fear of failure or saying/doing the wrong thing.
☐ Fear of change and needing to do things differently.
☐ Fear of giving up your position, power and space that you occupy.
☐ Fear of being cancelled.
☐ Fear of the impact of being seen as the "DEI police".

☐ _____
☐ _____
☐ _____
☐ _____
☐ _____

Unlearning

Let us first explore what unlearning is. In unlearning, we are trying to make what is familiar strange, and we are deleting prior knowledge that has become obsolete[11] or storing knowledge that we do not need now for use at a later time.[12] Unlearning can take place at the individual or group levels. To you as an individual, unlearning is the process of personal transformation with the aim to change ideas, attitudes or skills though personal effort. Unlearning can also occur at the group level when individuals in teams release or transform prior know-how, assumptions and mental frameworks in order to accommodate new information or values.

To lead through bias requires us to unlearn before learning. "Unlearning what?", you may ask. Unlearning the social conditioning that has contributed to the development of our bias and the norms that we consider to be acceptable.

Unlearning is about constantly challenging yourself to critically evaluate how you see the world and the people in it. Unlearning is about asking yourself on which socially conditioned norms you are basing your interaction with others at work. Unlearning is hard. We all have, over the many years of life experiences we have had, developed strong beliefs and biases. Unlearning these will take time and sincere effort.

To unlearn, the following guide can be beneficial for yourself and as a team in identifying and blocking the influence of bias:

1. Be critical of how you and your team see the world, and the decisions you make individually or as a group. Constantly question what bias could have played a role in leading to your or your team's beliefs about the world around you and the decisions you make.
2. Consciously and intentionally look at things from others' viewpoints.
3. Ask many "whys" until you and your team get down to the core assumptions driving your individual or collective thoughts, actions and decisions.
4. Seek out data and evidence to challenge yours and others' assumptions and bias.
5. Explore alternative options or solutions.

Self-Reflection: The Stories We Tell

We have all heard stories and may even have shared stories with others. Stories form an integral part of culture and are a powerful means through which human beings exchange their experiences across generations. Stories reflect our experiences. In organisations too, we share stories, and these stories reflect our experiences and the organisation's culture.

What do we talk about in our organisation? What are the main themes?

_____
_____
_____
_____
_____
_____
_____
_____
_____

What are the popular stories and narratives?

What do we not speak about? What topics are avoided? What do people stay silent about? And why?

What norms and values do these stories create? How do these stories construct the image of an ideal employee?

Is the way we speak, the stories we tell and the way the ideal employee is constructed excluding to some more than others? Who and how?

What alternative stories would I like my employees and colleagues to tell? How would they impact the organisation?

___

Learning

In the words of the nineteenth-century American writer Mary Roberts Reinhart: "When knowledge comes in the door, fear and superstition fly out". The best antidote to fear is a deep understanding that you now have from having read the previous chapters of this book through which you have developed a solid grasp of what bias is and what you can do to lead through bias to block the influence of them on your colleagues, yourself, your team and your organisation.

Learning requires you to continuously engage in the topic of DEI through opportunities to develop new understandings and neural pathways that challenge the bias that you hold (and, perhaps, still express, if only occasionally). While there may be learning opportunities that your organisation offers to leaders and employees, leading through bias and with strength requires you to take control and responsibility for your own learning. This should be seen as an important part of your own leadership growth journey, so set aside time regularly in your calendar for this.

In this learning stage, begin with identifying gaps in your understanding of the topic and seek out learning opportunities to address the gap. Review your learning gaps periodically and engage in learning opportunities regularly. It has after all taken us all life to lather on a thick layer of bias so it will take time for us to learn new ways of doing things that limit the impact of bias on others and our decisions.

Here are some of the ways you can take control of your learning efforts:

- Actively seek out knowledge and information. Subscribe to newsletters and articles on the topic of DEI and bias and carve out time to read them.
- Read widely. There are plenty of books on this topic that will provide rich insights to challenge the bias we hold.
- Attend trainings that are provided by your organisation or outside.
- Listen to podcasts or audiobooks. This can be an efficient way to use time on your regular commute, the gym, at airports and on airplanes, etc. There are plenty of audiobooks and podcasts with guests who bring diverse perspectives and experiences to this topic. We provide some recommendations at the end of this book.
- Attend events where you hear from people with different life experiences and identities from yourself.

Self-Reflection: My Learning Gaps

Now that you have read the previous chapters of this book and have a good understanding of the topic of bias and leading through it, identify the areas within DEI and bias that you feel confident that you have a good understanding of as well as areas that you need to know more about. Next, list the ways in which you are going to bridge the gap in your understanding (Image 7.5).

Growth

The growth mindset is a well-established topic. The term was made famous by Carol Dweck in her book *Mindset—The New Psychology of Success* in which she differentiates between having a growth mindset and a fixed mindset. Individuals who believe that their talents can be developed through hard work, good strategies and input from others have a growth mindset. On the other hand, those who believe that their talents are innate gifts have a fixed mindset. According to Dweck: "They [people with a growth mindset] tend to achieve more than those with a more fixed mindset… When entire companies embrace a growth mindset, their employees report feeling far more empowered and committed; they also receive greater organisational support for collaboration and innovation".[13]

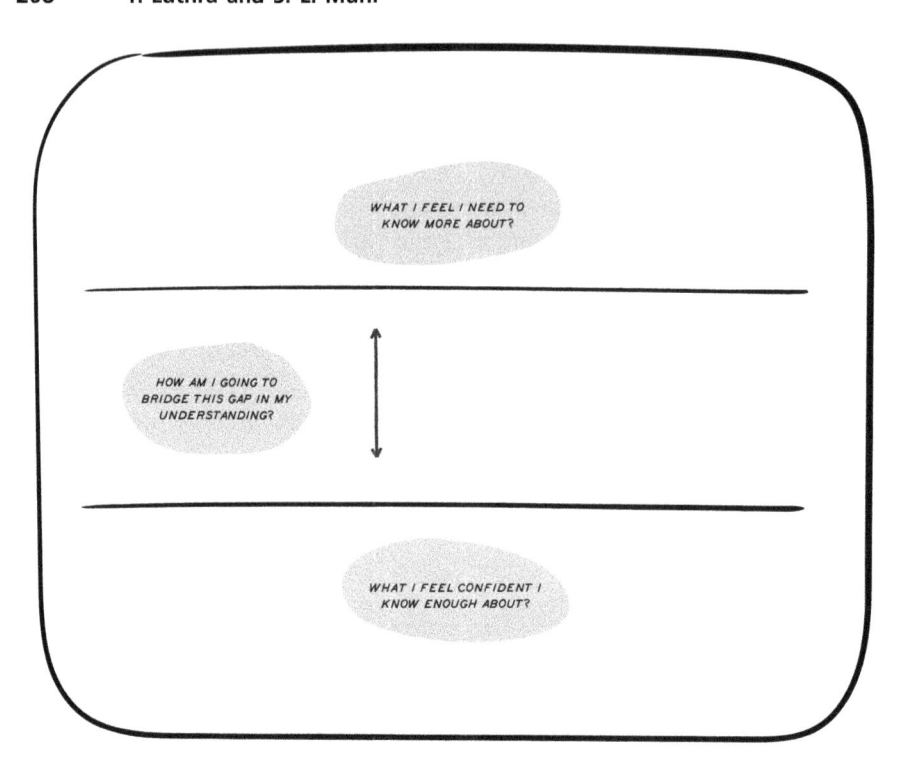

Image 7.5 Bridging the gaps in my understanding

In leading through bias, having a growth mindset is key to working through the fear and discomfort of this journey through unlearning and learning. A leader with a growth mindset sees the challenges of leading through bias as an opportunity for growth and development that will help them do things better than before. A leader with a growth mindset is not afraid of failure and getting things wrong. They see those situations as an opportunity to unlearn and learn.

At this stage of growth, reflect on your journey with leading through bias and being an inclusive leader, and then set goals for yourself moving forward. This growth stage of goal setting is extremely important to focus your efforts and to track progress periodically. Come back to the self-reflection exercises below and redo them every year, after reflecting on your progress against your targets.

Self-Reflection: Where Have I Got It Wrong in Leading Through Bias?

It is not uncommon to make mistakes in this journey. Reflecting on these experiences, understanding what went wrong and making a commitment to doing better are key. Reflect on instances where you felt you made mistakes in the area of DEI and active allyship. What went wrong?

_____

_____

_____

_____

_____

_____

_____

_____

_____

_____

_____

_____

_____

_____

What could you have done differently?

_____

_____

_____

_____

Self-Reflection: Setting Your Goals for Leading Through Bias

Having read the book up till this point, what would you like your goals for leading through bias to be? To help you decide on your goals and monitor progress, we draw on the goal-setting framework and leadership tool OKRs (Objectives and Key Results) that has gained widespread acceptance thanks to the work of John Derr in his book titled *Measure What Matters: OKRs: The Simple Idea that Drives 10× Growth*. OKRs help communicate what you want to accomplish and what milestones you will need to meet in order to accomplish it. They take this form: I will (Objective) as measured by (Key Results).

An Objective (O) is simply what is to be achieved. What are your objectives for leading through bias? Make these goals as specific as possible. In Chapters 5 and 6, you have been presented with multiple tools and strategies to block bias, and be an active ally to nurture inclusion. Let them inspire you to define your objectives. In your efforts to be an inclusive leader, some of these objectives may be less tangible than what you are used to in other aspects of your job. Some may seem fluffy. It's time to get comfortable with this.

When you set your objectives, you can find inspiration in the model from educational psychology called "the zone of proximal development". The model is composed of three zones (Image 7.6):

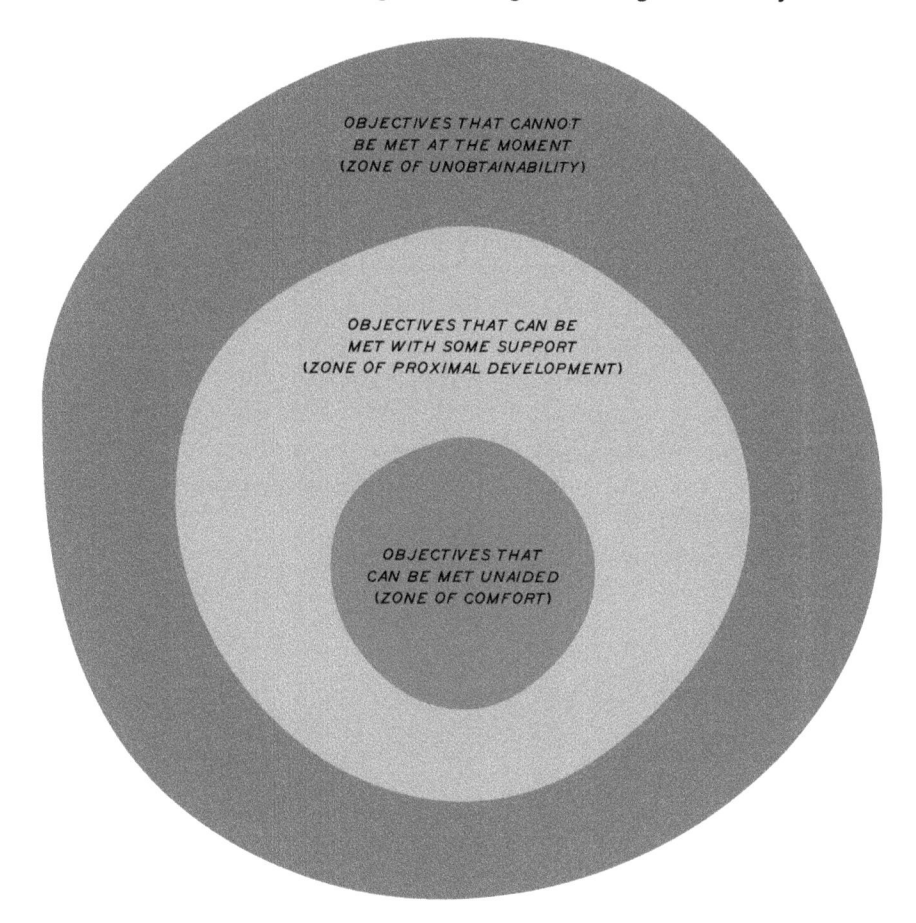

Image 7.6 Zones when setting objectives

- Zone 1: The first zone consists of objectives you can meet unaided. These are the low-hanging fruits, so to speak. They are the objectives you can initiate yourself and those that you don't need others' support or guidance to complete. The first zone consists of easy wins, but does not require you to grow and develop—this is the zone of comfort.
- Zone 2: The next zone is the zone of proximal development. In this zone, you find the objectives that you need others' support or guidance to meet. These objectives are the ones that might make you uneasy—not in a bad way—but in a way that pushes you out of your comfort zone. This is where you will grow and develop as a leader. The important thing in this zone is that you not only define the objectives but also the people you will need to collaborate with in order for the objectives to be met.

- Zone 3: The final zone consists of goals that you won't be able to meet at this point in time—either because you don't have (or can't access) the resources or because you can't (or prefer not to) push yourself this far out of your comfort zone at this point in time. This is the zone of unobtainability.

The important thing with the exercise below is that you pick objectives which are both in your comfort zone (the low-hanging fruits) and those that push you a little bit out of the comfort zone and into the zone of proximal development, but not all the way into the zone with objectives that you will not be able to meet. Envision this as a set of steps. Take the easy ones first and then step into the zone of proximal development. This will give you both the best chance of success and also the best chance of development—and maybe even the ability to extend your zone of proximal development to expand it into former unobtainable steps.

First list your objectives:

O1:

_____

_____

_____

_____

_____

O2:

_____

_____

_____

_____

_____

O3:

_____

_____

O4:

O5:

How would you know that you have met these objectives? Key Results (KR) help to benchmark and monitor how we get to the Objectives (O) that you have set. Effective KRs are specific, time-bound, ambitious yet realistic, measurable and verifiable.[14] What measures or outcomes could you use to determine the success of each of the objectives? Keep in mind that these measures or outcomes can be more intangible than you are used to in other aspects of your job.

KR1 (corresponding to O1)

KR2 (corresponding to O2)

KR3 (corresponding to O3)

KR4 (corresponding to O4)

KR5 (corresponding to O5)

Check that each of the Os and corresponding KRs link well together by applying the sentence structure as shown below for each OKR:

I will (O1) as measured by (KR1).

To be able to achieve the objectives that you have set above requires us to know what may hold us back. What do you see as challenges in your pathway that are holding you back from leading through bias effectively and meeting these objectives? These could be related to the fears you reflected on earlier in this chapter.

What could you do to address those challenges?

7.4 Engaging on the Tough Topics; Don't Hide From Them

Leading with strength will require you to respond to the tough topics that may come your way. This book should have prepared you for this and here are some common tough topics or questions that leaders get asked which may be good to consider in advance.

- "You have only chosen a woman/person of colour for that position because she is a woman/they are a person of colour. Let's see how long she/he/they last(s)".
- "If we are being inclusive, does it mean being inclusive to those who are racist, sexist and homophobic?"
- "It's so unfair that minorities are given priority. This is reverse discrimination. I have worked hard and now my chances of moving upwards in the organisation are limited".
- "Shouldn't we let meritocracy work its magic?"
- "We just can't find talent".

- "Hiring diverse talent will mean lowering the bar and we don't want to do that. They must be well qualified".
- "What do you do when you have two equally qualified candidates, but one also has a diversity thumbprint different from others?"
- "When is being woke too much?"
- "You talk about psychological safety, but I don't feel safe to be myself as a White man. I feel scared. How is that psychologically safe?"
- "Isn't DEI just making workplaces 'un-fun'? We can't say or do anything these days".
- "Companies now say that they want to hire engineers at a rate of 50% men/50% women. But 80% of the engineers in our field are male… Is it fair to try to hire 50/50?"
- "Isn't it too much when we start nit-picking everything we say and labelling it as being non-inclusive?"

We also occasionally come across leaders—often women—who say that they have dealt with bias in the workplace by brushing those instances of bias aside. They often say that hard work got them ahead (remember the myth of meritocracy?). They often make statements like: "I've been through it, why shouldn't they?", "What is the big deal? They are just being oversensitive and get easily offended. Women just need to toughen up. I have roughed it out and so can they".

The above comments or questions come from a position of power, privilege and potentially of insecurity or fear about what this means for their own role and value in the organisation. How would you respond to such comments or questions? Having read this book, you have the knowledge to be able to respond effectively to these comments and questions. Always respond with empathy, knowing that we are all biased, and draw on the following points to challenge the other person and their viewpoints:

- The workplace is not experienced in the same way by everyone. Some intersectional identities experience bias far more frequently and with greater intensity than others.
- Bias and discrimination are internalised and felt differently.
- Just because one generation had to rough it out doesn't make it right, and it doesn't mean others need to either. Surely, we can do better.
- Just because it has not been a "big" problem for someone, doesn't mean it isn't for others. That is the very definition of privilege, and such comments often come from people with privilege.

- Keep in mind that structures, systems and processes are rigged against those who are underrepresented. So, if others get offended, they may have a right to feel that way. Wouldn't you if you were in their place?

These topics are by no means exhaustive, and you may be confronted by topics that you don't know how to best address. Leading with strength means leaning into the discomfort and vulnerability of not always having the answers and being able to respond as such. In doing so, you appear authentic. Whenever you encounter a question or topic that you don't know the answer to within the DEI space, respond by saying something to the effect of "Thank you for your question/reflection. It is a question/area that I do not have a response to at this moment. DEI is a journey we are on together and I will need to learn more to be able to address that topic effectively". Come back to this book and your other resources to find the answer and then respond. In situations where you can't find the answer or appropriate response, seek advice from your DEI team, colleagues (who have different perspectives from yourself) and/or external experts.

Finally, and perhaps most importantly, leading through bias is challenging. It is hard and can take a toll on your mental and physical health. We are reminded of the 1997 Harvard Business Review article *The Toxic Handler: Organizational Hero—and Casualty*[15] in which Peter J. Frost and Sandra L. Robinson define the toxic handler as "a manager who voluntarily shoulders the sadness, frustration, bitterness, and anger that are endemic to organizational life". Toxic handlers listen empathetically, suggest solutions and work behind the scenes to prevent pain, carry the confidence of others and reframe difficult messages. These are all highly relevant to you as you lead through bias, addressing the inequity that exists. However, this comes at a cost. In leading through bias, you may experience resistance and even outright hostility from those unwilling to embrace inclusion. As we have seen in this chapter, you may be asked tough questions in aggressive or passive-aggressive tones. Toxic handlers shoulder not only the stress and frustration of those who are discriminated against, but their own stress caused by the very role they play. If this is you, here are some tips that you may find helpful:

- Be cautious of this stress. Be alert to its impact on your mental and physical health.
- Find your support network with whom you can share and vent in a safe space.
- Incorporate stress-relieving techniques that may include yoga, exercise or meditation.

- Take a break from this work when you need, to reenergise and heal so that you can come back stronger.
- Most importantly, be kind to yourself—and others—as you lead through bias.

> **What Can You Do Differently From Today? Leading With Strength Means:**
> - Leaning into the discomfort of leading through bias by showing vulnerability. You could share an instance when you got it "wrong", where bias influenced your actions or decisions and share with colleagues how you could have done things differently.
> - Nurturing psychological safety in your team meetings, ensuring that your colleagues and team members feel safe to make mistakes and address bias.
> - Making a conscious effort to address your fears, unlearn and learn, incorporating some of the suggested actions from this chapter.
> - Spending time reflecting on past experiences and planning for your journey of growth in leading through bias by setting your OKRs.
> - Engaging on the tough topics now that you have the know-how to support you, while taking care of yourself.

Notes

1. Brown, B. (2013). *Daring Greatly: How the Courage to Be Vulnerable Transforms the Way We Live, Love, Parent and Lead*. London, UK: Portfolio Penguin.
2. https://amycedmondson.com/.
3. Brown, B. (2018). *Dare to Lead: Brave work. Tough Conversations. Whole Hearts*. New York: Random House.
4. https://blog.ted.com/vulnerability-is-the-birthplace-of-innovation-creativity-and-change-brene-brown-at-ted2012/.
5. Carroll, B., Ford, J., & Taylor, S. (2022). *Leadership: Contemporary Critical Perspectives*. London: Sage.
6. DeRue, D. S., & Ashford, S. J. (2010). Who will Lead and Who will Follow? A Social Process of Leadership Identity Construction in Organizations. *Academy of Management Review*, 35, 627–647.
7. Fairhurst, G. T., & Uhl-Bien, M. (2012). Organizational Discourse Analysis (ODA): Examining Leadership as a Relational Process. *The Leadership Quarterly*, 23, 1043–1062. Uhl-Bien, M. (2006). Relational Leadership Theory:

Exploring the Social Processes of Leadership and Organizing. *The Leadership Quarterly*, 17, 654–676.
8. Drath, W. (2001). *The Deep Blue Sea: Rethinking Sources of Leadership*. San Francisco: Jossey-Bass & Center for Creative Leadership.
9. Meindl, J. R., Ehrlich, S. B., & Dukerich, J. M. (1985). The Romance of Leadership. *Administrative Science Quarterly*, 30, 78–102; Uhl-Bien, M. (2006). Relational Leadership Theory: Exploring the Social Processes of Leadership and Organizing. *The Leadership Quarterly*, 17, 654–676.
10. https://hbr.org/2022/11/7-ways-to-practice-active-allyship.
11. Hedberg, B. L. T. (1981). How Organisations Learn and Unlearn. In P. C. Nystrom & W. H. Starbuck (Eds.), *Handbook of Organisational Design* (pp. 1, 3–27). New York: Oxford University Press.
12. Klein, J. (1989). Parenthetic Learning in Organisations: Toward the Unlearning of the Unlearning Model. *Journal of Management Studies*, 26, 291–308.
13. https://hbr.org/2016/01/what-having-a-growth-mindset-actually-means.
14. https://www.whatmatters.com/faqs/okr-meaning-definition-example.
15. https://hbr.org/1999/07/the-toxic-handler-organizational-hero-and-casualty.

8

Final Thoughts

We would like to believe that our organisations are inclusive, equitable and that we hire and promote people solely based on hard work and merit. Sadly, this ideal is far from reality. Our workplaces favour some and not others, and bias is at the heart of the problem. Bias is everywhere—in us and others, in our interactions with each other and deeply embedded in workplace systems, structures, processes and policies. The pervasiveness of bias acts as a significant barrier to achieving the vision of diverse and inclusive workplaces for all. Therefore, leading through bias and knowing how to block this bias from influencing our words, behaviours and decisions is absolutely key to being able to nurture workplaces that are truly equitable and inclusive for employees with diverse intersectional identities.

We are firm believers that to enable sustainable change, we must address individual and systemic bias. Until now, our organisations have been applying band-aids on the challenges faced in nurturing inclusive workplaces. But these are short-term fixes and they do not lead to the long-term change we desire. We don't believe in giving people hammers to chisel away at the glass ceiling or tools to mould themselves to fit the current system, plagued by norms that favour some groups but not others. We believe that what is needed to move the needle towards inclusion is a redesign of our workplace so that it works for everyone. That redesign needs us all to step up. While diversity may be a managerial responsibility, nurturing inclusion is everyone's responsibility.

But the question that comes up time and time again is: how? How do we do this?

This book was written to address this question, while providing you with a more comprehensive and global view of the challenges we face and solutions that can be applied across multiple contexts. We adopt an intersectional lens that focuses on ensuring equity through behavioural change. We believe that by focusing on Knowledge-Attitude-Behaviour, we can enable this sustainable change to happen. Nurturing inclusion is not an easy process and there are no quick fixes. It takes time and commitment.

We began our journey in leading through bias by defining a purpose for DEI that is focused on achieving equity, making the case for you to lead with conviction. In unpacking what bias is and the many forms it takes while also introspecting on your own biases, you now have the know-how and right attitude to lead with clarity. We have also established that this is not enough. We need to act and so we have provided you with the tools that we believe you need to block bias across one of the most important organisational processes—the employee life cycle—to lead with accountability. But bias does not only manifest in the systems, structures, processes and policies. It also manifests in our relationships with others. To lead through bias requires you to lead with allyship by engaging with others in a way that nurtures inclusion. Finally, to lead through bias, you must lead with strength. We acknowledge that this journey is not an easy one. It is uncomfortable and it is challenging. To lead through bias, you will have to embrace vulnerability and lead from a place of deep strength. Through this book, we hope to have provided you with everything you need to do just that—in-depth knowledge, the right attitude towards bias and the behaviours to block bias in your interactions with others and your decision-making processes.

The five skills of leading with conviction, clarity, accountability, allyship and strength are crucial to being able to lead through bias and nurture inclusive workplaces. While there is plenty to be done, don't get disheartened by the magnitude of change needed. Start within your own spheres of influence and within your zone of proximal development. To make it easier for you, we leave you with a consolidated list of steps that you can take to lead through bias, extracted from the various chapters of this book. So if you are wondering—What can I do differently from today?—look no further.

8.1　As an Individual, You Can:

- Ask yourself if you wholeheartedly believe in the purpose of DEI and being honest with yourself.

- Recognise the need to make an effort to understand and believe in the purpose of DEI.
- Engage with colleagues with diverse perspectives across the organisation to understand what they believe the purpose of DEI is for themselves, their team and the organisation.
- Introspect deeply about where your identity-related cognitive biases lie.
- Do an Implicit Assumption Test (IAT) to identify where your biases may lie.
- Form a diverse bias compass circle.
- Prepare how you will respond respectfully when you are being biased.
- Address bias at work respectfully.
- Understand what it takes to be an active ally.
- Be clear about what active allyship is and is not, and why active allyship is needed.
- Reflect on the current phase of your allyship (denial, passive and active) and pushing yourself towards consistently active allyship.
- Reflect on the three components of allyship—knowledge, attitude and behaviour—and knowing where you stand now with each of them.
- Make a commitment to being an active ally and being clear about specific behaviours to engage in to demonstrate frequent and consistent active allyship including acknowledging and using your privilege to lift others.
- Lean into the discomfort of leading through bias by showing vulnerability. You could share an instance when you got it "wrong", where bias influenced your actions or decisions and share with colleagues how you could have done things differently.
- Make a conscious effort to address your fears, unlearn and learn, incorporating some of the suggested actions from this book.
- Spend time reflecting on past experiences and planning for your journey of growth in leading through bias by setting your OKRs.
- Engage on the tough topics now that you have the know-how to support you, while taking care of yourself.

8.2   As a Team/Organisation, You Can:

- Define the purpose of DEI for your organisation, team and individual employees. Be as specific as you can be and keep focused on removing barriers and increasing equity. Embed DEI within your company strategy.
- Clearly, frequently and consistently communicate the purpose of DEI to your employees.

- Conduct an analysis of your employee life cycle and assessing at which points your organisation or your team is most prone to bias.
- Commit to blocking bias at all points in the employee life cycle. It does not help to put all your resources into blocking bias in the beginning of the cycle, if bias nullifies the positive impact later on.
- Experiment with bias blocking. Some of the bias blockers may seem banal but try them out and observe the impact.
- Realise that you don't have to implement all of the bias blockers to make a difference, start with a few across different points of the employee life cycle, observe the changes they result in and then continue to implement more.
- Accept that bias blocking is a continuous process. Once some biases are blocked, others might pop up. So, continuously assess your employee life cycle. The best way to keep track is to talk to people about their experiences and conduct regular diversity and inclusion audits.
- Nurture psychological safety in your team meetings, ensuring that your colleagues and team members feel safe to make mistakes and address bias.

In the words of Albert Einstein, "The world we have created is a product of our thinking. It cannot be changed without changing our thinking". You have everything you need to lead through bias. Are you ready to enable the change you want to see?

Recommend Resources

Here are some of our favourite resources to help you further your journey in leading through bias.

Books:

1. *Inclusion on Purpose: An Intersectional Approach to Creating a Culture of Belonging at Work* by Ruchika Tulshyan
2. *So You Want To Talk About Race* by Ijeoma Oluo
3. *Caste* by Isabel Wilkerson
4. *It's About Damn Time* by Arlan Hamilton
5. *The Allyship Challenge* by Kimberly Harden
6. *Biased* by Jennifer Eberhardt
7. *Invisible Women by Exposing Data Bias in a World Designed for Men* by Caroline Criado-Perez
8. *The First, the Few, the Only: How Women of Color Can Redefine Power in Corporate America* by Deepa Purushothaman
9. *Take Back Your Power: 10 New Rules for Women at Work* by Deborah Liu
10. *Diversifying Diversity: Your Guide to Being an Active Ally of Inclusion in the Workplace* by Poornima Luthra
11. *The Art of Active Allyship* by Poornima Luthra
12. *Leading Global Diversity, Equity, and Inclusion: A Guide for Systemic Change in Multinational Organizations* by Rohini Anand
13. *White Fragility: Why it's So Hard for White People to Talk about Racism* by Robin DiAngelo

14. *Sexism in Danish Higher Education and Research: Understanding, Exploring, Acting*. www.sexismedu.dk
15. *DEI Deconstructed* by Lily Zheng.

Online resources and podcasts:

1. Harvard Business Review, hbr.org
2. HBR Women at Work
3. HBR IdeaCast
4. The Diversity Gap
5. Brown Table Talk with Dee C. Marshall and Mita Mallick
6. Inclusion Works
7. The Will To Change: Uncovering True Stories of Diversity & Inclusion
8. The Element of Inclusion
9. Code Switch
10. Untapped with Tariq Meyers
11. The Guilty Feminist with Deborah Frances-White.
12. Do You Know Sexism?

Index

A

Ableism 59, 89, 110, 137
Accentism 76, 77, 83
Active allyship 202, 206, 207, 211, 229, 236, 238, 243–248, 269, 283
Affirmative action 28, 29, 166
Age 10–12, 14, 29, 61, 68, 78, 80, 83, 84, 86, 87, 89, 90, 96, 116, 119, 137, 154, 155, 162–166, 169, 182, 212
Ageism 59, 83, 84, 137
Allyship xi, 4, 5, 31, 34, 142, 201–204, 206, 207, 245, 282, 283
Appearance 10, 11, 14, 30, 63, 68, 83–86
Appearancism/Lookism 84
Attraction 14, 156
Authenticity 253–255

B

Beliefs and practices 68
Bias awareness training 136
Binary 14, 31, 75
Board 25, 28, 30, 36, 88, 117, 194, 216, 243
Bonus 97, 160, 181, 189, 190, 196
Business case 24, 26, 27, 35

C

Class/socio-economic background 94
Classism 94, 98, 137
Colourism 76, 77
Confirmation bias 122–124, 167, 172, 173, 211, 232
Contrast bias 121, 173
Creativity 31, 34, 39, 69, 174, 253
Culture xiii, xiv, 1–3, 10, 11, 15, 17–20, 33–36, 39, 58, 61, 62, 65, 75, 83, 85, 92, 114, 115, 118, 124, 128, 145, 158, 171, 173, 174, 176, 178, 180, 184, 187, 189, 201, 208, 211, 221–223, 235, 243, 244, 252, 257, 258, 263
Culture add 116, 147, 148, 174

D

Decision-making xi, 50, 53, 54, 58, 116, 117, 128, 135, 137, 163, 186, 229
DEI strategy 9, 10, 20, 143, 244
Discrimination ix, xv, 1, 11, 12, 17, 28, 30, 31, 33, 59, 64, 65, 74, 76, 77, 80, 82–84, 86–90, 92, 94, 96–98, 106, 109, 136, 142–144, 167, 169, 179, 182, 187, 196, 203, 205–207, 209, 261, 276, 277
Diversity x, xi, 2–4, 10–15, 17–20, 24–27, 30–36, 44, 45, 62, 65, 66, 90, 99, 107, 108, 114, 116, 118, 127, 128, 138, 139, 142, 143, 145, 147, 153, 154, 157–160, 165, 174, 175, 179, 181, 187, 188, 190, 194, 195, 198, 203, 204, 214, 216, 223, 228, 244, 247, 281, 284
Diversity thumbprint 11, 12, 34, 65, 66, 99, 113, 119, 127, 214, 215, 218, 237

E

Education ix, 14, 29, 33, 55, 57, 69, 74, 75, 93, 94, 98, 116, 121, 126, 143, 144, 159–161, 196, 215, 222
Education bias 93
Employee life cycle 2, 3, 138, 145, 147, 187–190, 193, 194, 282, 284
Employee well-being 32, 33, 39, 127
Equality 21, 30, 42, 69, 70, 144, 180, 196, 201, 239
Equity xi, 3, 4, 21, 25, 30–32, 37, 39, 138, 147, 157, 179, 180, 195, 196, 201, 204, 237, 238, 282, 283
Ethnicity 10–12, 15, 82, 83, 116, 159, 178, 179, 194

Exclusion 1, 11, 19, 183
Exit interviews 187, 190
Expectation bias 119, 172
Experience ix–xi, xiii, 1, 3, 5, 10–12, 14, 15, 18, 19, 21, 25, 30, 33–35, 37, 39, 50–52, 56, 58, 59, 61, 63, 65, 66, 69, 72, 73, 75, 80–82, 84, 88–90, 92–94, 99, 113, 114, 116, 121, 123, 125–128, 135, 138, 142–146, 149, 151, 154, 157–160, 164, 174, 177, 178, 180, 187, 195, 202, 203, 207–209, 214–216, 222, 224, 230, 234, 235, 237, 255, 262, 263, 267, 269, 278, 283, 284
Experience bias 3, 65, 94, 99, 127, 277
Explicit bias 54–57, 64, 88, 136

F

Fairness 21, 27, 77
Father(hood) 127
Fatphobia 88
Focus bias 118, 119, 123, 172, 173, 194
Food 90, 117, 186, 240, 244

G

Gender x, 10–14, 21, 24, 25, 28, 29, 31, 32, 42, 43, 61, 68–72, 74, 75, 77, 82–85, 87, 88, 90, 97, 116, 118, 119, 125, 137, 140, 144, 151, 155, 159–166, 169, 179, 182, 186, 196, 198, 202, 203, 212, 216, 223, 236, 239, 252
Global majority global minority 78
Group conformity 233, 243

H

Hair 14, 61, 79, 86–88
Head hunter x, 161, 162, 189
Heterosexism 91, 111
Hijab 61, 90, 155, 223, 224
Humour 60, 62, 63, 224, 225

I

Identity 3, 11–14, 17, 27, 49, 54, 61, 65, 66, 68, 70, 77, 82, 91, 92, 99, 113, 118, 124, 126, 137, 169, 177–179, 186, 195, 214, 216, 218, 222, 223, 237, 245, 283
Implicit bias 54, 55, 57, 59, 90, 102, 114, 136
Inclusion x, xi, xiii, 1, 2, 4, 17–20, 22, 24, 26, 31, 33–35, 60, 62, 73, 89, 112, 116, 127, 128, 130, 138, 139, 145, 153, 176, 178, 179, 181, 184, 188, 190, 199, 201–204, 207, 221, 232, 235, 248, 258, 261, 270, 278, 281, 282, 284
Intersectionality 3, 11, 12, 42
Interviews 29, 33, 53, 73, 75, 79, 83, 87, 98, 114, 115, 119, 123, 124, 138, 154, 162–172, 189, 194, 197
Intuition bias xi, 114, 116, 147, 166, 237

J

Job add 53, 147, 151–154, 156, 157, 180, 188, 194, 198
Job description 153, 181, 188, 238

L

Language 15, 51, 52, 60–65, 76, 80, 82, 83, 117, 130, 144, 151–153, 177, 183, 194, 195, 202, 217, 223–225, 239, 240, 244, 247
Leadership ix–xi, xiii, xv, 3, 16, 20, 28, 30–34, 36, 39, 50, 61, 69, 70, 72, 73, 75, 84, 89, 95, 98, 114, 117, 123, 136, 140, 141, 143, 149, 153, 154, 161, 162, 171, 178, 188, 195, 196, 227, 228, 230, 231, 242, 251, 253, 255–258, 260, 266, 270, 279, 280
LGBT 25, 33, 111, 132
Location bias 98

M

Marital and parental choices 11, 96
Marital and parenthood choices 16
Meeting culture 236
Mental health 15, 73, 96, 127, 128, 182
Mental health bias 95
Meritocracy 136, 137, 144, 198, 276, 277
Microaggression 59, 60, 93, 128
Minority initiatives 139, 140
Mother(hood) 96, 97, 112, 126, 127

N

Nationality 15, 164, 177–179, 194, 212
Neurodivergent 95
Neurodiversity 11, 15, 62, 95, 182
Neurodiversity bias 137
Non-binary 13, 75, 119

O

Onboarding 145, 176–178, 189, 195

P

Parent(hood) 11, 16, 96–98, 119, 162, 169, 182, 194
Pay gap 81, 125, 131, 140, 180, 196
Personality 11, 15, 73, 94, 95, 118, 119, 169, 183, 219, 222, 227, 228, 236
Personality bias 94
Physical ability 89
Positive discrimination 28–30
Privilege ix, 11, 21–24, 31, 77, 209, 211, 219, 230, 254, 260, 277, 283
Proximity bias 122, 147, 150, 171, 172, 183, 237
Psychological safety 35, 207, 208, 211, 216, 224, 228, 230, 235, 236, 247, 252, 284

Q

Queer 13, 14, 82
Quotas 27–31, 44, 165, 166, 174, 189, 244

R

Race 10–12, 14, 29, 41, 42, 63, 68, 69, 72, 75–77, 104
Racism 12, 59, 75, 76, 82, 83, 92, 137, 144
Recruitment 29, 53, 63, 79, 87, 93, 97, 109, 114, 115, 119, 123, 125, 138, 145, 155–158, 160–162, 170, 172, 173, 175, 183
Relational leadership 242, 255, 279, 280
Religion 29, 79, 169, 194
Religious bias 90
Representation 15, 16, 26, 28, 29, 31, 32, 34, 124, 139–141, 158, 159, 161, 165, 166, 178, 194, 215, 233, 237, 244

Retention 18, 33, 138, 145, 176, 184, 190, 195

S

Salary ix, 69, 74, 96, 97, 119, 125, 126, 139, 140, 180, 181, 190, 196
Science, Technology, Engineering and Math (STEM) 27, 99, 103, 139, 158, 159
Selection 88, 97, 124, 131, 145, 156, 171, 217
Sexism 12, 59, 68, 75, 85, 92, 137, 183
Sexual orientation 10, 11, 14, 29, 62, 91, 92, 111, 131, 137, 155, 169, 179, 182, 194, 219, 220
Similarity bias 116–119, 121, 122, 130, 147, 148, 160, 167, 173, 183, 211
Sourcing 145, 156, 166, 189
Sponsor 229, 230, 243
Stereotype 63, 71, 72, 79–81, 85, 96, 100, 106, 108, 118, 119, 136, 139, 141, 144, 161, 167, 178, 224, 243

T

Talent x, 3, 10, 25, 31–36, 39, 64, 65, 69, 82, 83, 89, 93, 95, 99, 122, 127, 138–141, 145, 146, 149, 150, 152, 156–158, 160–162, 165, 175, 176, 179, 180, 186, 188, 189, 195–197, 218, 228, 232, 236, 244, 276, 277
Termite bias 59–64, 128, 184, 224
Tightrope bias 72, 86, 180
Transgender 13, 14, 75, 82, 126
Transphobia 66

U

Unconscious bias x, 54, 56, 57, 59, 60, 90, 114, 128, 136, 180

V

Vulnerability 5, 107, 108, 251–255, 260, 278, 282, 283

W

Weight 14, 68, 86–88, 110

X

Xenophobia 76